State Sovereignty and Intervention

This unique book contests sovereignty, a concept which until recently remained unchallenged within IR theory and international law.

Helle Malmvig offers a Foucault-inspired discourse analysis of the intervention in Kosovo in 1999 and the non-intervention in Algeria in 1998. The author explores sovereignty as a discursive construction and investigates the way sovereignty is affected by practices of intervention and non-intervention. The detailed contemporary case studies illustrate that state sovereignty has been constructed differently over time, and also highlight how sovereignty within the same historical period can be constructed in different and even contradictory ways; state sovereignty varies not only in time, but also in space. Explicitly building on previous constructivist studies (in particular, Walker, Bartelson, and Weber), this new volume pushes existing poststructuralist/constructivist literature on sovereignty one step further by investigating its spatial variations.

This accessible study will be a valuable tool for students and scholars of International Relations and Security Studies.

Helle Malmvig is a Senior Research Fellow at the Danish Institute for International Studies (DIIS), Copenhagen.

The New International Relations
Edited by Richard Little, *University of Bristol*, Iver B. Neumann, *Norwegian Institute of International Affairs (NUPI), Norway*, and Jutta Weldes, *University of Bristol*

The field of international relations has changed dramatically in recent years. This new series will cover the major issues that have emerged and reflect the latest academic thinking in this particular dynamic area.

International Law, Rights and Politics Developments in Eastern Europe and the CIS
Rein Mullerson

The Logic of Internationalism
Coercion and accommodation
Kjell Goldmann

Russia and the Idea of Europe
A study in identity and international relations
Iver B. Neumann

The Future of International Relations
Masters in the making?
Edited by Iver B. Neumann and Ole Wæver

Constructing the World Polity
Essays on international institutionalization
John Gerard Ruggie

Realism in International Relations and International Political Economy
The continuing story of a death foretold
Stefano Guzzini

International Relations, Political Theory and the Problem of Order
Beyond international relations theory?
N.J. Rengger

War, Peace and World Orders in European History
Edited by Anja V. Hartmann and Beatrice Heuser

European Integration and National Identity
The challenge of the Nordic states
Edited by Lene Hansen and Ole Wæver

Shadow Globalization, Ethnic Conflicts and New Wars
A political economy of intra-state war
Dietrich Jung

Contemporary Security Analysis and Copenhagen Peace Research
Edited by Stefano Guzzini and Dietrich Jung

Observing International Relations
Niklas Luhmann and world politics
Edited by Mathias Albert and Lena Hilkermeier

Does China Matter? A Reassessment
Essays in memory of Gerald Segal
Edited by Barry Buzan and Rosemary Foot

European Approaches to International Relations Theory
A house with many mansions
Jörg Friedrichs

The Post-Cold War International System
Strategies, institutions and reflexivity
Ewan Harrison

States of Political Discourse
Words, regimes, seditions
Costas M. Constantinou

The Politics of Regional Identity
Meddling with the Mediterranean
Michelle Pace

The Power of International Theory
Reforging the link to foreign policy-making through scientific enquiry
Fred Chernoff

Africa and the North
Between globalization and marginalization
Edited by Ulf Engel and Gorm Rye Olsen

Communitarian International Relations
The epistemic foundations of international relations
Emanuel Adler

Human Rights and World Trade
Hunger in international society
Ana Gonzalez-Pelaez

Liberalism and War
The victors and the vanquished
Andrew Williams

Constructivism and International Relations
Alexander Wendt and his critics
Edited by Stefano Guzzini and Anna Leander

Security as Practice
Discourse analysis and the Bosnian War
Lene Hansen

The Politics of Insecurity
Fear, migration and asylum in the EU
Jef Huysmans

State Sovereignty and Intervention
A discourse analysis of interventionary and non-interventionary practices in Kosovo and Algeria
Helle Malmvig

Culture and Security
Symbolic power and the politics of international security
Michael Williams

Hegemony and History
Adam Watson

State Sovereignty and Intervention

A discourse analysis of interventionary and non-interventionary practices in Kosovo and Algeria

Helle Malmvig

LONDON AND NEW YORK

First published 2006 by Routledge
2 Park Square, Milton Park, Abingdon, Oxon, OX14 4RN

Simultaneously published in the USA and Canada
by Routledge
270 Madison Avenue, New York, NY 10016

Routledge is an imprint of the Taylor & Francis Group, an informa business

First issued in paperback 2011

© 2006 Helle Malmvig
Typeset in Times New Roman by
Bookcraft Ltd, Stroud, Gloucestershire

All rights reserved. No part of this book may be reprinted or reproduced or utilised in any form or by any electronic, mechanical, or other means, now known or hereafter invented, including photocopying and recording, or in any information storage or retrieval system, without permission in writing from the publishers.

British Library Cataloguing in Publication Data
A catalogue record for this book is available from the British Library

Library of Congress Cataloging in Publication Data
A catalog record for this book has been requested

ISBN10: 0-415-39314-0 (hbk)
ISBN10: 0-415-66389-X (pbk)
ISBN10: 0-203-96945-8 (ebk)

ISBN13: 978-0-415-39314-0 (hbk)
ISBN13: 978-0-415-66389-2 (pbk)
ISBN13: 978-0-203-96945-8 (ebk)

To Erik

Contents

List of figures		x
Foreword, by Jens Bartelson		xi
Preface, by Richard Little		xiv
Acknowledgements		xvi
Introduction		xvii
1	Sovereignty as discourse	1
2	Analytical strategies	23
3	From object of observation to object of intervention	45
4	Sovereignty and intervention	77
5	From object of concern to object of non-intervention	105
6	Sovereignty and non-intervention	138
7	Contrasting constitutions	156
8	Sovereignty intervened	170
	Notes	172
	Bibliography	185
	Index	196

Figures

1 The diachronic and synchronic analyses: Kosovo 35
2 The diachronic and synchronic analyses: Algeria 35
3 Practice and discursive object: Kosovo 37
4 Practice and discursive object: Algeria 37

Foreword

It is a great honour to be invited to present this book by Helle Malmvig to what I hope will be a large and receptive audience. It would be fully possible to start a foreword like this by lamenting the fact that sovereignty for a long time remained virtually uncontested within International Relations theory and international law, and then go on to celebrate the fact that the present volume achieves such a contestation, and does so with a vengeance. But this book does something more than merely criticize traditional understandings of sovereignty, and therefore deserves to be situated and read in a different and more demanding context.

Today, when the meaning of the concept of sovereignty has been contested for quite some time, knowledge of the consequences of this contestation is needed if we want to be able to make sense of our present predicament. This kind of knowledge cannot primarily concern the theoretical meaning of the concept of sovereignty, but has to pay systematic attention to the actual function of this concept within political and legal practice. Whatever semantic and political consensus there once was as to the proper meaning of sovereignty, and however contested that consensus later became in a first wave of critical scholarship, recent scholarly attention has been focused on the changing functions of this concept within a variety of historical and political contexts.

It is against this backdrop that this book should be read. Helle Malmvig has written a book that takes us beyond existing critical and historical analyses of the concept of sovereignty, and right into the realm of contemporary political rhetoric. In her book, she describes how the concept of state sovereignty takes on different meanings depending on its different usages in justifying actual practices of intervention and non-intervention in the international system. A main upshot of this argument is to show that sovereignty and intervention not only are mutually constitutive concepts, but also are hierarchically arranged insofar as sovereignty can be regarded as normal only by virtue of intervention being considered pathological, and vice versa. In order to substantiate this bold claim empirically, she analyses how the Algerian conflict came to demand justifications of non-intervention in the international community, and how the largely simultaneous conflict in Kosovo came to call for justifications of intervention from the same community. Helle Malmvig pursues this line of inquiry with great theoretical ease and considerable attention to empirical details, and in the end delivers important conclusions about how and why the meaning of sovereignty varies across spatially distinct but temporally overlapping contexts.

At first glance, these conclusions could serve to reinforce the belief that the meaning and applicability of the principle of sovereignty are wholly contingent upon political and legal practices, and that there is no hard core of philosophical meaning left that could function as an uncontested foundation of those practices. Seen from this perspective, and when understood in its traditional senses, the concept of sovereignty is either redundant or incoherent, and would seem to lack any explanatory power and normative relevance in the present. Attributes like indivisibility and discreteness are but fetishes of an age which now is drawing to a close: hence there is no need to suffer from *le mal de Bodin* any more. Today, when sovereignty simply is what we make of it through our linguistic conventions and discursive practices, any attempt to define the meaning of this concept independently of those practices is nothing but a concealed attempt to seize the rhetorical initiative, and thereby political power as well.

This latter contention has some disturbing implications for our ability to study different aspects of the global political order we see emerging today. Although Helle Malmvig does not discuss these implications in principal terms, her book testifies to the moral importance and legal salience of the problem of sovereignty through its choice of cases. The conflicts in Algeria and Kosovo were harbingers of the new global order that emerged after the end of the cold war. The relationship between sovereignty and intervention has been inverted: intervention gradually became regarded as a normal state of affairs, whereas state sovereignty increasingly was considered pathological. In the ensuing efforts to define and defend new sources of legitimate authority internationally, claims of cosmopolitan justice clash not only with those of traditional state sovereignty, but with those of American imperial lawmaking as well, making the different loci of sovereignty claims even harder to pinpoint than before. Apparently, we have not moved beyond sovereignty simply because states no longer are its principal and prima facie equal claimants anymore. Rather, claims to sovereignty have proliferated in the global polity, now being raised with respect to the principles of cosmopolitan law as well as in the context of imperial ideologies. In the final analysis, it seems as if *le mal de Bodin* has successfully mutated into a new and even more contagious version that is able to infect not only states, but other forms of political life as well, ranging from guerrillas to international organizations. To complicate things further, the transition from territorial to functional differentiation has created a new distinction between territorially specific claims to sovereignty and functionally specific ones in the world polity. Not only is territorial sovereignty today contested, but jurisdictions between functional domains are equally hard to demarcate in the absence of a shared *Grundnorm*.

So sovereignty is not only what we make of it, but equally that which constitutes the identity of its makers by virtue of being the main bone of contention in their recognition games. By exposing the mechanisms that connect claims to sovereignty with justifications of intervention, Helle Malmvig shows us what we can expect from this new global order in terms of its possibilities and limits. Being a generalized state of exception, this order constantly generates new opportunities for intervention, which demand urgent responses from different agents within the world polity. Yet simultaneously, this order requires the resulting interventions to be legitimized in such a way that they can be rendered meaningful within at least *one* if not all of the available legal vocabularies – statist, cosmopolitan, imperial – that compete freely for normative supremacy within this world polity in the absence of a common structure of authority. Thus, in order to understand this new order more fully, we must pay attention to the *evolutionary* aspect of the relationship between intervention and sovereignty, and how the identity of agents is shaped precisely by its reflexive and evolving character. The war against terror and its various territorial manifestations have testified to this need – and Helle Malmvig has provided an indispensable theoretical foundation for fulfilling it.

I would like to end this foreword by pointing to what I take to be the chief virtue of this book. This lies neither in its theoretical sophistication nor in the valuable empirical results it delivers, but in its very constructive attitude to social constructivism. In this book, key insights from the linguistic turn are used in order to actually *solve* scientific problems rather than merely to tear down existing solutions to these. This is the way to go when intellectual curiosity rather than the desire for recognition is allowed to determine the search for knowledge.

Jens Bartelson
Copenhagen, November 2005.

Preface

One of the most significant developments in the post-cold war era is the putative change in attitude to third party intervention into the domestic affairs of sovereign states. After the Second World War, assessments of intervention were largely dictated by cold war considerations and were heavily overlaid with cold war rhetoric. East and West persistently traded accusations that the superpower on the other side of the iron curtain was violating the sovereignty of independent states around the world. By the same token, both the United States and the Soviet Union insisted that they wished to defend state sovereignty. But this position was deeply compromised by their mutual hostility. Following American intervention into the Dominican Republic, the Johnson Doctrine enunciated in 1965, stated that the United States would intervene militarily if necessary to prevent the spread of communism within the Western hemisphere. Three years later, following the Warsaw Pact's intervention into Czechoslovakia, the Brezhnev Doctrine echoed back to the United States the right of the Soviet Union to intervene militarily within the Soviet Bloc to defend communism. When the cold war came to an end, there was some optimism that the era of intervention and counter-intervention would give way to a new world order where the sovereign rights of states would be universally respected.

The idea of a new world order was almost immediately greeted with scepticism. Moreover, although the East–West ideological divide has gone, internal conflict has persisted throughout the post-cold war era and it continues to create the potential for external military intervention. But the rationale and the discourse surrounding whether or not outside states should intervene into domestic conflicts have changed very dramatically. Now the discussion focuses on the need for humanitarian intervention and whereas during the cold war, the United States and the Soviet Union frequently came under criticism for meddling in the internal affairs of other states, throughout the post-cold war era attention has recurrently been drawn to the reluctance of the international community to confront internal conflicts. There has often been widespread criticism of the international community, identified in the form of the United Nations, for the failure to step in and prevent the wholesale and indiscriminate violence that has regularly been perpetrated against innocent civilians.

Helle Malmvig in this book specifically examines the response of the international community to events in Kosovo and Algeria during the course of the 1990s. The detailed and fascinating case study chapters reveal that in both cases the international community displayed a marked reluctance to become involved in the internal conflicts. Nevertheless, at the end of the day, there was a very different response in these two cases. Events in Kosovo eventually precipitated the intervention by NATO, whereas despite the deaths of more than 100,000 people in Algeria, there was no international response. By focusing on the language that was employed within the international community during these two cases, Malmvig is able to demonstrate that over time, the nature of the discourse changed dramatically. But whereas in the case of Kosovo, the discourse eventually took a form that was permissive of intervention, in the case of Algeria, despite changes in the discourse, it continued to prohibit intervention. The key point that Malmvig wants to make, however, is that the discourses not only reveal important differences between these two cases, but they also open an important window on sovereignty and provide a way of interrogating the concept. What the case studies demonstrate is that sovereignty was constructed very differently in these two sets of discourses, opening the way to intervention in the case of Kosovo and closing the route to intervention in the case of Algeria.

The poststructural approach adopted in this book, therefore, succeeds, first, in focusing on the way that sovereignty is constituted, articulated and practised, and, second, on the fact that sovereignty can be constituted, articulated and practised in very different ways within the international arena at any given time. Moreover, because of the divergent ways that sovereignty can be articulated, it follows that intervention can be legitimated in some circumstances and not in others. Malmvig reveals that the sovereignty discourse manifested in the two cases under study was, at the start, sufficiently open to permit a variety of responses to the internal conflict. However, with the passage of time, the room for manoeuvre permitted by the articulation of sovereignty became increasingly circumscribed with the consequence that the international community was manoeuvred in the direction of either intervention or non-intervention.

Not everyone will be convinced by the interpretation that Malmvig draws from the case studies. Indeed, the case studies could be used to support the realist notion of "organized hypocrisy". According to this approach, states are driven by self-interest and they will violate international norms whenever it improves their position by doing so. The hypocrisy emerges because states will also draw on a discourse that legitimizes their actions. But Malmvig is not persuaded by this line of argument, in part because it fails to account for the complex way that discourse evolves over time and maps onto developments on the ground, and in part because it presupposes that policymakers possess an inherently implausible ability to "shape" reality so that their account of what is happening in the international arena coincides with and legitimates their preferred policy.

Whether or not Malmvig's account is accepted, it cannot be denied that this book represents a very serious and important attempt to move beyond established poststructural theory and engage directly with empirical material. And it is also significant that Malmvig identifies and confronts the methodological problems that arise in the process. Although the book follows in the wake of other poststructuralists, there is no doubt that it moves on their discussion of the theory and practice of sovereignty and intervention some considerable distance and in a direction that makes it increasingly difficult for poststructural sceptics to ignore.

Richard Little
University of Bristol

Acknowledgements

By providing timely portions of academic encouragement and critique several people and institutions have made this project possible. In particular, the Institute of Political Science at the University of Copenhagen, the Watson Institute of International Studies at Brown, and the Danish Institute for International Studies (DIIS) mark my journey of institutional affiliations.

From my time at the University of Copenhagen I wish to thank colleagues and staff: especially then fellow PhD candidates Tina Pipa, Helle Johansen, Mikkel Vedby Rasmussen, Anders Wivel, Carsten Bagge Laustsen, Anders Berg-Sørensen, Anders Esmark, Jørgen Staun and – not least – Henrik Breitenbauch, whom I also thank for translating the many French quotations. Jens Bartelson has provided invaluable and continued support for this project and his mind-wrecking comments have caused both intellectual frustration and great inspiration. Without his pioneering work on sovereignty, this book could not have come into life. Thanks also go to Ole Wæver for his always constructive comments along the way, and for fruitful advice on how to position and present my own work, to Lene Hansen for her sound methodological reflections and "no-nonsense" attitude to poststructuralism, and to Ulla Holm for her encouragement and enthusiasm – and for great intellectual discussions. Today, I am privileged to work with Ulla at DIIS.

Niels Åkerstrøm Andersen and Asmund Born from the Department of Management, Politics and Philosophy at Copenhagen Business School deserve credit for creating inspirational and much needed courses on how to make sound analytical strategies. They provided me with apt analytical comments and questions on several chapters of this book.

When the project was at an early stage, I was fortunate to spend a research semester at the Watson Institute of International Studies. I am particularly grateful to James Der Derian and Thomas Biersteker for giving me that opportunity, and for stimulating conversations and company. Special thanks also to the staff at Watson, who were always forthcoming and ready to help.

Finally, I wish to thank the series editor, Richard Little, and also Harriet Brinton at Routledge for all their help and constructive advice.

Introduction

In the 1990s the Balkans drew world attention. Just on the border of Europe, so it was told, people were being killed, persecuted, raped and repressed on the basis of an anachronistic and barbaric ideology, which power-seeking and opportunistic political leaders skilfully used to proclaim that the people of the Balkans could only live in clean ethnic states; that divergence was a source of enmity and hatred, rather than a source of richness and prosperity.

On another of Europe's borders, just across the Mediterranean basin, dreadful massacres were simultaneously being perpetrated, these, however, drawing much less attention. By 1998, up to 100,000 Algerians had been killed in an incomprehensible bloodbath carried out by fanatics and extremists who, it was argued, shed political and democratic means and aimed their violence at innocent civilians, including women and children.

With reference to these images, the French Foreign Minister was asked: "Why don't we do something about Algeria?" This seemingly innocent question appeared to demand an authoritative lesson about who we are, where our responsibility resides, on the proper locus and limits of political authority, on the realm of foreign politics versus the realm of domestic politics. "What do you want?" Charette asked, and answered himself:

> That the government tells the Algerians what to do? Algeria is not France: it is necessary to understand and admit this fact once and for all. Algeria is a sovereign nation. It has to solve its own problems; it is up to the Algerian people to choose its destiny. Moreover, the different leading Algerian politicians do not ask us to intervene. As for me, I have not been given responsibility for Algeria's destiny, but for France's foreign policy and for offering my part to the security of the French.
>
> (Charette, 30 January 1997)[1]

The same seemingly innocent question was asked in relation to Kosovo. Here politicians, however, answered: we have to do something. We have to intervene. Extrajudicial killings and gross violations of human rights can never be an internal affair. It is our obligation to act as moral human beings. How can we turn our backs on Kosovo, lingering passively when innocent civilians are massacred, persecuted and repressed; when human rights are perpetually violated and the rule of law has been exchanged with the law of rule? The international community has to act when state power is brutally abused. This is our responsibility too.

The events in Kosovo and the events in Algeria seemed, in other words, to produce two very different answers to who we are, who is to guarantee our future, what our responsibilities are and where they reside; where the boundary is to be drawn between internal and external, the foreign and the domestic.

How are we to approach these seemingly different articulations? From a specific, and undoubtedly dominant, discourse on International Relations, these articulations do not give rise to questions about the status or nature of sovereignty, but rather to questions of when and why states intervene, of the possibilities of creating a society of states where humanitarian principles override national interest, or of the impossibility of justice and ethics in the international sphere. The immediate puzzle and disciplinary controversy at hand does not appear to revolve around the reality of sovereignty, but over the reality of international politics. By swiftly applying a range of well-known disciplinary dichotomies of truth and rhetoric, might and right, realism and idealism, the research agenda is moved to its proper place, and International Relations theorists can engage in the appropriate debates over the dictates of interest versus values, or the effects of the absence of an overarching authority.

Yet, whether in the guise of realism or idealism or somewhere in between, longing for a middle position, these debates rely on, and hence (re)produce, a certain meaning to the concept of state sovereignty. To speak of the hypocrisy and inconsistency with which states enforce their ethical standards upon others (see, for example, Chomsky 1999; Krasner 1999; Weller 2000, 1999a; Mccgwire 2000), or to contend that NATO's intervention in Kosovo signified one more step in the direction of creating an international society grounded in common norms and values (Knudsen 1999a, 1999b), to argue that the West turned a blind eye to the Algerian atrocities due to economic interest and quest for oil, or conversely that the West did not do anything about Algeria due to a lack of national and/or strategic interest, is already to operate within the confines and logic of state sovereignty and its purported effects upon political life (see, for example, Martinez 2000; Stora 2001; Spencer 1998). In other words, sovereignty is already inscribed through the backdoor, not as object of investigation but as a necessary foundation. Only through a prior conceptualization of sovereignty do these debates and contentions become intelligible and important. Sovereignty can only disappear as a question, as something to be investigated, if state sovereignty already is treated as given and settled.

The ever-expanding literature on humanitarian intervention that purports to tackle head-on questions of sovereignty's current meaning, potential change or frequent transgression, also tends to assume the content of sovereignty (see, for example, Hoffmann 1996; Wheeler 1997; Knudsen 1999b; Ramsbotham and Woodhouse 1996; Lyons and Mastanduno 1995b). By engaging in endless disputes over how humanitarian intervention can be defined, which acts qualify as real humanitarian intervention and what the dangers are of engaging in such endeavours, not only is the meaning of state sovereignty presupposed, but intervention is a priori inscribed as a problematic and deviant act, whereas state sovereignty is positioned within the realm of the good and the normal (see also Malmvig

2001b). Thus, when much of the literature on humanitarian intervention emphasizes that humanitarian intervention risks being based on particular and ulterior motives; that great powers much too easily will abuse a right to humanitarian intervention and that such a right will be enacted with inconsistency; that it is problematic, or even morally wrong, to endanger the lives of one's soldiers for the sake of others or that humanitarian interventions may set a dangerous precedent for the future thereby undermining state sovereignty in the long run, this body of literature inscribes sovereignty with a specific meaning (see especially Wheeler and Morris 1996). State sovereignty is reproduced as the unquestioned foundation of international politics, which silently tells us who we are, where we belong, and with whom our responsibilities and moral obligations rest, while itself being withdrawn from investigation. Characteristically, Ramsbotham and Woodhouse (1996: 33), for instance, argue, echoing Hedley Bull's seminal dictum: "to approach the classical debate about forcible humanitarian intervention, the natural place to begin is with the core concept of state sovereignty." But why is it the natural place to start? And what are the implications of starting with state sovereignty? Such questions are often answered by sovereignty itself.

But what happens if we wish to question the evident being of sovereignty? What happens if state sovereignty is turned into a question rather than the natural point of departure, thus no longer constituting that silent and unquestioned foundation allowing us to move on to seemingly more precarious issues? We will then have to circumvent most theories of International Relations. If we wish to turn sovereignty into an object of investigation, refraining from assuming sovereignty and hence granting sovereignty a prior meaning, most International Relations theories will turn out to be less helpful. Since the very discipline itself is one of those sites where sovereignty is stabilized and practised, since International Relations reproduces sovereignty just as much as explaining it, while simultaneously being a product of, and dependent on, sovereignty, existing theories might be badly equipped to carry out this task. In other words, International Relations is prevalently blind to its own circular logic of being and representation – that which the discipline purports to represent (sovereignty), it produces at the moment of representation, while frequently forgetting that the very possibility of this representation is dependent on that which it (the discipline) claims to represent.

How are we then to determine what sovereignty is, what it has been or might become? A few scholars have – for over a decade now – answered that the very question is wrongly phrased. The question is itself founded on a modern episteme that assumes the sovereignty of the knowing subject and installs this subject as the source of all knowledge (see in particular Bartelson 1995; Ashley 1996). Rather than asking to the static being of sovereignty we should ask how sovereignty is constituted, articulated and practised; rather than asking what sovereignty is, we should ask *how* sovereignty is. These studies have accordingly looked towards the multiple sites and daily practices which participate in the production and reproduction of sovereignty. Instead of turning sovereignty into a unitary object of the world, they have addressed how sovereignty is spoken of, known and practised (see, for example, Ashley 1987; Ashley and Walker 1990a; Walker 1993; Bartelson

1995; Weber 1995; Dillon 1995). Sovereignty, it is argued, is nothing in itself, it has to be continuously enacted and re-enacted.

While the pioneering work of Ashley and Walker primarily investigated state sovereignty via disciplinary practices and the theories and assumptions of International Relations, emphasizing how the very discipline is a product of a specific modern spatio-temporal solution to questions of political identity and history, while at the same participating in the continuous reproduction of sovereignty, later studies have embarked on historical analyses of sovereignty's constitution and change (Walker 1993; Ashley and Walker 1990a; Ashley 1987, 1988). By further explicating the relationship between practice and meaning, these later studies have been able to account for sovereignty's emergence and changing meanings over time, and have disrupted the common narratives of sovereignty's ceaseless continuity (Bartelson 1995; Weber 1995). State sovereignty has thus been divested of its unitary existence, and, in its place, poststructuralists have installed always contingent, competing and shifting articulations of sovereignty. As Weber has argued:

> Sovereignty marks not the location of the foundational entity of international relations theory but a site of political struggle. This struggle is the struggle to fix the meaning of sovereignty in such a way as to constitute a particular state – to write the state – with particular boundaries, competencies and legitimations available to it. This is not a one time occurrence which fixes the meaning of sovereignty and statehood for all time in all places; rather, this struggle is repeated in various forms at numerous spatial and temporal locales.
>
> (Weber 1995: 3)

In which sites or through which practices are these struggles over sovereignty's meaning played out? Which practices participate in the production and reproduction of sovereignty? Bartelson has in his *A Genealogy of Sovereignty* focused on the intimate and historical relationship between knowledge and sovereignty. He has shown how sovereignty only becomes meaningful and intelligible in the background of knowledge, and how knowledge in turn can only be produced in the background of sovereignty. By an investigation of this historical circuit between knowledge and sovereignty over three historical epochs from the early Renaissance to Modernity, Bartelson has demonstrated how sovereignty's meaning has changed over time and how changes in discourses on sovereignty have been closely intertwined with changes in knowledge.

According to a similar logic Cynthia Weber has argued for the mutual dependence of sovereignty and intervention. Intervention, Weber has contended, is normally understood as a transgression or violation of sovereignty within International Relations theory. This understanding, however, implies that intervention can only be defined on the basis of a prior – albeit often hidden – conceptualization and assumption of sovereignty. The meaning of intervention is in this way dependent on sovereignty, but sovereignty is equally dependent on intervention;

intervention being one of those practices that stabilizes and fixates meanings of sovereignty. On the basis of a historical analysis of five cases of intervention legitimations, starting with the European Concert's intervention in Naples and Spain in the early nineteenth century and ending with the American interventions in Grenada and Panama in the late twentieth century, Weber demonstrates how sovereignty has been invested with various meanings across time and how interventions have participated in the construction and change of sovereignty. Bartelson and Weber have accordingly both approached meaning and practice as a productive circuit – although by different analytical strategies – and opened up this circuit for temporal change. They have both undertaken historical investigations of sovereignty, accounting for its shifting meaning and foundations across historical epochs or across different cases of intervention situated in different historical epochs.

This book is much indebted to the work of these authors, as will become clear in the following chapters. Yet, whereas Weber and Bartelson have primarily studied the temporal contingency of sovereignty, showing how sovereignty's meanings have been grounded and produced over time, they have not studied sovereignty as a concept open to various articulations within the same time. On a theoretical basis Bartelson (1995: 3) as well as Weber (1995: 2) emphasize that sovereignty differs in form and content through space and time. But they have confined their studies to differences across time. The implication is, as I will argue for in more depth in Chapter 1, that the content of sovereignty emerges as relatively fixed within different historical epochs; that the continuous struggles to stabilize sovereignty's meaning disappear, as it were, across space. In short, although poststructuralists on a general level contend that meaning always is essentially contested, provisional and political, and although Bartelson and Weber specifically argue that what counts as sovereignty is not the same in all places, these contentions have remained mainly theoretical.

This book proceeds along the route opened up by Bartelson and Weber. It shows how sovereignty can be articulated, grounded and justified in several, even conflicting or incompatible, ways within the same time, but across different spaces. Thus, this book will venture into a hitherto unexplored field, emphasizing variations in space rather than in time.

With Weber's study of the sovereignty/intervention nexus as a point of departure, I argue that sovereignty and intervention are not only to be seen as mutually dependent but also as hierarchically arranged. Sovereignty/intervention constitutes a binary pair, where sovereignty resides on the side of the good and the normal, whereas intervention belongs to the problematic and pathological. Sovereignty just is, whereas intervention always seems to need justification. By legitimizing interventions the meaning of sovereignty is not merely produced and stabilized, as suggested by Weber, but sovereignty is at the same time recognized and (re)produced as part of the good and normal, whereas intervention is recognized and reproduced as a problematic act in need of justification. No one, in other words, questions or is puzzled by the fact that interventions are followed by justifications. On the basis of the assumption of sovereignty's normality, this only appears as natural and evident. Legitimations of interventions are in this sense, I argue, inherently paradoxical. They simultaneously violate and assume sovereignty, and recognize and produce sovereignty.

The converse implication is, of course, that normally non-intervention does not demand legitimations. This is presumed to be a healthy state of affairs: a sign that international life works as it is supposed to. Yet can we find instances where the practice of non-intervention indeed was problematized and therefore in need of legitimations? Situations where politicians and officials engaged in the curious practice of justifying sovereignty and non-intervention? This book claims that Algeria is an example of such a situation; that politicians, officials and others by the end of the 1990s were justifying why the international community could not possibly intervene in the Algerian conflict, and that these very legitimations *equally* constituted, relied on and gave meaning to the concept of state sovereignty. Thus, I suggest that we can study fixations of sovereignty through practices of intervention as well as non-intervention. Through an investigation of how the intervention in Kosovo and the non-intervention in Algeria were justified, sovereignty can be studied across different spaces, but within the same time. In other words, this book is able to focus on differences in articulations of state sovereignty in space since the two types of legitimations as well as the two conflicts run parallel in time. The main theoretical question of this book can accordingly be formulated the following way: *how do interventionary and non-interventionary practices in different spaces but parallel time rely on and constitute meaning to state sovereignty?*

To answer this question demands more than a synchronic study of the two types of legitimations. A mere synchronic investigation of the constitutions of state sovereignty would not allow for an analysis of how Algeria emerged as a situation which demanded that politicians and officials engage in the abnormal practice of legitimizing non-intervention and sovereignty. The reader would still be left in the dark as to why what usually does not need to be justified appeared as a necessity in the case of Algeria. A diachronic analysis of those prior discursive struggles and selections that conditioned the legitimations of non-intervention in Algeria and intervention in Kosovo is indispensable, if we are not to situate these legitimations in an ahistorical vacuum. Through the diachronic studies of the cases of Kosovo and Algeria I analyse those shifts and turns in the representations of the two conflicts, which came to convey Algeria as a murky conflict with no clear lines – a distinct space marked by unspeakable massacres and brutality, while also being a responsible, independent and sovereign subject, who for itself and by itself was able to solve its own problems of fundamentalist terrorism, and create its own future of democracy and peace, and yet a situation which required that non-intervention was legitimized. Kosovo, instead, emerged as a clear case of ethnic cleansing and mounting genocide, planned and ordered by a power-seeking dictator, who was unwilling to walk down the path of peace and negotiation; who had left his people without representation, truth, freedom and protection, a situation therefore demanding international action. By tracing those discursive battles and shifts in the articulations of the two conflicts over the 1990s, the diachronic analysis is able to answer how Algeria was constituted as a situation in which intervention was impossible, while Kosovo appeared as a situation in which intervention was a necessity.

The theoretical *problématique* outlined above can thus more specifically be divided into three empirical sub-questions: How did the Algerian conflict over the course of 1992–1998 emerge as a situation that demanded legitimations of non-intervention? How did the Kosovo conflict over the course of 1991–1999 emerge as a situation that conversely demanded legitimations of intervention? And how did these divergent legitimations constitute meanings to state sovereignty in different spaces but parallel time?

By adopting a dual strategy of diachronic and synchronic discourse analysis this book proceeds into a relatively unknown terrain within International Relations. It constructs and applies a set of analytical strategies unfamiliar to most theorists in International Relations. This demands, as I will argue in the chapters to come, that a thorough explication of analytical assumptions and choices is carried out. In contrast to the prevalent "tradition" within poststructuralist studies, this book intends to engage in explicit deliberations and elaborations of what predominantly are considered tedious and even dangerous methodological questions. This also means that I will explicitly relate this book's *problématique* to existing poststructuralist work on sovereignty. Conversely, however, one will look in vain for lengthy summaries or reviews of what could be called "mainstream" literature on sovereignty/intervention and its presumptions about truth and representation. This terrain has already been traversed many times before me, and since this study proceeds from an altogether different perspective, I have found it expedient not to repeat the poststructuralist critique of this literature. Neither will one find ready-made policy recommendations, predictions about the future or explanations of the past. Instead, I hope that my study will prove a bit disturbing to those who much too readily assume that state sovereignty belongs to the abstract thoughts of political theorists; to those who already have claimed state sovereignty's obsolescence and to those for whom politics does not make sense without it. Hopefully, this book will also add new insights to those studies before me that travelled the unsafe waters of discourse analysis, as well as to those who have already explored the contingency of sovereignty.

The structure of the book is as follows. It is divided into three main parts and eight chapters. In the first chapter I shall spell out the epistemological and ontological implications of approaching state sovereignty as a discursive construct rather than a timeless being and engage in an extensive review and discussion of Walker's, Bartelson's, and Weber's studies of sovereignty, on the basis of which I argue for the importance of opening up sovereignty in space, and the possibility of studying constitutions of state sovereignty through legitimations of intervention and non-intervention. Chapter 2 explicates what is to be understood by an analytical strategy and why it is warranted, and it specifies the analytical categories, questions and assumptions that guide the diachronic and synchronic analyses of this book.

The second part is composed of the four main empirical chapters, where the first two are devoted to the diachronic and synchronic analyses of Kosovo and the last two to the corresponding analyses of Algeria. On the basis of the analytical strategy developed in Chapter 2, it is argued that the shifting articulations on Kosovo and Algeria over the course of 1991–1999 can be analysed in terms of a "funnel" signifying a gradual process of discursive selections and elevations conditioning and excluding future articulations and possibilities. Chapter 3 studies this historical and contingent process with respect to the case of Kosovo, ending with the discursive stabilization of Kosovo as a case of ethnic cleansing and mounting genocide, which seemingly could only be remedied by an intervention. Chapter 4 addresses the specific content of intervention legitimations. It is guided by three analytical questions: first, it asks what meaning is given to intervention; second, which community these legitimations produce; and third, what are the conditions of possibilities for this community. Chapter 5 turns to the diachronic analysis of Algeria ranging from 1992 to 1998. Here it is shown that although the discursive processes of selections and exclusions did not "end" with an intervention, as in Kosovo, it did come to a situation where politicians, officials and others had to legitimize why intervention could not be undertaken. In Chapter 6 these legitimations of non-intervention are accordingly investigated through the same three analytical questions as in the synchronic analysis on Kosovo.

The third and last part is composed of a summarizing comparison of Algeria and Kosovo and a conclusion. Chapter 7 compares explicitly the diachronic and synchronic chapters. On the basis of the prior chapters it highlights similarities and differences between the two cases, showing how the two processes had their own distinct dynamics and histories and how state sovereignty was articulated differently in the two cases. Chapter 8 concludes the analysis, discussing alternative positions and perspectives on the status of state sovereignty today.

1 Sovereignty as discourse

This book approaches state sovereignty as a discursive practice rather than an already given entity in the world. It seeks to answer how state sovereignty is granted meaning rather than what state sovereignty is, and the focus therefore shifts from an essentialist question of *being* to a constructivist question of *becoming*.

Below I will spell out some of the main epistemological and ontological assumptions linked to this proposition and question. Yet, one will not find a lengthy justification of the poststructuralist position, since this book does not aim to bring new insights to the field of International Relations through a philosophical critique of the foundationalist theories that flourish within it.[1]

Instead, this chapter will devote considerable space to a discussion of three existing poststructuralist works on state sovereignty: Walker, Bartelson, and Weber.[2] It will show how the concept of sovereignty is progressively opened up in time by the three authors, but that the full implications of their analyses have not been explored, since they have not examined the contingency of sovereignty in both time *and* space. In short, the extensive review is to highlight how the *problématique* of this book builds on, but also adds to previous poststructuralist studies. Simultaneously, this account will serve to illustrate how the three scholars employ the concepts and insights of particularly Foucault and Derrida in practice, and what the analytical consequences of this are.

The chapter is divided into three parts. In the first part some of the basic epistemological and ontological assumptions that guide this book will be addressed. In the second part I will briefly turn to the reception of poststructuralism within the discipline of International Relations, focusing in particular on questions of methodology. On this basis, the third part will turn to the discussion and critique of the three major poststructuralist works on sovereignty.

From reality to discourse

Turning to the first question: why should state sovereignty be studied as a discursive practice, rather than as an objective reality; as a question of how it is spoken of, rather than what it is? The short and declaratory answer is that state sovereignty cannot be investigated independently of our theories, language, thoughts and practices. We cannot know, define or grasp the reality of sovereignty from a position prior to, or outside of, our appropriations and interpretations. Sovereignty is nothing in itself before speech and practice. Moving from a question of being to a question of becoming, thus, means that one studies how state sovereignty is practised and spoken of, rather than what the reality and essence of sovereignty is, or might be. It implies that state sovereignty is approached as a historical and ongoing practice – always in the making – rather than as an already fixed and ahistorical entity. Accordingly, one will not find a definition of state sovereignty within this book. Not only because this would evade the historicity of state sovereignty – as Nietzsche so famously argued, "only that which has no history can be defined" – but also because this book claims that state sovereignty's meaning has not changed "merely" over time (Nietzsche 1956: 212). Even within the same time, multiple meanings and usages of state sovereignty coexist. By making a prior definition of sovereignty I would hence close, on the level of definition, that very object which this book intends to study.

From the contention that the world – for example, state sovereignty – is only present to us and only becomes intelligible through discourse, it does not, however, follow that the world does not exist independently of language and thought. The rather different assertion is that the world (reality) cannot be accessed, understood or rendered meaningful in the absence of speech and interpretation and that reality therefore ceases to constitute an already given empirical referent which knowledge and truth must correspond and refer to. Thus, the poststructuralist assertion is not – at least in the version of this book – that, for instance, "the Holocaust" or "the Gulf War" did not happen, but that we can only know what the Holocaust is through discourse. The Holocaust, to put it bluntly, does not entail any meaning or being before articulations, but comes into being through articulations. As Laclau and Mouffe often are quoted:

> The fact that every object is constituted as an object of discourse has *nothing to do* with whether there is a world external to thought, or with the realism/ idealism opposition. An earthquake or the falling of a brick is an event that certainly exists, in the sense that it occurs here and now, independently of my will. But whether their specificity as objects is constructed in terms of natural phenomena or expressions of the wrath of God depends upon the structuring of a discursive field.
>
> (Laclau and Mouffe 1985: 108)

Similarly, whether the Gulf War constituted an attempt to create a new world order, to protect the territorial integrity of Kuwait from aggression, or to secure the West's strategic interest in the Middle East; which kind of subjects (the international community, neo-colonial imperialists, or a new hegemonic superpower) were involved; with which motivations, interest and intentions this subject acted; and how "we" – for instance, International Relations scholars – are able to know and assess these motivations and justifications distinguishing them, for instance, from rhetoric and manipulations, is – just as in the case of the earthquake – dependent on how the Gulf War has been and continues to be discursively structured and restructured. This does not imply that discourse is to be equated with mere opinions or ideas. Neither is discourse to be seen as synonymous with language as a signifying tool.

What then is to be understood by the concept of discourse? Albeit no unanimous definition exists, it seems fair to claim that discourse is generally taken to denote an order, or a field, that makes specific beings and practices intelligible and knowledgeable, and makes us who we are, and what we do and think (see, for example, Foucault 1984b; Milliken 1999; Åkerstrøm Andersen 2002; Simons 1995). Or more specifically along the Foucauldian definition, a discourse is a group of statements, which govern the production of objects, concepts and subjects (Foucault 1972). Thus, a given discourse orders the production of a number of subject positions, which grants individuals or groups a position to speak authoritatively and meaningfully about certain objects and concepts and delineates these individuals as acting and wilful subjects. For instance, discourses on international politics typically organize the production of sovereign states, diplomats, heads of states or international organizations as purposeful and acting subjects who are allowed to act and speak about certain objects and concepts, for instance, war, peace and cooperation. Yet, these subjects cannot speak in any way they like if their statements are to be taken seriously. A discourse will similarly entail criteria, which makes it possible to differentiate between, for instance, true and false, normative and objective, invalid and valid, absurd and reasonable statements (Foucault 1972: 115). To use an example from the chapter on Algeria, not just any kind of propositions were taken to be legitimate when Western leaders, officials, commentators and intellectuals were speaking about the Algerian crisis. Notably, a sharp boundary was drawn between judgemental/punitive enunciations on the one hand, and empathetic and understanding enunciations on the other. One had to speak in terms of the latter rather than in terms of the former, if statements were not to be disregarded and rejected as improper and untimely.

To counter a common (mis)perception, it should hence be emphasized that studying the world as discourse does not imply that the world can simply be constructed in a different image according to our instrumental preferences or aesthetic likings. As Negri and Hardt also caution, having recognized that identities are contingent and arbitrary constructs does not mean that they evaporate into thin air. "They are real illusions and continue to function as if they were essential" (Hardt and Negri 2000: 129). To argue that the world is discursively constructed does not mean that we willingly and self-consciously can make up, for instance, alternative subject positions. For example, a housewife will not easily be accepted as an acting subject in international politics nor as an authoritative speaker on the object of International Relations. Similarly, showing that, for instance, national interest is a discursive construction does not imply that the very concept of interest ceases to constrain how we can talk, know and practise international politics. Poststructuralists, in other words, view the world as relatively rule-bound and regulated. Albeit knowledge and identities always are, in principle, regarded as contingent and arbitrary, which specific identities an individual might occupy in a given situation, or which kinds of statements that are accepted as meaningful are relatively restricted (Jørgensen and Phillips 1999: 14). Discourses set specific limits for being and knowledge; limits for what we can possibly think, say and do, and who this "we" might be. Studying discourse is, hence, in this Foucauldian version, a matter of identifying those conditions of possibilities under which we can say, think and do, as we do, of analysing and reflecting upon the limits of being and knowing (Foucault 1984b, 1972).

Yet, in contrast to Kant, Foucault – and poststructuralists in general – do not view these limits as necessary, transcendental or universal, but as contingent, open and historically produced. This is one of poststructuralists' most crucial points. It makes it possible to show how what we presently take for granted has been different, how the world is open to various discursive fixations and how we have thought differently about, for instance, health, punishment, international politics or state sovereignty. This in itself constitutes a political intervention and a specific form of critique.[3] As Johnson explains in Derrida's *Disseminations*:

> The critique reads back from what seems natural, obvious self-evident or universal, in order to show that these things have their history, their reasons for being the way they are, their effects on what follows from them, and that the starting point is not a (natural) given but a (cultural) construct, usually blind to itself.
>
> (Johnson in Derrida 1981: xvi)

This type of critique should, however, not be seen as yet another attempt to transcend discursive limits, or as a new form of ideology critique where only the poststructuralist analyst seemingly is able to access the truth and disclose the hidden workings of power. The analyst does not stand in a point outside of, or "uncontaminated" by, discourse. Poststructuralists rather work with and use the concepts of discourses, operating on the border of our historical constructions. No attempts are made to transgress what is said, thought and done, or to dominate the said from an exterior sovereign position. It is not a matter of creating an exterior space from where the schisms of modernity can be evaluated, criticized or escaped. Whether in the form of "Derridean deconstruction" or of "Foucauldian discourse analysis", such textual strategies do not claim to hold a privileged access to the world. They do not attempt to evaluate the truth and rightness of competing representations or to disclose particular discourses as rhetoric or fraud. As Derrida emphasized:

> We have no language – no syntax and no lexicon – which is foreign to this history: we can pronounce not a single deconstructive proposition which has not already had to slip into the form, the logic and the implicit postulations of precisely what it seeks to contest.
>
> (Derrida 1978: 280)

Hence, poststructuralism does not offer a new solution or foundation upon which we can be directed to better policies or proceed towards a superior version of the world.[4] Walker's analysis of sovereignty, as we will see on p. 12, is a good example of how a poststructuralist reading can unravel the conceptual linkages between sovereignty and the core concepts of International Relations. Walker shows how the conceptualization of sovereignty has profound consequences for the way we perceive politics and identity, but his analysis cannot escape or transcend itself (for example, by pointing to alternative forms of political organization than the sovereign state).

While poststructuralists, thus, depart from the modern foundations of Enlightenment, they do not offer a new (postmodern) safe haven, from where we can point to new directions and redeem modernity's promises of freedom, truth and emancipation.[5] This has often led to accusations of political nihilism and scientific relativism. Yet, emphasizing the contingency and discontinuity of our historical constructs, pointing to the politics involved in what often appear as innocent and self-evident discursive practices – be they scientific discourses, the drawing of a map, or legitimations of intervention – do not necessarily lead to a blasé posture of indifference. Poststructuralist studies may make us less prone to accept self-evident truths and the powerful invocations of the good, the moral, the true and the right – this often is referred to as the nihilistic or relativistic side of poststructuralism – but the other side of that coin should be underscored as well. If we believe, as Torfing has emphasized, that

> what is ethically good or morally right is guaranteed by God, rationality or the essence of Man, we might be less inclined to participate actively in the preservation of those ethical and moral values than if we realized that only our responsible defence of what is good and right will ensure the persistence of our ethical and moral standards.
>
> (Torfing 1999: 288)

Or as Ole Wæver has argued with reference to Nietzsche – the supposed nihilism of Nietzsche does not equate to "demolishing values". Rather, since "there is no stable foundation for given values ... we must create values" (Wæver 1989b: 40).

The implication of "constructivism" is, in other words, itself a source of construction! The consequences of the disappearances of any assured foundations is itself a matter of interpretation and appropriations, which can equally turn into despair and passivity as rejoicing and activism. Without taking a grand detour into the Habermas/Foucault debate, I will argue that Habermas' critique of Foucault and poststructuralists in general is conditioned on this grand contention of Enlightenment, which tells us that political activism and critique must be based on a solid foundation of universal moral and communicative reason. Without it, Habermas cannot contemplate any reason "to take up the fight", or engage in academic practices. The absence of safe foundations must translate into paralysis and indifference (Habermas 1987: 287; see also Simons 1995: 110–16; Campbell 1998b: 502).[6] Dreyfus and Rabinow (1982: 95) surprisingly voice a somewhat similar critique, arguing that Foucault's archaeological description of discourses "prevents him from offering any account of which social issues should be taken seriously and what might be done about them. Archaeology ... can never enter the debates which rage around the moments it studies". Foucault and Derrida are, however, both good examples of poststructuralists who personally took the latter consequence of "constructivism", working for prison reforms, Médecins sans Frontières, the rights of Algerian immigrants in France and Czech Charter 77 dissidents, and against apartheid in South Africa (see also Campbell 1998b). Although this book does not, and has no intentions of, providing a manual for political action or a safe foundation upon which the truth or rightness of prevailing discourses can be judged, the political is not absent or removed from the analysis. I do not offer any policy advice or normative prescriptions; neither do I draw lessons from Kosovo, nor evaluate the legitimacy of intervention and non-intervention. Yet the analysis of the discourses on Kosovo and Algeria may, for instance, serve to emphasize the depoliticizing effects of a moral language of humanitarian intervention, the power involved in invocations of threats or the seemingly neutral delimitation of who are fundamentalist terrorists. Hopefully, this book will also display those discursive strategies and conditions of possibilities, which served to portray the conflict in Kosovo as an international responsibility where "our" future and identity was at stake, and those which served to tell us that Algeria's problems never could be ours; that our primary identity and obligations reside within territorial boundaries. Revealing the fluidity of the boundary of national and international, the contingency of the definition of the competencies and authorities of states, and the unquestioned foundations of sovereignty, may also caution those International Relations theorists and commentators who often too readily reproduce these divides.

Receptions

These epistemological assertions and discussions are obviously not new to the discipline of International Relations, although they arrived conspicuously late. A relatively small number of International Relations theorists have over the span of two decades sought to push this agenda into the discipline, setting some of International Relations' core concepts in motion. They have contributed to shaking disciplinary boundaries and hitherto agreed assumptions (see, for example, Der Derian 1987; Shapiro 1988; Ashley 1987; Walker 1987). Through genealogical studies or deconstructive readings, poststructuralists within International Relations have asked a new set of questions and turned theories into discursive practices rather than neutral representations or explanations of an already given reality. Asking how, for instance, diplomacy, security or sovereignty have been discursively produced and sustained over time, poststructuralists have displayed how International Relations theories themselves participate in the construction and re-construction of international politics as a specific realm of power, anarchy and insecurity; as the very negation of the domestic community, marked by an absence of progress, truth and freedom. Deconstructing the seemingly stable divides between, for example, realism and idealism, national and international politics and relations, these works have sought to denaturalize or politicize what has most commonly been

Sovereignty as discourse 7

agreed upon. Since the 1990s several new empirical studies have also emerged, for example, on European foreign policy, immigration or relief aid (see Bigo 2001; Wæver 1995a; Hansen 1998; Dillon 1995; Der Derian 1992; Williams 1998; Bartelson 1995; Campbell 1992; Weber 1995; Huysmans 1995, 2000; Doty 2000; Edkins 2000).[7] This diverse set of studies have opened up the discipline to a new space of investigation, where the world can be studied as text, as a continuous construct always in the making, rather than as a timeless essence to be represented and defined most accurately.

This book's claim to novelty does therefore neither rest on the introduction of poststructuralist thoughts nor on a sketchy philosophical critique of foundational theories. Rather, as I will spell out further below, the claim to novelty can only be made with explicit reference to existing poststructuralist literature – by an overt attempt to draw on and discuss the existing poststructuralist works on sovereignty.

While what is in International Relations somewhat oddly referred to as "constructivism"[8] has now gained a relatively firm hold within the discipline – embracing the notion that "propositions can be tested against evidence" (Krasner 1999: 49) – this rapprochement between rationalist and constructivist has in many ways contributed to further radicalization and marginalization of poststructuralists who, just as in the 1980s, can claim to constitute dissident voices situated on the border of the discipline (Milliken 1999: 227; Wæver 1996: 168). This in turn also makes it much easier to discharge poststructuralists, at best through readings of secondary literature, and at worst not at all (Smith 1996a). Oversimplifications and outright misunderstandings are evident results. Poststructuralist studies are often disqualified as idealist or relativist which, in the case of the former, merely explain the harsh realities of international life by inter-subjective values and ideas where the forces of power and materiality have become completely absent (Mearsheimer 1995; Walt 1991), or in terms of the latter, as a set of obscure destructive writings, which have sawed off the very branch they are sitting on. Especially the latter studies have gained momentum and served to distinguish constructivist from poststructuralist, ontology from epistemology, and the subjective from the objective (see, for example, Jackson and Sørensen 1999: 237; Krasner 1999: 47; Katzenstein 1996: 67).[9]

These superficial and stereotyping accounts are by no means helped by an unfortunate tendency within poststructuralist studies themselves to resurrect old ghosts, refusing to engage in discussions of shared assumptions and means to carry out discourse analysis for example (Ashley and Walker 1990a; Ashley 1996; George 1994; Campbell 1996; Der Derian 1989). Rather than positioning one's study in relation to already existing poststructuralist work on the subject, poststructuralist writings often seem more preoccupied with outlining a so-called traditional or orthodox approach. Characteristically, in a recently edited volume on *Sovereignty and Subjectivity*, the concluding chapter spends ten pages out of eleven criticizing what is described as the "mainstream and neo-orthodoxy" of International Relations theory rather than attempting to spell out which alternative insights the various contributions have produced (Persram 1999). Applying labels such as "traditional", "mainstream" and "orthodoxy" of course serves, just as the application of "nihilism" and "dangerous science" (Walt 1991), to exclude and stigmatize, while rendering one's own position superior, thereby undermining the often proclaimed virtues of diversity and pluralism. Yet, that is not to say that positioning can or should be avoided. I will, however, argue that as long as poststructuralists mainly define their research projects in relation to foundationalist literature – through definitions of "what they are not" – debates among poststructuralists and between poststructuralists and "foundationalists" are seriously restrained, and this in turn comes to substantiate the frequently voiced critique against poststructuralism, as an "anything goes" approach.

There are indeed good reasons for poststructuralists' resistance in terms of proceeding along the lines of defining a "research programme", engaging in methodological disputes, and departing from the ritual critique of foundationalism. The most pressing reasons are, which I will return to in more depth in the next chapter, that poststructuralists generally view questions of methodology as attempts to silence, exclude and normalize, hence rendering only *one* perspective valid. By granting priority to methodological rules, poststructuralists argue, the seemingly innocent rules of procedure come to sneak ontology in through the backdoor. Rules of method come to decide what exists and does not exist, thus producing the very object of investigation (Åkerstrøm Andersen 2002). As I will elaborate on in more detail in the next chapter, the "anything goes approach" can be avoided without this leading to homogenization and ontologization.

In an attempt to steer free of the above-mentioned pitfalls and misunderstandings, the remaining part of this theoretical chapter will not take a long journey through the "traditional" literature on sovereignty. Since the already existing poststructuralist studies have accounted meticulously for the assumptions and epistemology that mark the foundationalist literature, I will not repeat this manoeuvre or apply it to the latest studies on sovereignty and intervention. I will instead start from the three monumental poststructuralist writings on state sovereignty: Walker's (1993) *Inside/Outside*, Bartelson's (1995) *Genealogy of Sovereignty*, and Weber's (1995) *Simulating Sovereignty*. The discussion of their work will function as a means to traverse many of those assumptions that guide much of the current literature on sovereignty. Moreover, the works of these three authors will also be treated as instructive examples of how state sovereignty can be, and has been, analysed when we ask how sovereignty is produced, rather than what sovereignty is. Finally, introducing these theorists is a way to bring in some of the thoughts and analytical strategies of Michel Foucault and Jacques Derrida in particular. Hence again, rather than engaging in a long summary of the differences and various receptions and interpretations of Derrida and Foucault – which have flooded the humanities in the last decades – I will focus on how Walker, Bartelson, and Weber concretely apply their works and how that shapes their analytical frameworks (see, for example, Deleuze 1988; Dreyfus and Rabinow 1982; Simons 1995; Edkins 1999).[10] In short, the aim is to display how the analytical and theoretical decisions made bear consequences for what each study can and cannot answer, and hence what might be overlooked or excluded due to the different theoretical and analytical starting points.

Three works on sovereignty

The following part will be divided into three large sections: the first focusing on the strategy of deconstruction applied by Walker as well as Bartelson, the second and third on two different Foucauldian strategies, genealogical and archaeological, employed by Bartelson and Weber.[11] To each of the three authors I will ask three straightforward questions: What is the object of analysis, and which more or less implicit analytical strategy is employed to study that object? What are the main insights of the analysis? And what do the questions asked inhibit each study from analysing? Moving from Walker to Bartelson and finally to Weber it will be argued that sovereignty is "progressively" opened up, but that none of the three authors combines an analysis which takes account of contingency of state sovereignty in time as well as space.

Walker and Bartelson – deconstructing a discipline, deconstructing its core concepts

Through a reading of International Relations texts, especially the modern Anglo-American theories associated with realism, Walker sets out to investigate those assumptions, concepts and principles that the discipline is predicated on, notably the concept of state sovereignty. International Relations theory is in this way approached as a discursive practice. Rather than being seen as explanations of international politics, they are seen as discursive articulations of those international processes, which they claim to explain (Walker 1993: 159). To put it differently, rather being representations of what is already there, theories of International Relations are seen as "participators" in the continuous production and reproduction of what state sovereignty means.

Walker views the discipline as a practice simultaneously relying on the unquestioned foundation of state sovereignty, while at the same time reproducing this very concept. State sovereignty and the discipline of International Relations hence function as simultaneous objects of investigations in Walker's analysis.

This means that there is an inevitable yet productive circular logic involved, which we will also find in Bartelson's and Weber's studies: International Relations is both seen as a practice that (re)produces sovereignty, and as a practice made possible by sovereignty. Sovereignty is constitutive of International Relations and International Relations is constitutive of sovereignty. Walker does not, however, raise or tackle this circular logic on an analytical level. Similarly, neither does he spell out explicitly which poststructuralists' concepts and ideas he employs or is inspired by. One can, however, argue that his study can mainly be read as a Derridean deconstruction with a touch of Foucault. The aim is to expose a range of the discipline's binary opposition founded on the principle of sovereignty. This serves to: "destabilise the assumptions take[n] for granted, then show[ing] how other ways of thinking might be opened up" (Walker 1993: 23).

Deconstruction is, in a very condensed form, a reading of texts which asks to the premises, possibilities and binary oppositions whereby meaning is produced. By the use of the text's own concepts and hierarchies, the deconstructive move consists of reversing the binary oppositions. What is treated as a negative, marginal or supplementary version of the first privileged term is proven to be the condition of possibility for the first term (Culler 1983: 213). This is an immanent form of critique, which does not stand outside the text, and which does not relate the text to reality or sign to signified. The reversal is, however, only the first move. Merely to reverse the hierarchy would be to stay within the logic of the oppositions. It would only be a move "from one concept to another". In a second move, the deconstructive strategy is therefore to displace the conceptual order and subvert the text's oppositions. It is still a reading within the text, but it draws attention to the marginal and silenced, which folds the text back on itself (Derrida 1978: 21; Culler 1983: 213). Deconstruction is, in this sense, a double-gesture or double-writing. Furthermore, deconstruction can, according to Derrida, be carried out in two ways. It can either take the form of an ahistorical demonstration, which through a formal, logical analysis of texts points to tensions and paradoxes, or it can take the form of a more interpretative and historical reading, which Derrida, for instance, has carried out in relation to Plato, Freud, Rousseau and Marx (Derrida 1992; Edkins 1999: 65).

I will contend that Walker uses both strategies. In *Inside/Outside* one will find careful readings and (re)interpretations of Max Weber, Machiavelli and Hobbes; readings that are carried out against the dominant interpretations of these authors within International Relations and aim to undermine the discipline's seemingly innocent reference to a three-century-long intellectual "tradition", or even a tradition stretching all the way back to the Greek city states and Thucydides (Walker 1993). Yet one will also find the more formal and logical way of deconstruction, where Walker through his reading of present debates, unravels the premises, paradoxes and binary oppositions that these debates continue to reproduce. Although the two are intimately linked, it is in many ways through the latter strategy that Walker analyses sovereignty and its political effects.

Having outlined Walker's object of study and the "analytical strategies" by which this object is studied, we can now proceed to some of the main insights produced by Walker's analysis of the sovereignty/International Relations nexus, first addressing sovereignty.

Sovereignty, Walker shows, is a powerful modern resolution to questions of political identity and the tension between universality and particularity, unity and diversity. This tension is not new, Walker argues. In the Middle Ages it was, however, solved differently by a hierarchical rather than horizontal subordination. Sovereignty is a modern articulation of universality/particularity, and a very elegant and powerful one. Sovereignty is, in Walker's terminology, a spatio-temporal resolution that effectively answers who and where we are. It is a spatial resolution, in that it has confined political identity within an exclusive territorial boundary. Within this boundary the good and the true can be realized. But is it only within particularistic communities that the universal can be achieved; only within that politics can occur. The absence of community and authority on the outside, rising from the primacy and monopoly of political identity on the inside, predicates an anarchy of radical difference and continuous insecurity. The Other, as a spatial Other, takes the form of an enemy thereby leading to "an ethics of absolute exclusion", where ethical principles can only be applied within the bounded space of the sovereign state. This spatial side of sovereignty also bears temporal consequences. Universal and ethical principles can only be realized within the spatially confined community. It is here that progress, development and politics can be actualized. On the outside, in contrast, improvements, history and politics are impossible. The outside is characterized by mere repetition and recurrence, being a sheer realm of relations.

State sovereignty, according to Walker, is a modern solution which produces a whole set of binary pairs that are woven into one another in a long chain of equivalence: inside/outside, self/other, politics/relations, realism/idealism, International Relations/ethics, presence/absence, progress/repetition, self/other, the empirical/normative.

Walker reverses several of these hierarchies. I will here very briefly describe two such deconstructive moves, the first concerned with the perhaps most important pair – inside/outside. Walker shows that the outside in International Relations theories is read only as a *negation* of, rather than as different from, the domestic community. Through this negation all other characteristics come to follow in the form of absence. The international, as absence, is predicated on the national, as presence. Only through a prior conceptualization and assumption about political life within, is it possible to say something about life on the outside. The inside becomes the condition of possibility for the outside. This reversal also allows Walker to deconstruct a whole number of other binary oppositions, for instance, between realism/idealism. Usually, realism is read as the dominant tradition in International Relations. It is taken to be the privileged position from where one can speak about the "real" dynamics of International Relations. Walker, however, reverses this hierarchy by showing how realism and idealism are predicated on the same notions, and hence how idealism in fact is the dominant tradition of International Relations (Walker 1993: 74). Realism's claims about plurality, difference and anarchy on the outside can only take place in the background of the proclaimed universalism by idealism. Realists and idealists differ in terms of whether or not it is possible to realize an international community, but they both rely on the same domestic analogy. For both realist and idealist, the international (community) can only be conceptualized as the domestic community writ large. The foundation of realism and idealism is, in short, the same.

Turning to Walker's investigation of the International Relations discipline, I will focus on his analysis of what could be called "history and sovereignty", and the so-called "division of labour between International Relations theory and political theory". Walker argues that by leaving sovereignty unquestioned, International Relations theories have come to read the future as well as the past on the basis of the principle of state sovereignty, thereby inscribing a continuity on the present, past and future. Since sovereignty always constitutes the point of beginning, present changes or future directions become matters of whether sovereignty is defunct or as present as ever. Without an (historical) understanding of "where we come from", it becomes impossible to envisage alternative trajectories or identities. The unquestioned foundation of sovereignty does not only have significant consequences for the way in which contemporary and future paths are written, but equally have significant consequences for the writing of the past. History comes, in International Relations theory, to take the form of continuities, from the Greek city-states to the Renaissance and the modern codification of sovereignty. This allows the discipline to draw a long uninterrupted line of permanence from Thucydides to Machiavelli and Hobbes, where similar patterns of international conflict can be detected again and again. By forgetting the history and contingency of sovereignty, sovereignty emerges as a static phenomenon, which can be grasped by making the correct definition. Or rather, by the repeated attempts to treat sovereignty as a question of finding that definition which most accurately corresponds to its essence, "a certain amnesia about its historical and culturally specific character" has been encouraged (Walker 1993: 166).

Through the discipline's continued evasion of sovereignty's historical contingency, the apparent natural division of labour between political theory and International Relations theory continues to be reproduced. This has crucial consequences for the way in which legitimate research questions can be asked and answered by International Relations theory, as well as of course political theory. It also carries important implications for the way in which sovereignty is defined and addressed. When sovereignty is read from the inside – as a centralization of power and authority within a given territory – the issues to be tackled, or questions to be answered, come to revolve around the convergence between people and state, the proper democratic procedures by which this is to be secured, or the possible erosion or strengthening of the state; read either in terms of its (increasing) capability to regulate civil society or its decreasing capability to control economic processes and capital flows under the sway of globalization. When sovereignty is read from the outside – as both an absence of a centralized authority (of sovereignty) and the presence of a plurality of (sovereign) states in an anarchical condition – such questions, however, disappear. Instead, debates become centred on questions of the relative importance of national interest versus the importance of international society, of the status of law and norms in the face of the ever-present possibility of conflict, or of the tensions between the principle of sovereignty and cosmopolitan claims of human rights. On the basis of sovereignty's spatial separation of inside and outside, political theorists "forget about the particularity of the community that is shown to be capable of reason, justice, democracy and liberty", while International Relations theorists in turn forget about "the extent to which their theories are coloured by the positive aspirations that are deemed to be legitimate within states" (Walker 1993: 177). The principle of sovereignty, Walker (1993: 177) concludes, "says all that is to be said, indeed all that can be said about the character and location of modern political life. *All* contradictions are resolved, and they are resolved with great elegance, style and simplicity" (italics added).

Yet, if sovereignty functions as such an elegant and powerful solution, providing us with answers to who we are, where we come from, even predicating the alternative trajectories of the future, how can we then think and practise anything different? How are we, if at all, to move away from those predefined alternatives and binary logics which sovereignty imposes? How are we to imagine alternative political identities? Or in Derrida's terms, how does Walker move from reversal/neutralization to subversion and replacement? Walker (1993: 179–83) admits, although not in these terms, that this is difficult. He seems, to a large extent, captured by his "fascination" with and formulations of sovereignty as an elegant, powerful and simplistic solution that resolves *all* modern contradictions (see also Hansen 1997a). This obviously inhibits him from envisaging alternative political identities. However, Walker does suggest tentatively that gender, culture and class can be introduced into the theories of International Relations without reading these identities through the concept of sovereignty. That is to say, without turning culture into nations or values, gender into sovereign Man, or subordinating class to nation (Walker 1993: 179–83).

In Bartelson's *Genealogy of Sovereignty*, a deconstructive strategy is similarly applied. The aim is, as with Walker, to take on a critical investigation of "empirical discourses on sovereignty", exposing what is taken to be first, privileged and original, and what conversely is read as secondary, supplementary and absent (Bartelson 1995: 18–20). Bartelson's deconstruction is, in particular, concerned with what International Relations theory and macro-sociology respectively attempt to explain, and what they assume in order to explain. On the basis of this reading, Bartelson's main argument is that International Relations theory and macro-sociology function as mirror images of one another. What the former renders as problematic and as something to be explained, the latter treats as unproblematic and given and vice versa. One, thus, finds a certain similarity with Walker's analysis of the division of labour between political theory and International Relations theory as accounted for above. Yet, Bartelson primarily draws attention to how the two perspectives explain the empirical formation of the international system and the formation of state sovereignty. He shows how macro-sociologists can only "bring the state back in" and grant the state an autonomy from society by carving out anarchy as an already given structural context, just as International Relations theory can only explain the emergence of the international system by presuming the prior presence of the sovereign state. Common for both macro-sociology and International Relations theory is that they ask ontological questions. They assume the possibility of representation and sovereign Man as subject of representation. The result is that a prior demarcation between domestic and international is presupposed. Bartelson instead suggests that sovereignty should be studied as a discourse of demarcation; as a discourse framing objects on the inside and the outside without itself being part of either. As we will see this framing varies over time and with knowledge.

To sum up, the deconstructive strategy employed by Walker and Bartelson enables them to expose what normally is treated as evident and given, to display those binary oppositions the discipline is founded on and continues to reproduce. In particular, Bartelson and Walker showed how the scientific community in its eagerness to explain must also leave something unexplained. The presumptions of presence and representation have crucial implications for how International

Relations theory accounts for change, writes the past, or envisages alternative political identities, in the case of Walker, or studies the formation of sovereignty in terms of Bartelson. The deconstructive strategy, however, is not able to substantiate its theoretical claim about sovereignty's historical contingency or the continuous variation of framing over time. This can only remain a mere claim. Walker very effectively analyses the present – especially disciplinary – effects of sovereignty and suggests how politics and political life might be analysed by concepts other than those associated with the sovereign state. But he cannot show how it has been different, or how it may become different.[12] Sovereignty, especially in Walker's analysis, comes to suck everything in. It tends to explain and solve everything. In Walker's reading of the discipline, there are no competing articulations, no "great many meanings", neither in space nor in time (Nietzsche 1956). They all seem to be expressions of the same modern resolution. Consequently, it becomes difficult to propose change, or rearticulate space and time in other ways than the powerful resolution of state sovereignty has, and possibly continues to do. To be able to account for difference, contingency and historicity one has to turn to other analytical strategies. This leads us, at first, to Bartelson's *genealogy* of sovereignty.

From deconstruction to construction

Bartelson's aim is to write a history of sovereignty, but a history that does not assume a prior meaning or referent. The object must, in Bartelson's (1995: 53) words, be "held in suspense" in order to refrain from any prior ontologization of sovereignty. The powerful distinction between inside and outside is accordingly turned into an object of investigation. Asking how this distinction came into being, and how it was drawn and redrawn inside knowledge, Bartelson's main contention is that the transformation of sovereignty takes place in close interdependence with transformations of knowledge. Knowledge produces, sustains and legitimizes a certain conceptualization of sovereignty, and sovereignty produces, sustains and legitimizes a certain form of knowledge. Knowledge and sovereignty are mutually constitutive. Hence, again we find the poststructuralist circuit between the object of investigation and the discursive practice through which this object is produced. Whereas Walker did not raise this as an analytical issue, Bartelson elaborates on the circular relationship. The sovereignty/knowledge circuit is held open for various meanings and there is accordingly no fixed conceptual relationship between the two. Bartelson also explains how this productive relationship of sovereignty/knowledge works through reproduction (supplementation), production (articulation) and duplication (Bartelson 1995: 6–7). In short, where Walker assumes a particular modern relationship between sovereignty and knowledge, Bartelson turns this into an object of investigation.

How can such a history without an object be written? How does one write a history of a fluid sovereignty/knowledge nexus? In order to do so, Bartelson suggests a combination of Foucault's *archaeological* and *genealogical* strategies, however, employing both with some minor modifications. A Foucauldian archaeology, to recap some of my initial remarks, seeks to *describe* the formation of discourses. It studies language as specific types of statements – different from propositions, sentences and speech acts. Statements are not analysed as representations of an object, or as expressions or thoughts of a sovereign subject, but as discursive *events*, which constitute objects, concepts and subjects. A statement is analysed as an event, because it brings something into being. It makes something appear and discourse analysis is accordingly "about pure descriptions of these discursive events" (Foucault 1972: 27). Being descriptive, a discourse analysis is not a commentary. It is not an effort to reduce statements to something else, be they intentions, structure or context. Statements must be accepted at face value (Foucault 1972: 109). How are statements and discourse related? Discourse is, in Foucault's definition, a group of statements that are linked to one another by those general *rules* that govern the production of object, subject and concepts. "Whenever one can describe between a number of statements a system of dispersion, whenever between objects, types of statements, concepts or thematic choices, one can define a regularity ... we are dealing with a discursive formation" (Foucault 1972: 38). This is the first point where Bartelson chooses to depart from Foucault's archaeology and turn to Foucault's genealogy. Bartelson's critique is, in brief, that it remains uncertain whether the rules that "govern" discursive formations are part of discourse or residing outside of discourse; being a form of causal laws which determine – and are able to explain – the emergence of subjects, object and concepts (Bartelson 1995: 72; Dreyfus and Rabinow 1982: 79ff). The former interpretation seems most consistent with Foucault's break with structuralism as well as with the conscious and intentional subject, but makes Foucault unable to account for the transition from one discourse to another (Bartelson 1995: 72).[13] In order to explain transformations of discursive formations, Bartelson chooses to combine an archaeological strategy – describing what we could call discursive spaces of regularities – with a genealogical accounting for temporal discontinuities.[14] I will very briefly point to some of the main assumptions and aims of a genealogical analysis necessary in order to appreciate Bartelson's study as well as the diachronic analyses of this book.

Genealogy was originally outlined by Nietzsche in his *The Birth of Tragedy and the Genealogy of Morals* and further explored by Foucault (Nietzsche 1956; Foucault 1977a). Genealogy is a specific way of writing and approaching history, which abandons the quest for ever knowing the past as it really was, writing history from a perspective outside of history, and presupposing the very object, subjects and concepts, whose emergence is to be explained. A genealogy is, Foucault (1977a: 153) explains: "A history without constants. Nothing in man – not even his body – is sufficiently stable to serve as the basis for self-recognition or for understanding of other men".

Accordingly, a genealogy does not claim to be able to represent the past as it actually unfolded and progressed. It rather proceeds from the assumption that the past is always interpreted by present concerns – that any writing of history is formed by the present and carried out within the present, including its own. As Bartelson (1995: 78) also puts it, "it is we and only we who do the interpretations [of earlier interpretations]. If genealogical history happens to be rewritten, it is because the present changes. If the present changes, it is partly because history is rewritten". A genealogist is, in this sense, more interested in the present than the past. The aim is to problematize the present by constructing a counter-memory. A genealogy is to question and historicize current discourses and their appropriation of objects, subjects and concepts tracing them back to those relations of power and knowledge under which they were formed.[15] History is, in other words, studied as a series of battles between different interpretations. Not in the form of a gradual "progress from combat to combat", but as a "violent and surreptious appropriation of a system of rules, which in itself has no meaning" (Foucault 1977a: 151–2).

Genealogy constitutes a break with history written as progress; as a succession of continuous events moving towards a telos, as well as history as a search for origin and timeless essence – a break with finalism as well as with presentism. History is neither written as a great totality of monumental high point, imposing a continuity of similarities and analogies between past and present where the past is recognizable and all too familiar, nor is it written in order to conserve the past in an ever-restless attempt to maintain our roots in the present. A genealogy is to cut off roots and traditions, writing a different history of our source and identity and directing itself against reality, identity and truth (Foucault 1977a: 160–4). In other words, a genealogy must disturb the recognition of the past in the present. It introduces discontinuities rather than continuity, dissolves origins of identity, uproots traditional foundations and ceases to judge the past in terms of a truth only available in the present (Foucault 1977a: 160–4).

Starting from the identification of a present *problématique* and our present discourse on sovereignty, Bartelson (1995: 54) asks: "how and by what means the differentiation between inside and outside, sameness and otherness was carried out. How sovereignty in its modern guise, became both an empirical and transcendental concept?"

Bartelson divides his writing of sovereignty/knowledge into three epochs – the Renaissance, the Classical Age, and Modernity – distinguishable by different regularities governing statements. His aim is to describe each discursive formation as well as the transitions between them.

Starting in the Middle Ages and early Renaissance, Bartelson shows how knowledge and political rule derive from God and how everything outside of the state is beyond political knowledge. In fact, state sovereignty itself is a concept without meaning in the Renaissance. With the so-called Classical Age, the concept of sovereignty, however, enters political discourse. Sovereignty becomes linked both to the immortal state as a whole – as a space of power and interest – and to the King. The King is identified with the state and the state with the King. Simultaneously, a new episteme of knowledge is formed. In this new episteme, knowledge is based on representation. Truth is a matter of accurate representation; of the exactness of naming. This exactness is no longer guaranteed by God but by the sovereign. The sovereign emerges as a source of truth as well as of present peace in that the sovereign protects the state from its violent past. Classical theorists are also able to perceive a world of states and to draw a distinction between foreign and domestic policy; a distinction unavailable to Renaissance knowledge. Yet, this world of states is not to be conflated with the modern notion of the state system. It is not a system entailing more than the sum of its parts. Rather, Bartelson suggests, it is a "table of states" that permits the theorists to measure power and calculate interest. By Modernity in the late eighteenth century, the "international" emerges as a new concept. The "table of states" is replaced with the notion of an international system composed of sovereign nation-states. This change in the discourse on sovereignty is again conditioning, as well as conditioned by, the epistemic change in the discourse on knowledge. Bartelson argues that representation no longer constitutes an unquestioned foundation of knowledge. With Modernity Man becomes the sovereign creator of his representations while also being an object of these representations. Man takes the place of King and the discourse on sovereignty becomes centred on the relationship of Man and state rather than King and state. Sovereignty ontologically and ethically distinguishes the (nation-)state from the international and furnishes these two spheres as opposed yet mutually constitutive realms, which must be studied as separate political realities. The sovereign state can now, as we have become used to, be investigated from two vantage points: that of macro-sociology or that of International Relations theory.

Arriving at our present modern condition, Bartelson (1995: 236) rhetorically asks, as did Foucault, who is to kill Man after Man had killed the King, and the King had killed God, hence once again rendering sovereignty incomprehensible.[16] Bartelson predicts that we may expect that sovereignty will change as a result of the current critique against the foundation of modern knowledge. Yet, in contrast to earlier forms of critique, the critique directed against Modernity does not tell us what to put in the place of sovereignty, progress and transcendence. We are only, Bartelson (1995: 248) contends, left with the idea that such decisions are inherently political.

Bartelson's genealogy provides us with the "missing historical link" of Walker's analysis of the present discursive relationship between International Relations theory and sovereignty and the conditions of possibility for reading sovereignty from the outside and the inside. Much of the power and novelty – but at the same time limitations – of Bartelson's genealogy reside in his detailed and fairly abstract historical delimitation of the sovereignty/knowledge nexus. I will here very briefly raise two such limitations. First, because sovereignty in Bartelson's analysis only transforms in concurrence with transformations of epistemes, the process of change is granted an overwhelming inertia. Change it seems does not come easy.[17] As a result, sovereignty appears as a relatively closed concept whose meaning is discursively fixated (closed) over several centuries. Sovereignty, in fact, emerges as a rather solid point of reference within the three epochs. Although Bartelson (1995: 3) initially contends that sovereignty in form and content differ across space and time, we only see variations in terms of time. Second, focusing on knowledge as the "producer of change" is of course an analytical choice which legitimately excludes other forms of discursive practices that also may participate in the production and reproduction of sovereignty. Yet, by that choice it becomes much more difficult to envisage or appreciate how sovereignty is reproduced (or possibly changed) outside disciplinary discourses. Sovereignty comes to take on an endurance of elusive philosophy; a discursive practice open to political scientists and philosophers alone. Confined within a philosophical discursive realm, it remains difficult to imagine how politicians, commentators, diplomats and a whole range of other subjects entitled to speak in the name of sovereignty are also engaged in continuous struggles over sovereignty, and hence also may change and fixate meanings of sovereignty. In order to show how sovereignty is enacted – out of lack of a better term – in "everyday political life", and how it also serves as a powerful foundation within a multiplicity of political practices – besides discourses on knowledge – we will need to open up the concept further and propose a new set of analytical strategies. This will, as a first step, lead us to engage with Cynthia Weber's analysis of the intervention/sovereignty nexus.

Sovereignty/intervention

Cynthia Weber proceeds from the poststructuralist argument that there does not exist only one type of sovereignty – or one discourse on sovereignty – in modern political life. Rather multiple forms of sovereignty coexist. Sovereignty may refer to different types of rules (democratic, authoritarian, totalitarian), and to different forms of economic systems (capitalist, socialist). It may also refer to a variety of state competencies, privileges and responsibilities, and it may be grounded in changing foundations, such as God, King and people. Meanings of state sovereignty, in short, fluctuate not only across time but also across space. Sovereignty is a continuous "site of political struggle" (Weber 1995: 3). Weber also forcefully argues that meanings of sovereignty are settled – however temporally – through a range of discursive practices and fixations of sovereignty can accordingly be studied through a number of distinct political practices. Weber chooses one, namely intervention. The aim is to study "how the meaning of state sovereignty is fixed historically via practices of international relations theorists and practices of political intervention" (Weber 1995: 3).

On the basis of an examination of the conventional literature on intervention, Weber shows how sovereignty and intervention function as conceptual opposites. Intervention is usually understood as a violation of state sovereignty and the meaning of intervention therefore comes to be derived from state sovereignty. As a consequence, International Relations theorists already operate with an – albeit often implicit – conceptualization of state sovereignty when speaking about intervention. When a certain act is defined as an intervention, it is presumed that it is already known what state sovereignty is. Short of state sovereignty, it seems impossible to speak of intervention in international politics: since "who would be the target of intervention and what would be violated or transgressed?" (Weber 1995: 11). Whether any given event constitutes an intervention or a non-intervention, is hence dependent on what meaning sovereignty is attributed in advance. In order for something to be portrayed as an intervention, there must always already be an idea of what falls and does not fall within the sovereign sphere of the state, who is and is not a member of the domestic community of the target state, who can speak on the community's behalf, and which authorities, competencies and responsibilities rest with that sovereign state. Although intervention, in principle, is open to many forms of definitions and interpretations, these definitions will all rely on and constitute a particular conception of state sovereignty.

The relationship, however, works both ways. Just as intervention is dependent on sovereignty, so is state sovereignty dependent on intervention. Intervention is one of those practices that fills out the meaning and content of state sovereignty. When state leaders justify a given intervention they are simultaneously (re)producing what is to be understood by state sovereignty. Through legitimations of intervention, boundaries are drawn between inside and outside states. Interventionary practices decide what counts as respectively international and national concerns, settle questions over the location and foundation of sovereignty and grant the target state specific authorities and competencies, while stripping it of others. The content of state sovereignty is thus not given in advance – prior to interventions – but is temporally constituted during the very process of intervention.

Sovereignty and intervention do not only function as conceptual opposites; they are also mutually constitutive. Intervention is one of those practices that gives meaning to sovereignty, while the practice of intervention at the same time only gives meaning on the backdrop of a prior conceptualization of sovereignty. Thus, we here find again the circular and productive relationship between the object of investigation – sovereignty – and the discursive practice – intervention – through which sovereignty is studied.

Which analytical strategies does Weber employ in order to investigate the historical production of sovereignty? Weber chooses three historical epochs and five cases of "intervention": European Concert's intervention in Naples in 1820, the Wilson administration's interventions in Mexico in 1920 and Siberia in 1917, and the Reagan-Bush administrations' interventions in Grenada in 1983 and Panama in 1989. Inspired by Foucault's archaeological and genealogical work and Baudrillard's work on simulation, Weber asks three broad questions of each of the five cases: (1) What is represented? (2) What are the conditions of possibility for these representations? (3) What happens when it is no longer possible to represent? The third question is justified with reference to Baudrillard's critique of Foucault's power/knowledge nexus. Based on the assumption that we have moved on to a post-representational order characterized by simulation, Baudrillard – and Weber – claim that Foucault is only able to operate within a logic of representation where truth still can be produced, because Foucault's conceptualization of power depends on the ability to refer to truth. In order to answer what happens when representation no longer is possible, Weber's analysis of the last two cases is therefore supplemented with Baudrillard's order of simulation.[18]

Starting with the European Concert's intervention in Naples, Weber shows how intervention legitimations (re)produced the monarch as the proper location and foundation of sovereign authority. The European Concert argued that if a state was constituted any differently than in the form of absolute monarchy, or if a revolution was threatening to overthrow the monarchy, the state could no longer be regarded as sovereign. According to this logic, the Concert could contend that it was, in fact, not violating the sovereign authority of Naples, but rather preserving it, because the popular revolt in Naples aimed to depose the only legitimate foundation of rule. Proceeding to the Wilson administration's interventions in Mexico and Siberia, Weber identifies a shift in the representations of the foundation and location of sovereignty. Sovereignty now resides with the people rather than the King, and the people are now the ultimate referent of sovereignty to be accurately represented via government.

In the 1980s the foundation of sovereign authority still resided with the people and it still presumed that the people ought to be represented politically by government. Yet, who the people are, could only be answered by invoking a community of judgement (Weber 1995: 92). With respect to the Reagan administration's intervention in Grenada, it was the regional Organisation of East Caribbean States (OECS) which was inscribed as the proper community of judgement. Since this community had requested military assistance from the United States and since this community included the people of Grenada, justifications could once again argue that this did not constitute an intervention. The people of Grenada are rendered synonymous with the people of the OECS and the territorial sovereignty of Grenada is replaced with the regional sovereignty of the OECS. The Panama invasion was similarly justified by the use of "the Wilsonian strategy", whereby Noriega was portrayed as an unrepresentative dictator, and the people as potential democrats to be protected by the United States.

Having analysed the question of "what is represented" in terms of Grenada and Panama, Weber moves on to the Baudrillardian perspective, arguing that the discourses on the two interventions operate according to logics of simulation rather than logics of representation. Showing how the OECS's request to the United States was fabricated in advance and how the governor general of the OECS did not possess the authority to make such a request, Weber argues that the OECS and the people of Grenada both constituted *black holes*, rather than solid ground upon which judgements or interpretations could be made. The OECS and the Grenadian people were mere artificial referents, which readily could be exchanged with other referents.[19] Similarly, in terms of the Panama invasion, Weber argues that the Endara government simulated rather than represented the will of the Panamanian people. The Panamanian people, General Noriega, the Endara government and the Bush administration all have claims to sovereignty and meaning therefore implodes. Meaning is both everywhere and nowhere.

In conclusion, Weber asserts that sovereignty does no longer have a foundation such as people or God. Sovereignty and intervention have ceased to constitute oppositional terms. They can be endlessly substituted and replaced with one another. Yet, although sovereignty no longer can be produced, it can, however, be simulated, and diplomats and state leaders continue to invoke and speak in its name. Practices of intervention, in this sense, remain one of those sites where sovereignty is produced (simulated).

Cynthia Weber very powerfully opens up the concept of sovereignty. By stressing the multiple practices that participate in the stabilization of sovereignty and by originally linking the practice of intervention with sovereignty, Weber takes the argument of sovereignty's contingency one step further than Bartelson and Walker. Simultaneously, she makes an important contribution to the conventional literature on intervention/sovereignty, which has tended to read intervention either in terms of transcendence or hypocrisy. This book is indebted to and draws much inspiration from Weber's analysis. Partly because of this inspiration, it is, however, necessary to raise a number of theoretical problems and uncertainties, which the analysis suffers from. I will here stress three issues to be further discussed and tackled in the following chapter.

The first question relates to Weber's object of investigation and the practice through which she studies that object. Weber explicitly states that it is meanings of sovereignty that are to be studied. Yet the empirical analysis also examines the fixations of the boundary of intervention and non-intervention, spelling out what in each discourse comes to be articulated as non-intervention and intervention. Through what Weber terms "interventionary practices", meanings of sovereignty, intervention and non-interventions are all turned into objects of investigation. This spurs certain analytical problems. Although I agree that it is necessary to study what counts as respectively intervention and non-intervention – qua the mutual constitutive character of sovereignty/intervention – Weber, in fact, comes to settle the meaning of intervention prior to her analysis by determining Naples, Mexico, Siberia, Panama and Grenada as examples of intervention. Second, and related to that point, it is not entirely clear how Weber defines and understands "interventionary practices". It might be argued that sovereignty, intervention and non-intervention in Weber's analysis all are constituted through official *legitimizations,* rather than through "interventionary practices". In order to untangle such questions the relationship between legitimations and intervention may need to be more thoroughly spelled out.

The third question relates to Weber's conceptualization of time and historical change. Weber aims to show "how state sovereignty has been fixated historically" and the analysis very powerfully demonstrates historical differences in fixations of sovereignty across the five cases of interventions. But we do not see how these changes come about. Each historical epoch appears to serve as an example of radically different conceptualizations of sovereignty. Yet, there is no historical account for the conditions of possibilities for this change or for how the transition between each epoch/discourse takes place. In this sense, Weber's study should perhaps foremost be seen as a *synchronic* rather than *diachronic* analysis of five intervention legitimations and their various fixations and reproductions of sovereignty. I will address some of these analytical questions in the next chapter. This chapter will end with a short conclusion on the works of Walker, Bartelson, and Weber, pointing to this book's distinct approach and main aims.

From contingency in time to contingency in time and space

This chapter's extensive survey of Walker, Bartelson, and Weber was undertaken for several purposes: first, in order to show what happens to our understanding and analyses of sovereignty when we ask how sovereignty is constituted and sustained rather than what sovereignty is; second, as a means to unravel the consequences of taking sovereignty for granted which Walker, Bartelson, and Weber all exposed through deconstructions of the existing literature; and third, as a way to point to this book's specific *problématique*. The review also serves to illustrate how the three authors' emphasis on different parts of especially Foucault's work, and the various discursive practices through which they studied sovereignty have enabled them to focus on different aspects of how sovereignty is constituted, while evidently omitting others. Walker's largely deconstructive strategy especially focused on the modern discourse on sovereignty and its effects on International Relations theory, but it could not account for how "we" became caught by this powerful resolution. Bartelson's genealogy, however, traced the conditions of possibilities of our modern episteme, and hence also of International Relations theories' dependence on and reproduction of sovereignty. It showed how sovereignty has come to work as an unthought foundation of political knowledge, just as knowledge has come to function as that ground which renders sovereignty intelligible. Cynthia Weber, on the other hand, brought constitutions of sovereignty outside of practices of knowledge, arguing for the mutually constitutive character of sovereignty and intervention. When compared one might say that each of these three authors has opened up the concept of sovereignty one more step. Bartelson "released" sovereignty from Walker's powerful modern articulation by asking how we arrived at our modern predicament and answering this question by tracing genealogical roots, mutations and transformations of a closed circuit of sovereignty/knowledge. Bartelson's detailed analysis, however, left us with a discourse on sovereignty that only very slowly changed as a result of sovereignty's dependence on transformations in epistemes. Weber "released" sovereignty from practices of knowledge, showing how intervention is one of those practices participating in the production of sovereignty.

This book will pursue some of the implications of Weber's analysis of the sovereignty/intervention nexus. It will also attempt to open up sovereignty even further by studying constitutions of sovereignty across space, but parallel time via practices of legitimations of intervention and non-intervention. In other words, the objective is to take existing poststructuralist literature on state sovereignty further by: first, embarking on a diachronic study of those prior historical processes through which respectively non-intervention and intervention were constituted as necessary acts; second, studying the hitherto unexplored practice of non-intervention legitimations; and third, studying how state sovereignty is open to various articulations within the same time.

How can such an analysis more specifically be carried out? What is to be understood by the practice of non-intervention legitimations and by synchronic and diachronic analyses? Which questions and assumptions will guide my study of discourses and how are Kosovo and Algeria to be compared? These are all important analytical, rather than theoretical or epistemological questions, to be the theme of the next chapter.

2 Analytical strategies

This book argues that constitutions of sovereignty can be studied across space but within the same time by combining a diachronic and synchronic analysis of two cases running parallel in time. Which analytical assumptions and strategies will inform such an analysis? This is the theme of this chapter. It will fall in three parts. The first part will spell out what is to be understood by an analytical strategy, why it is needed and how it is differentiated from positivist methodology. The second part engages in a brief discussion of case selection and comparison, and the third addresses the individual elements of the analytical strategy.

From positivist methodology to analytical strategy

As argued in the last chapter, it is indeed possible and necessary, also from a poststructuralist perspective, to reflect upon how one's research is carried out and how it can be discussed and criticized, without being subjected to what Feyerabend (1975) called the tyranny of positivist methodology. This fear of the "tyranny" involved when engaging in methodological disputes has been echoed by many poststructuralists within International Relations. Der Derian (1989: 7) has, for instance, argued that formal approaches to the study of discourse are too close to "the methodologism of which there is already a surfeit in international relations theory" (see also Ashley and Walker 1990b; Campbell 1996; George 1994). And, of course, Foucault (1972: 17) famously stressed "Do not ask who I am, and do not ask me to remain the same; leave to our bureaucrats and our police to see that our papers are in order."

The unwillingness to engage in considerations and discussions of "how to questions" has generally been predicated on an argument which says that such considerations over rules and methods serve to normalize, exclude and dominate. Raising methodological discussions and demands is seen as "police work", undertaken in order to discipline and control scientific borders. By spelling out criteria and assumptions, the scholar, it is argued, participates in the dominating structures of the academy and thereby comes to bring closure and silence to alternative perspectives (Ashley and Walker 1990b; Campbell 1996; George 1994).

Refusing to address issues of "how to" deliberations is, however, also a powerful means of closure, which can function to render poststructuralists immune from criticism. It may moreover give credence to "the anything goes critique" and preclude fruitful and critical dialogue among poststructuralists.[1] Recently a number of poststructuralist authors have, however, drawn attention to this, going against the tide by spelling out the many possible and different ways whereby discourse analysis can be conducted and raising some of the problems and assumptions which the various analytical choices might imply (for example, Neumann 2001a; Milliken 1999; Diez 2001; Hansen 1998; Wæver 2000, 2003). As Milliken (1999: 235), in this respect, has argued, such methodological considerations may in fact help the analyst by making it easier to read and organize one's work. This is often needed because the rather abstract theoretical notions and concepts of discourse analysis elaborated by, for instance, Foucault and Laclau and Mouffe do not give much guidance in terms of how to carry out discourse analysis in practice (for a similar point, see Jørgensen and Phillipsen 1999; Dyrberg et al. 2000). Thus, the reader as well as the analyst may benefit from more thorough explications of which analytical choices have been made in order to study the object in question.

Following a number of Danish writers I will here call such analytical reflections an *analytical strategy* (see, for example, Pedersen 1983; Åkerstrøm 2000; Kjær 1996). The term is foremost to direct attention to the fact that *how* objects of investigation are studied is an analytical choice – strategy – made by the analyst. It is not the objects of observation in themselves, which tell us how they are (wish) to be studied, but the analyst who makes objects appear, who constructs the objects of investigation. Therefore, discourses *do not exist* prior to our investigations of them, as it sometimes unfortunately seems to be implied. It is the analyst who constructs them through the analytical choices and definitions made in order to identify them in the first place. This awareness of the construction involved in any study safeguards us from the implicit ontologization made by positivist methodologies. It also serves to underline that there does not exist a set of pre-given methodologies rules, which dictates how discourses are to be investigated. From the perspective of the analytical strategist, the hesitations expressed by many poststructuralists over the effects of methodologization in terms of normalization and exclusion of alternative perspectives also become less relevant. If objects do not exist prior to our construction of them, and hence do not tell us how they are to be investigated, an infinite number of analyses and research strategies can in principle be employed. This point does not, however, preclude us from specifying how we conduct our analyses. On the contrary, it becomes all the more important.

Yet an analytical strategy does not conform, and does not aim to conform, to the positivist methodologies applied by most theories of International Relations. It cannot meet the criteria and demands, which Keohane (1988) so (in)famously outlined in his presidential address to the ISA. An analytical strategy is neither to be seen as a means to *test* poststructuralist approaches, nor as a way to furnish a set of *universal criteria* upon which poststructuralist work can be evaluated. The problem is, however, that the poststructuralist critique of Keohane's response to "reflectivism" seldom has given rise to alternative proposals or reflections over how poststructuralists more specifically conduct their analysis. It has rather served as a powerful basis from which poststructuralists once more could assure each

Analytical strategies 25

other that critique and evaluation always is synonymous with positivist science and that dialogue among "rationalists" and "reflectivists" is inherently impossible. Many poststructuralists have thus continued to render their work immune from criticism. In accordance with the incommensurability positions of the 1980s, poststructuralists have safely been able to announce: "Don't criticise me we speak different languages" (Guzzini quoted from Wæver 1996: 158).

Having said this, however, I do not believe that it is possible for any (poststructuralist) studies to account in full all of the meticulous details of the research process, or all the analytical choices made. It is an illusive quest to achieve complete methodological transparency. Neither do I believe that poststructuralists ought to construct a "normal science of discourse analysis" furnishing a Lakatonian common research programme, or spelling out the "best ways to study discourse" as Milliken (1999) proposes. To do so would exactly run counter to the poststructuralist argument about the importance of openness and plurality when conducting research. It would lead to an implicit embrace of the positivist notion that there exists a set of superior methodological means and criteria for discourse analysis. The analytical strategy, which will be outlined in this chapter, may serve as an inspiration for others, but it is certainly not to be seen as a prescription. It does not constitute a set of methodological *rules*, which signify the best way to conduct discourse analysis.

The analytical strategy has, on a more idiosyncratic level, served as a means to structure that large body of textual material which this book engages with. But even more importantly the analytical strategy commits me to the analytical choices made, opening up the analysis for critique. Hereby, it becomes possible to question the specific analytical delineations made and to unravel conceptual relations, for instance, between discourse and practice, change and reproduction.

Case selection and comparison

This book proposes to open up sovereignty in time and space by studying and comparing two cases that run closely parallel in time. Which cases, we might ask, can be employed to that purpose? Why have I chosen to compare Kosovo and Algeria and what can be achieved by such a study if we are not to be guided by prior hypotheses and theories? And can such types of questions be asked and answered at all from the epistemological perspective of this book?

While comparative studies within the social sciences usually are undertaken either in order to use the case-specific to extract something general, or in order to show how the case-specific departs from the general, this is not the intention of this book. Kosovo and Algeria are neither selected in order to infer a set of inductive propositions about the world, nor in order to conduct an empirical test of a set of theoretical hypothesis (see, for example, Lyons and Mastanduno 1995a). Accordingly I have not chosen the cases of Kosovo and Algeria because they enable me to verify or falsify a hypothesis. Classifying and justifying the selection of Kosovo and Algeria on the basis of their status as "exemplary", "paradigmatic", "extreme", "critical" or "deviant" cases hence does not make much sense (see, for example, Flyvbjerg 1991: 137ff). To categorize and select cases with reference to these typologies would have demanded that I already operated with a theory which delineated what is normal, likely and predictable, and what is abnormal, unlikely and unexpected. Only on the basis of such prior theoretical assumptions can a given case be characterized as, for instance, critical or paradigmatic. Thus, although my aim is to show how sovereignty can be articulated in several ways within the same time, I do not aim to *test* the "poststructuralist *hypothesis*" about the openness of sovereignty in space, or to *falsify* the common proposition about sovereignty's unitary existence through the finding of a "black swan". If this book were to engage in such a project it would have to employ an entirely different epistemology and methodology.

Albeit my selection of Kosovo and Algeria cannot be grounded with reference to the case typology above, I have chosen to study these two cases for two other reasons – first, and primarily, because the legitimations of the intervention in Kosovo and the non-intervention in Algeria, when briefly compared, did not only seem to differ, but also to conflict, in terms of state sovereignty's meaning. Thus, at the end of the 1990s newspapers and human rights organizations continually reported on suppression, gross violations of human rights and extrajudicial killings in Algeria as well as Kosovo; on authorities abused and on an absence of freedom and protection. But while massacres, repression and extrajudicial killings were determined as acts and events that clearly did not constitute an internal affair of Yugoslavia, this seemed much more dubious in the case of Algeria. Although the death toll of Algerian civilians had mounted to tens of thousands and the government had been accused of neglect or outright complicity in these killings, constant references were made to the need of respecting Algeria's independence and sovereignty, and the according impossibility of international involvement. In short, where the boundary was to be drawn between national and international, state authority and legitimate international responsibility, national identity and the essence of humanity, internal affairs and international obligations, did not appear to yield a similar answer in the two cases. The second reason that the two cases have been chosen is because the conflicts and the two types of legitimations run parallel in time, both undergoing a process of what we might term conflict escalation and gradual internationalization over the 1990s, and both coming to involve questions of state sovereignty and intervention, hence making it possible to undertake a parallel analysis of how state sovereignty was constituted within the same time, but across different spaces.

I am, however, not the first to have been struck by the differences as well as similarities between the cases of Kosovo and Algeria. A few scholars have contrasted Kosovo and Algeria, primarily seeking to draw international attention to events in Algeria by comparing them with events in Kosovo. Albeit these authors have not made comparative studies of the two conflicts, they have stressed differences in the way that the two conflicts have been responded to, mainly criticizing the international community for acting inconsistently by responding vigorously to the massacres in Kosovo, while responding with indifference and passivity to the massacres in Algeria. Yet to advance this type of criticism, it has to be assumed that the two conflicts in fact were similar. Only on the basis of an underlying claim about the two situations *really* being identical, can scholars ask in the name of universality (and hence identity) "why here and not there?", and accordingly replay the old chestnut of Western double standards, power politics, and rhetoric (see, for example, Spencer 1998: 127; Stora 2001: 58). Spencer, for instance, argues:

> What at first sight is puzzling, however, is that the abandonment of Algeria is without parallel in international responses to other conflicts so close to western Europe in the Mediterranean, most notably in Kosovo and the wider Balkans. External responses to the Kosovo crisis have been far from perfect, but have taken up considerably more diplomatic and military energies than Algeria, even though there is a clear parallel between the two. Both conflicts taking place within the boundaries of sovereign states, in which the governing authorities have neglected their duties in safeguarding the lives of their citizens.
> (Spencer 1998: 127)

Spencer's puzzlement, in other words, derives from the dual assumption that the two conflicts were similar and that sovereignty must mean one thing only. Both conflicts, Spencer determines, take place within the spatial confines of sovereign states and both conflicts display evidence of governing authorities having transgressed their duties towards their citizenry. On this basis of sameness, what is to be explained is the differences in the international responses leading to an intervention in Kosovo and non-intervention in Algeria. But it is only by presuming that sovereignty must be the same and the two conflicts are identical that the two responses appear as curious and puzzling.

From another and just as dominant perspective, the intervention in Kosovo and non-intervention in Algeria does not emerge as a puzzle at all. Instead, it serves as a forceful reification of the fact that international politics works as it has always worked – according to interest and power. Comparing the response of the West to the predicament of the Kosovar Albanians with that of the Kurds in Turkey – equally on the presumption of sameness – Chomsky (1999: 13), for instance, writes: "again the factors that drive policy does not seem hard to discern ... Serbia is one of those disorderly miscreants that impede the institutions of the U.S. dominated system, while Turkey is a loyal client state that contributes substantially to the project." In other words, Chomsky has no difficulty explaining the differences between the two responses, since the workings of interest and power are already assumed. Krasner is similarly not surprised by the fact that states sometimes choose to violate state sovereignty while not in others:

> At times rulers adhere to conventional norms and rules because it provides them with resources and support, at other times rulers have violated the norms, and for the same reasons ... following the conventional practices of Westphalian and international legal sovereignty might or might not be an optimal policy.
> (Krasner 1999: 24)

In short from this perspective, and in contrast to Spencer and Stora above, no anomalies are readily apparent. The cases of Kosovo and Algeria are simply versions of the same international reality; a reality that is already known – where great power interest dictates when intervention is "optimal" and when it is not – and which therefore does not give rise to puzzles or questions, but only to affirmations of the same.

This book does not attempt to analyse Kosovo and Algeria in terms of a moral puzzle or in terms of a paradigmatic reaffirmation of power politics corresponding to the arguments of respectively Spencer/Stora and Chomsky/Krasner. Instead of claiming that the two cases in fact were identical and should have been treated identically by the international community, this book aims to study how the two conflicts were discursively constructed and which international actions were taken to be possible in response to the two conflicts; how Kosovo came to be portrayed as an international affair, whereas Algeria largely came to be defined as an issue resting well within the boundaries and authorities of Algerian sovereignty.

The point is therefore not to reveal that the events in Algeria and Kosovo were equally monstrous and brutal, and yet that the international community – or alternatively the great powers – chose to approach them differently out of, for instance, hypocrisy or vested interest. Neither is the point to propose that the two cases in fact were inherently different and that it was only natural and necessary that they were responded to in different ways. Instead, articulations related to Kosovo and Algeria will be analysed at their manifest level. This implies foremost that enunciations are not seen as expressions of something else; as mere surface phenomena underneath or behind which one will find their true cause or real explanation. Statements will neither be studied as mere expressions of latent forces – be they power, intentions, interest or the unconscious – nor will distinctions be drawn between true and false statements, between what is said and what is really meant in spite of the said. By taking articulations seriously and analysing them at their manifest level, this book's point of departure is very different from that of, for instance, Chomsky and Krasner. Instead of equating articulations with rhetoric, and subsequently appealing to some extra-discursive ground – notably interest and power – from where differences between the cases of Kosovo and Algeria can be explained (away), the analysis will remain on the level of discourse; investigating those, sometimes minor, processes of articulations and selections, which conditioned the different types of legitimations; showing how these very legitimations, in turn, produced meaning to state sovereignty.

To sum up, I propose that the conflicts in Kosovo and Algeria mark out interesting cases, neither because they are essentially similar or inherently different, nor because they diverge or correspond to existing hypotheses or dominant theories, but because both conflicts came to involve questions of sovereignty and intervention and both took place at roughly the same time

Just as the justifications for selecting Kosovo and Algeria do not conform to the usual categories of case selection, neither does the analysis of the two cases correspond to what is usually understood by comparative studies. In contrast to most comparative studies, even those that employ an explicit constructivist framework,

I do not have a set of prior categories through which Kosovo and Algeria will be compared (see, for example, Kuusisto 1999). No predefined series of variables, be they, for instance, history, national characteristics, or regime type, guide the writing of the two cases. The comparison of Kosovo and Algeria is only made in the final empirical chapter *after* the analysis of each case has been carried out, and it is hence only on the basis of the prior empirical analyses of the two cases that similarities and contrasts are made between them. The reason for not carrying out a comparison throughout each chapter, but only a concluding comparison in the final chapter, is primarily – in line with the arguments above – that Kosovo and Algeria are to emerge in their own historical specificity, instead of being forced into a common narrative.

Yet the final comparative chapter will, of course, also come to install a specific perspective upon the two cases. Not by way of theory but by the very attempt to compare the two. By explicitly comparing Kosovo and Algeria, the specificities and contingencies of each case easily come to serve as a foundation for the other. That is to say, the discursive articulations and fixations related to Kosovo are analysed through the "looking glass" of Algeria, just as the articulations related to Algeria are analysed through the "looking glass" of Kosovo. In this way one might say, Kosovo is constructed – from an extra-discursive position – as that foundation or yardstick through which Algeria is evaluated and vice versa. Although this is surely not the objective of the comparison, the concluding comparison of the two cases will unavoidably install a specific (comparative) perspective upon the two cases; a perspective that was not part of the articulations related to the two cases. The strength of the comparison is, however, that it can show how those articulations, which appeared as universal, natural and evident, when compared emerge as contingent, political and specific, and hence that alternative perspectives and articulations are possible. Foremost, the comparative perspective is the means by which this book shows how state sovereignty can be articulated in multiple ways even within the same time.

We can now proceed to the third section. Here the main elements of the diachronic and synchronic strategy will be discussed.

Diachronic strategy

It should first be stressed that the diachronic strategy resembles and echoes some of the main assumptions of Foucault's genealogy. However, I have chosen *not* to use the term "genealogy" for two reasons: first, genealogical work is undertaken in order to study historical transformations of concepts (discourses) such as sovereignty, security, punishments or diplomacy; studies which usually span several centuries. Yet the historical analysis, which is carried out in relation to Kosovo and Algeria, only covers a period of less than a decade. This implies that I follow minor variations in articulations much more closely and that the description of discursive shifts and exclusions is much more detailed than those one will usually find in genealogies. Second, the purpose of the diachronic analysis is not to account for ruptures and transformations of discourses, but to account for the conditions of possibility for the legitimations of non-intervention in the case of Algeria and intervention in the case of Kosovo. The diachronic analysis is concerned with the constitution of a specific discursive event, showing the contingency of the discursive process of selections and mutations that gradually but not inevitably constructed Kosovo as an object of intervention and Algeria as an object of non-intervention.

Yet, similarly to a genealogy, the diachronic analysis is to be seen as a history of the present. It starts from a *problématique* of the present, asking how we arrived at that present situation. A history of the present – in contrast to a history of the past in terms of the present – does not only situate itself within a specific perspective or *problématique*, it also attempts to refrain from the common practice of writing history from retrospect, granting past meaning its present significance (Foucault 1977a). For example, from hindsight it easily appears as if the international community chose to ignore Kosovo although it was readily apparent that Milosevic was an unaccountable thug who could not be negotiated with, and who only waited to unleash his project of ethnic cleansing against the Kosovar Albanians. This inscription of the international community as partly complicit in the suppression of the Kosovar Albanians qua its passive stance and refusal "to do something" throughout the 1990s, is, however, an inscription which can only be made by drawing on a *present* discourse surrounding the events in Kosovo, and by inscribing passivity and "doing something" with its present significance. Similarly, in respect to Algeria, the articulations of "silence" and the arguments of the impossibility of intervention are easily written all the way back to the annulment of the parliamentary election in 1992, thereby portraying silence as a conscious policy of the West adopted right from the start. In both cases, history comes to be written and judged from a presentist position relying on a discourse that was not available at that time. Or to put it slightly differently, one reads present interest and politics back into history. Interpreting the history of Kosovo and Algeria over the 1990s as a continuous presence of passivity and silence, pretending that silence, passivity or neutrality had the same meaning, is of course equally to write history in the form of *continuities*.[2] Thus, instead of determining what was really taking place, in spite of the said; instead of writing history from hindsight, whereby it comes to erupt as a series of continuities, the diachronic analysis seeks to problematize the present. It intends to show how it could have been, and how it has been different, tracing those discursive battles and strategies that have established present meanings (Foucault 1977a).

So what constitutes my present starting point; which *problématique* do I read Kosovo and Algeria through? The two diachronic chapters on Kosovo and Algeria will be guided by the two questions briefly outlined in the Introduction. Based on the contention that intervention is recognized and reproduced as a problematic act in need of justification, I ask: *how did Kosovo come to emerge as a situation that demanded intervention*? Based on the contention that Algeria constituted an instance where the practice of non-intervention was problematized and therefore in need of legitimations, I ask: *how did Algeria emerge as a situation that demanded non-intervention?* In short I ask: what are the conditions of possibility for the emergence of Kosovo as an object of intervention and Algeria as an object of non-intervention?

From this diachronic or genealogical perspective, the "end-situations" of intervention and non-intervention are neither seen as inevitable outcomes of progressive processes, nor as obvious results of the events in themselves. Rather they are approached as outcomes of a number of contingent processes of discursive selections, which each conditioned what Kosovo and Algeria was, and was not, and how they could be responded to. As it will be specified further below, the cases of Kosovo and Algeria are analysed as going through two phases, or stages, in the 1990s. The first phase is named *object of observation* and *object of concern*; the second *object of problematization*; the analytical endpoint of the two processes of constitution being *object of intervention* and *object of non-intervention*. This analytical construction of two phases directs us to two important and interrelated questions: How can such a process of discursive selection and conditioning be studied?; How are the two phases constructed?

In terms of the first question, although I do not study transformations of discourses in the genealogical sense, I do diachronically study a specific process of constitution, which hence also must address the question of how articulations move; how change is possible. As it will be spelled out shortly, I believe that from a poststructuralist perspective one can indicate on a very general level how change is possible, but one cannot and should not explain change, find the causes of change, or delimitate beforehand what that change might consist of.[3] The latter must remain an empirical question.

As we saw in Bartelson's genealogy, transformation is, in a Foucauldian perspective, taken to occur through battles of interpretation (Bartelson 1995; Foucault 1977a). History is moved by interpretations of earlier interpretations (Dreyfus and Rabinow 1982). This is, however, a fairly elusive proposition, although Foucault attempts to specify it at times (for example, Foucault 1978a). In order to appreciate what enables meanings to change Laclau and Mouffe might serve as a fruitful addendum to Foucault's Nietzschean "play of wills" or the archaeology's regulating structure. As Laclau and Mouffe have stressed, meaning is always only partially fixed. It is always contested. Discourses are never closed totalities. They are not equivalents to Saussure's language system. Rather than being closed structures, discourses are unstable and open-ended, always challenged from what Laclau and Mouffe (1985: 111ff) call the *field of discursivity*. As Doty (1997: 6) also puts it: "A discourse's exterior limits are constituted by other discourses that themselves are open and inherently unstable." But how is meaning partially fixed, as well as changed? How is meaning constituted and re-constituted? Laclau and Mouffe (1985) in this respect make an important distinction between articulations and discourse. Articulations are those practices that partially fixate relational identities. Articulatory practices, in other words, constitute meaning. Yet, articulations always work with *moments* of existing discourses, reproducing some while excluding others. Articulations draw on, reformulate and challenge discourse. As Diez has pointed out, this invests change with a circular character. "Articulations transform discourse, but then again they are emerging from specific discursive contexts" (Diez 2001: 31). But as Diez also correctly argues, this is the only way to study change within a poststructuralist perspective! As we saw in the last chapter, Walker's, Bartelson's, and Weber's studies of sovereignty are all guided by the same – although sometimes implicit – assumption. They study fixations of sovereignty through various discursive practices that construct meanings of sovereignty while at the same time being dependent on sovereignty.

While Laclau and Mouffe direct us to the possibility of change by their emphasis on articulation and the open-ended character of discourse, they do not attempt to explain change or identify cause(s) of change. This does not constitute a problem or hindrance. On the contrary. Describing how specific discourses move can never be seen as an equivalent to furnishing a theory of change. As Foucault (1978a: 11) stressed "I am a pluralist. My problem is to substitute the analysis of different types of transformation for the abstract, general and monotonous form of 'change'." In other words, we are not to look for universal or underlying causes of change. Rather we are to study how specific articulations produce and reproduce meaning, and conversely how specific discourses enable various articulations. Thus, how articulations, for instance, pick up and draw upon elements of an already established discourse, how certain articulations succeed in questioning hitherto agreed assumptions or how tensions and paradoxes might displace a previous discourse altogether is exactly what is to be studied, rather than being turned into a prior theoretical contention about the causes of change. To give some examples from the empirical analyses of this book: when Kofi Annan in 1997 voiced his concern over the international community's apparent unwillingness to do something about the massacres in Algeria, and its pretence of not knowing what was really going on, his speech came to serve as a powerful reference point and was widely used as an authorized reading on the international community's failed stand towards Algeria. It, for instance, enabled journalists and commentators to ask politicians what the international community intended to do about Algeria. Previously this form of questioning had been almost unthinkable, quickly being inscribed as partisan and biased. In conjunction with the doubts that had been raised ever since 1997 over who was actually behind the killings, it moved Algeria from a concern into an international problem, which had to be solved. Yet, as I show, it was only on the basis of a numerous range of prior articulations and selections, which had depicted terrorism and human rights violations in Algeria as international concerns and questioned the unconditioned support to the Algerian government, that it was possible to ask when and what the international community would do in relation to Algeria, and hence to convey Algeria as an international problem. To recapture the logic of Laclau and Mouffe, the articulations of an international problem drew on as well as reformulated prior discursive fixations. It was these specific sets of prior articulations, selections and exclusions that made up the conditions of possibilities for speaking about Algeria in terms of an object in need of international solutions. This analysis is accordingly not made on the basis of a prior theoretical contention about the causes of, or universal character, of change. Neither can it be used as general proposition dictating that something has to be formulated as a concern before it can be articulated as a problem, or that Kofi Annan has to raise a certain agenda, before similar articulations will follow suit. The findings are a result of my empirical analysis, not of prior theoretical elaborations. It was, for instance, as we will see, another type of discursive conditions that enabled articulations on Kosovo to move from an object of observation to an object of problematization.

This, however, also implies that the diachronic analysis is not able to delineate a set of causal and necessary factors, which shaped the intervention in Kosovo and non-intervention in Algeria. Neither can it rank certain articulations and shifts as more or less crucial for "the end result". It can, as pointed out, trace all those discursive selections, variations and elevations which gradually, but not inevitably, came to necessitate legitimations of non-intervention in the case of Algeria and intervention in Kosovo, but it does not allow for a determination of certain discursive moves as necessary factors. For instance, I do not intend to make counterfactual propositions such as: if Kofi Annan had not raised the issue of Algeria, then Algeria would have remained a mere international concern, or that if Kosovo had not been portrayed as a case of ethnic cleansing and mounting genocide, then intervention would have been excluded as a possible course of action. This argument also hinges on the ongoing discussion of the linkage between representations and policies. As Lene Hansen has argued, there is a tendency within constructivist studies to view representations as shaping policy responses causally. In relation to Bosnia it has thus been suggested that constructing the war as a result of ancient ethnic hatred resulted in a policy of non-involvement, whereas representations of Serbian aggression called for international sanctions. However, Hansen (2006) shows both theoretically and empirically that this cannot be treated as an evident policy outcome. Similarly this book, for instance, also points out that in spite of the continuous references to brutal massacres and atrocities of innocent Algerian civilians, international involvement did not automatically follow suit, just as the representation of ethnic war in Kosovo, carried out by two equally guilty parties did not give rise to recommendations of non-involvement. In short, neither massacres nor ethnic war constitute magic words which in themselves condition certain actions. It should be stressed, however, that I do not only claim that causal policy deductions cannot be made on the basis of representations, but, as noted, also refrain from making causal explanations at all. If this were the purported aim of this book, it would need to proceed from a very different epistemological position, as well as adopting a very different analytical strategy.

Turning to the second question, I divide the diachronic study of Algeria and Kosovo into two phases. Object of observation/object of concern, and object of problematization ending with object of intervention/non-intervention. These phases are meant to indicate a process of discursive selection, but they are not ontological headings. Neither are they necessary or universal phases of constitutions, to repeat the argument from above. Yet they structure the rather detailed narration of the two cases and direct the reader's attention to the way in which articulations on Kosovo and Algeria shifted and narrowed over the years of 1991–1999. However, by the three headings I also mean to emphasize that the diachronic

34 *State sovereignty and intervention*

analysis is focused on how Algeria and Kosovo were articulated as *objects*. That is to say, it focuses on how international actors commented upon, responded to and addressed Kosovo and Algeria; how they constituted Kosovo and Algeria as objects of international discursive practices. Not everything that was ever mooted, uttered and said in relation to the two cases is therefore included. It is through a specific perspective and analytic that I narrate and structure the analysis of Kosovo and Algeria.

Albeit the two phases dictate this structure, dividing it into seemingly neat stages, it should be stressed that they are empirically rather theoretically generated. They have been constructed by paying meticulous attention to my empirical material, yet they are analytical constructs, in the sense of not being ontological propositions. In other words, I can only justify my division of the multiple articulations on Kosovo and Algeria by appealing to an ever-shifting and inherently undeterminable process of induction and deduction. As Bartelson (1995: 84) similarly has noted: "periodisation is an activity both inductive and deductive; one abstracts from one's familiarity with a material, and uses this abstraction to comprehend the material itself".

The diachronic study of the gradual constitution of intervention in Kosovo and non-intervention in Algeria is subsequently used as the basis for the synchronic study. Having showed how we got here, how we arrived at a situation where unspeakable killings in Algeria demanded that politicians had to legitimize why intervention could not be undertaken, and the mounting genocide in Kosovo demanded that politicians legitimized the necessity of intervention, the synchronic study is able to investigate how these legitimations of intervention and non-intervention produced meanings to sovereignty. It should be stressed that it is this prior diachronic study that allows me to compare Kosovo and Algeria in the first place. Only on the basis of the diachronic analysis can it be shown how politicians were placed in a situation where they had to legitimize non-intervention in Algeria and intervention in Kosovo, and subsequently these forms of legitimations can be studied.

However, having said this, the main focus of this book is the synchronic analyses. It is here that I study constitutions of state sovereignty across different locales, but within the same time. Graphically the dividing line between the diachronic and the synchronic analyses can be illustrated the following way, in terms of a funnel (see Figures 1 and 2).

As the figures display, the diachronic analysis of Kosovo begins in 1991 and ends in 1999, whereas the analysis of Algeria begins in 1992 and ends in 1998. This should again be seen as an analytical choice. Since history does not tell us where it begins and ends, beginnings and endings are always discursive constructions. Accordingly "points" of emergence and closure can neither be justified with reference to history itself, nor to an extra-discursive foundation outside of history, but must be justified with reference to one's specific *problématique*. It is the analytical question asked which shapes one's writing of history, and hence of endings and beginnings, not the nature of history or the events in themselves. Since my *problématique* departs from the present – by asking how Kosovo emerged as an object of intervention and Algeria as an object of non-intervention – the point of beginning is in fact the end. That is to say I

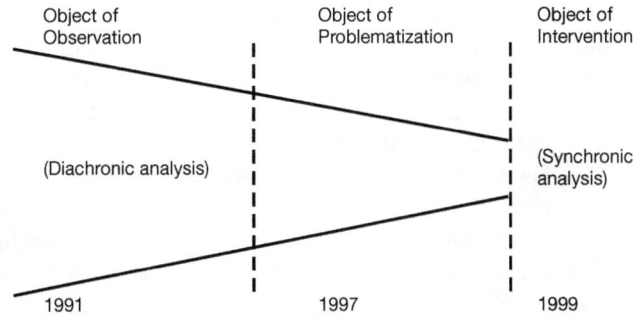

Figure 1 The diachronic and synchronic analyses: Kosovo

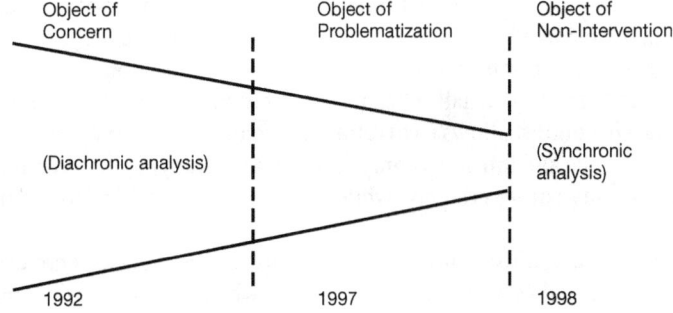

Figure 2 The diachronic and synchronic analyses: Algeria

do not proceed from a single point in the past – 1991 or 1992 – from which the source of intervention and non-intervention can be found. At the beginning one does not find the origin or roots of the present, but disparity (Foucault 1977a: 142). At the beginning, as the figures show, the discursive field is very open. It does not start in one point or one event, but in multiple possibilities and potentialities. It is this very openness that makes the political possible and allows for alternative articulations, different interpretations and various trajectories.

Synchronic strategy

Whereas the diachronic strategy enables me to describe a temporal process of constitution, showing how intervention and non-intervention rest on contingent and historical processes of selection, the synchronic enables me to show how these conditions of possibilities were actualized and enacted through the legitimations of intervention and non-intervention. In short, where the diachronic analysis has a dynamic perspective, the synchronic has a static perspective. It does not analyse how legitimations of intervention and non-intervention changed over time through discursive exclusions, selections and elevations, but how legitimations were discursively structured within a specific time, and hence how they gave meaning to sovereignty. The synchronic analysis is, in this sense, frozen in time (Kjær and Åkerstrøm 1996).

This does not mean that legitimations did not change over those four months of 1999 with respect to Kosovo or over the year of 1998 with respect to Algeria.[4] The purpose of the synchronic analysis is not to study such changes, but to study how meanings of state sovereignty were produced.

The synchronic study, however, demands that the relationship between sovereignty, intervention, non-intervention and legitimations is disentangled. Once again it is necessary to elaborate on the circular character of practice and meaning.

In accordance with Weber I contend that intervention and sovereignty are mutually dependent. The meaning of intervention is dependent on a prior conceptualization of sovereignty, at the same time as sovereignty's meaning is (re)produced when intervention is defined. The dominant readings in International Relations define intervention, as Weber has pointed out, as a violation of sovereignty, hence giving rise to interpretations of intervention as just one more symptom of the gradual obsolescence and erosion of the sovereign state; as one more move in the direction from particularity to universality; or as organized hypocrisy, as a sign that nothing much has changed, states still talk cheap while abiding to power and interest. Weber's analysis in contrast allows us to refrain from studying intervention only in terms of transcendence and transgression. It opens up for studying interventionary practices as constitutive of sovereignty, while at the same time being dependent on sovereignty.

Yet some analytical confusion arises, I argued, because Weber does not clarify which practice(s) she studies sovereignty through and whether these practices themselves are held open for investigation. On the one hand, Weber suggests that it is intervention which produces sovereignty, on the other hand, she turns the meaning of intervention/non-intervention into a product of discursive articulations; these articulations in turn being synonymous with legitimations of intervention. Further unclarity is added because what Weber terms "interventionary practices" in all five cases are discursively articulated (legitimized) as in fact not being interventions.

To remedy this, it is necessary to be more explicit in terms of the objects that are to be studied and in terms of clarifying the practice–meaning relation. What counts as non-intervention or intervention cannot be treated as given, as Weber's study indeed demonstrates. The meaning of intervention and non-intervention has, just as sovereignty, to be studied as discursively established. This also implies that Weber's notion of "interventionary practices" has to be substituted with legitimations: first, because it is unclear what interventionary practices indicate, second – and related to that – because it seems to be legitimations of intervention which Weber in fact uses to study constitutions of sovereignty, rather than what might be called intervention in itself. In other words, I choose to view legitimations as that articulatory practice which constructs meanings of sovereignty/intervention. Yet, since I also claim that the hitherto overlooked practice of non-intervention legitimations equally constitutes sovereignty, it is through the dual legitimations of non-intervention and intervention that the production of sovereignty and intervention's meaning is studied. Figures 3 and 4 depict this idea graphically.

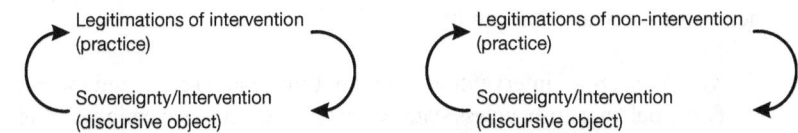

Figure 3 Practice and discursive object: Kosovo

Figure 4 Practice and discursive object: Algeria

But why did non-intervention as well as intervention need to be justified at all? The answer in terms of intervention perhaps seems obvious, but yet gives rise to a curious paradox inherent in all legitimations of intervention. Again, we will need to turn to Weber's study in order to render the argument intelligible. In terms of intervention legitimations Weber suggests that interventions are accompanied by justifications because diplomats assume that there are norms that regulate state behaviour and that a community of sovereign states which respects and abides by these norms already exists. Yet, I will suggest that there is something else at play than prior existing subjects – such as diplomats – that are restrained by commonly held norms and rules. In order to understand the need to provide justifications it is not necessary to turn this practice into a question of which norms or which community diplomats think exist. Such a question would turn discourse analysis into a hermeneutic or sociological project. It would shift the analysis to one of subjective or inter-subjective beliefs. Moreover, deriving justification from (inter)subjective norms would easily lead us to Krasner's (1999) conclusion that the norm of non-intervention is merely a token of "Organized Hypocrisy" having always been broken when interest and power dictated so. Instead of attributing legitimations to a divergence between norms and interests, rhetoric and behaviour, where power and interest always gain the upper hand, I will suggest that it is intervention and sovereignty's constitution as binary oppositions that demands legitimations. This does not lead to incongruence between words and deeds, but to a paradox inherent in all forms of intervention justifications.

I, therefore, proceed from the somewhat understated logic in Weber's (1995: 4) conceptual analysis of intervention and sovereignty; that interventions always already are determined as problematic. Sovereignty is taken to belong to the normal affairs of international life, whereas intervention is construed as the abnormal and pathological. Intervention is positioned as that phenomenon or anomaly that needs to be explained, discussed and justified, whereas sovereignty just is and must be. It is this hierarchical relationship between sovereignty and intervention, I argue, which necessitates that interventions are legitimized, and which, as will be explained further on p. 38, similarly makes legitimations of non-intervention abnormal. By conversion, this also implies that legitimations of intervention presuppose state sovereignty and reproduce intervention as problematic acts that need to be justified! By the very acts of justification, state sovereignty is reinscribed as a crucial fact of international life. If state sovereignty was not presumed to be part of the normal order of international politics and interventions were not seen as

38 State sovereignty and intervention

problematic violations, then there would be no need in the first place to legitimize such acts. As Parekh also has put it:

> The very concept of intervention would not make any sense, and the need to justify it would not arise, unless states were assumed to be sovereign and entitled to immunity from external interference. Justifying intervention on strictly humanitarian grounds alone also makes sense only on such an assumption.
> (Parekh 1997b: 56)

Parekh, however, overlooks that intervention at the same time is understood as a violation of state sovereignty. This does not make a case for the argument that legitimations of interventions merely function as organized hypocrisy. It instead points to a reversal, in Derrida's terms, of the binary pair and to the paradoxical character of intervention legitimations. Justifications of intervention do not only construct meanings of state sovereignty, but they also participate in the (re)production of state sovereignty as a vital and necessary fact of international politics. This implies that the hierarchical relationship between sovereignty and intervention is reversed. Intervention is not a problem to be solved or a derivative term of sovereignty. Intervention becomes sovereignty's condition of possibility. Intervention becomes one of those very practices through which sovereignty is produced as a vital fact of international life. It becomes that very practice, which enacts and hence assures sovereignty's continued existence. And yet, simultaneously, by the very understanding of the act, sovereignty is violated! Legitimations of intervention are in this sense always paradoxical, entailing an inherent tension, in that they at the same time pay tribute to and violate state sovereignty (see also Malmvig 2001b).

But if non-intervention is presumed to be the normal state of affairs, then the legitimations of non-intervention in Algeria can indeed also be said to entail a paradox. Normally there is no need to justify non-intervention. So why did politicians, officials and commentators become enmeshed in the curious practice of justifying non-intervention in Algeria? To answer this question demands an analysis of those prior discursive articulations and stabilization that conditioned these legitimations, and this analysis will be carried out in the diachronic chapter. On a general level, the answer hinges on those discursive processes which, over the course of the 1990s, gradually came to question the boundary between internal and external, and the very extension and content of Algerian sovereignty. By 1997, it will be shown, it was no longer settled what resided within the sovereign boundaries and competencies of Algeria, and what did not. It was repeatedly asked, why does the international community not become involved? Why is nothing done? And by answering this question politicians and others became engaged in the curious practice of legitimizing what normally does not need to be legitimized. They were pointing out what normally does not need to be pointed out: that Algeria was a sovereign state.

On the one hand, by making references to the need of respecting Algeria's sovereignty, sovereignty was hence treated as a given. Sovereignty was seen as something already in existence, its invocation being a mere innocent and nominal practice, which just designated what was already there. On the other hand, by legitimizing non-intervention and invoking the concept of sovereignty politicians were, in the very same move, recognizing that the meaning and boundary of sovereignty was in dispute, that they – through their very references to Algeria's sovereignty – were enmeshed in a political practice where they constituted and decided its meaning and content. When politicians and others were invoking Algerian sovereignty, they were, at one and the same time, referring to sovereignty as a given, and yet recognizing that sovereignty no longer resided within the obvious and non-political. Sovereignty was something that needed to be emphasized and demonstrated. If it was not "acknowledged" that non-intervention and sovereignty were contested, there would be no need to invoke the two and no need to point to their existence. At the same time, this "recognition" could never be displayed; if so, the invocation would lose its power. If the contingency of sovereignty were to be revealed, then sovereignty would be open to political manipulation and decision, hence creating intervention as a viable political option. Conversely, if sovereignty was displayed as a given, there would be no need to justify why intervention could not be carried out! Politicians were therefore caught in a paradoxical practice, where they simultaneously constituted sovereignty as something given and natural, and as something contested and political.

This paradoxical character of intervention as well as non-intervention legitimations constitutes the starting point of my synchronic analyses of Kosovo and Algeria. Yet, to investigate the discursive constructions of the content of sovereignty/intervention, the analysis is further aided by a set of analytical questions. The first of these consists of three sub-questions: (1) How is the violation of sovereignty represented?[5] (2) Which community is constituted through that representation? (3) What are the conditions of possibilities for this community? These three analytical questions are inspired by Foucauldian discourse analysis, in particular *Archaeology of Knowledge and Discourse on Language* (Foucault 1972). Thus, the first question focuses on what is represented as an object of discourse, which subject positions are granted the right to speak about these objects, and which criteria and differentiations make for distinctions between valid and invalid, objective and subjective, true and false, statements. The second analytical question focuses on how the relationship between objects and subjects is articulated, how, and if, objects can appear simultaneously as both objects and subjects, and how subjects are inscribed with a given identity. The third question focuses on how subjects are differentiated from other subjects in time and space; by distinctions drawn, for instance, between us and them, inside and outside, presence and absence, potential and actual. These three questions are, of course, both related to and dependent on one another. How subjects are installed with a given identity, as asked in the second question, is evidently also dependent on how the spatio-temporal distinctions constitute the subjects at play, as asked in the third question, on which subjects are invested with an authority to speak, and on how they claim to make true and valid statements, as asked in the first question.

Having spelled out the basic lines of the diachronic and synchronic strategy, we can now turn to the third section, addressing the question of text selection and reading.

Reading strategies and text selection

When Foucault (1998: 263) once was asked about the choices that informed his selection and reading of texts, he answered: "One ought to read and study everything." By this ambitious proposition Foucault meant to indicate several things, some of them worth underlining, before spelling out my own selections of texts. First, since the boundaries of discourses cannot be delimitated beforehand, our reading should not be guided by a prior theme, or a fixed referent, such as madness, punishment, security or sovereignty. Instead, we ought to follow how statements refer to other statements and how these statements refer to others in turn, until we end up with a structured whole; with a regularity in the dispersion of statements, in the terminology of Foucault. Second, to read everything also means that we should not only study the canonical texts of an age, those texts and authors which, for instance, today are singled out as important, or those that obviously appear as significant, for example, Hobbes in respect of sovereignty, the speeches of Prodi in relation to European integration or the UN Security Council resolutions in respect of the intervention in Kosovo, but also marginal ones and those that did not make it (see also Bartelson 1995; Neumann 2001a; Åkerstrøm Andersen 2002). And third, we should read everything in the sense that we are not to make a prior distinction between official and private sources or, in the context of International Relations, between, for example, foreign policy announcements and private conversations between diplomats, between popular/journalistic writings and those of the academy. Neither of these texts resides outside of discourse, nor are we to attribute a greater importance to certain authors or sources beforehand (see also Åkerstrøm 2002). This does not imply that all texts are equally important or that all voices are equally significant. The point is to turn such questions into a matter of discourse, for example, subject positions in terms of authors and monuments in terms of importance, rather than a question of prior theoretical distinctions (for example, Foucault 1978a, 1972).

While I agree with Foucault in terms of the importance of not delineating beforehand which texts should or should not be read and which texts and authors are most significant, the ideal of reading everything is – in particular today – an impossibility. When Foucault (1998: 263) emphasizes, in connection with the questions about text selection, that he "read every medical work *of importance* for methodology of the period 1780–1829" to write the *Birth of the Clinic*, one might argue that he sneaks a criterion – "of importance" – in through the backdoor and that the body of textual material at that time probably was far smaller than it is today (italics added). Those who attempt to analyse current discourses are today confronted with an archive that has "exploded". Moreover, to read everything, abandoning any form of prior selection, is of course an unreachable ideal, which Foucault of course did not fulfil himself. Foucault's work was always very much focused on French discourses and the pre-selections of empirical material were most likely made by the curators at the Bibliothèque Nationale (Dreyfus and Rabinow 1982: 59). Hence, although we should not engage in a prior definition and demarcation of discourse through text selection, we may legitimately ask which texts have been read and when one can say to have read enough?

In terms of the first question, it should be stressed that I have attempted to read very broadly, to read as many different texts as possible and thus in a sense strived to reach the unreachable ideal of reading everything. My archive is thus composed of multiple texts on Kosovo from 1991 to 1999 and Algeria from 1992 to 1998. These being official French, British and American foreign policy statements; debates in national parliaments and sub-committees; statements, reports, resolutions and discussions of international organizations, the EU, OSCE, the Contact Group, the UN Security Council, and various sub-committees of the UN; press releases and reports of NGOs, especially Amnesty International and Human Rights Watch; newspaper articles, editorials and magazines, in particular the *Washington Post*, the *New York Times*, the *Guardian, The Times, The Economist, Le Monde*; news broadcasting especially BBC and CNN; and finally academic articles and commentaries by intellectuals.[6]

The broad selection of texts has been made for three reasons in particular. First, in accordance with Foucault's argument above, I hold that it is necessary to read as much as possible – albeit not everything – in order to be able to describe and identify discursive correlations, references' references, key concepts, battlefields and boundaries. Second, and related to the first point, to gain a general knowledge or familiarity with a discursive field one has to read very broadly, particularly in the "first phase" of one's "explorations" of a field (see also Wæver 2000; Holm 1999). Even if one only chooses to study one discourse, the boundary of that discourse cannot be identified without this general knowledge of alternative discursive positions, reached by a prior reading of a very broad range of texts. Third, if we wish to avoid hegemonization and monolithization of discourses, or too easily jumping from discourse to foreign policy statements and vice versa, reading in breadth is again imperative (see also Hansen 1998; Wæver 2000). By focusing solely on a very narrow range of texts, for example, US presidential statements, one does not only risk overlooking important concepts, relations and struggles, but also deriving discourse from their authors, thereby being exposed to the traditional critique against idealism and subjectivism (see also Malmvig 2001a). As Milliken (1999: 234) similarly has pointed out, when International Relations scholars only analyse articulations by, for instance, US officials and US intellectuals in order to invoke the notion of a homogeneous Western security discourse, this is simply not sufficient. Discourse analysis cannot be carried out on the basis of a few texts only. Although Wæver (2000) and Neumann (2001a) argue that in principle one only needs to read one text carefully, because the discursive structures must be apparent in any text, they also admit that in practice this is not the case. If this were to be true, discourse would be the equivalent of a Saussurean language system – *langue* – where only one signified corresponds to every signifier, thereby turning discourse into a fixed unchangeable structure, which articulations always only reproduce. We would, in short, come to operate according to a structuralist, rather than a poststructuralist, logic. In order to avoid some of these pitfalls, I have therefore attempted to include and read as many texts as possible.

I have in particular drawn my texts from British, American and French sources. This choice should, however, not be seen as reflecting a prior differentiation between, or expression of, British, American or French discourses. The aim is not to conduct an analysis of competing national discourses. Discourse might be structured around national-territorial lines, but this will not be the theoretical basis of my analysis. Neither should discourses, according to the Foucauldian perspective adopted in this book, be delineated according to extra-discursive subjects, nor should meaning be derived and correlated with prior subjects such as nation-states. Or to put it differently, articulations are not to be seen as expressions of, for instance, "the national identity of France", or "the national interest of US". This also implies that when I write "Clinton argued" "Jospin explained" or the "UN resolution spelled out" this does not signify "Clinton's discourse" or "Jospin's articulation" (see also Holm 1999), neither is it to be interpreted as respectively American or French discourses. Articulations do not, to put it bluntly, belong to their authors. While national differences in this way are downplayed, one could argue that the archive is constructed and defined according to another subject, namely the West (see, for example, Campbell 1993; Weber 1995; Diez 2001; Holm 1999). This is arguably the case to some extent. Yet, since debates and resolutions of UN sub-committees and the General Assembly, Contact Group statements, reports of NGOs and the OSCE also have been included, the archive might not even correspond to the elusive subject of the West. If anything perhaps the selection of texts reveals a "Western bias", which is impossible to escape.

However, one will undoubtedly notice a prevalence of French statements in the diachronic and synchronic analyses of Algeria. This is not to be seen as a choice regarding text selection. Neither is it to be seen as based on a theoretical contention about the relative importance of France in relation to Algeria, although admittedly France and Algeria do have a curious bond. The prevalence is rather based on the simple fact that at various points through the 1990s I have only been able to find very few "non-French texts" on Algeria. In particular in the early and mid-1990s, Algeria was predominantly commented upon by French politicians, journalists and intellectuals. The near absence of statements by British, American and EU officials may not cause much surprise. After all it seems obvious that France qua her historic, cultural and linguistic ties to Algeria should entertain a special relationship with her former colony. But what kind of meaning this special relationship should be attributed was not in any way given. As the diachronic analysis will show, how the special relationship was articulated indeed varied over the course of the conflict in the 1990s. Thus, although the predominance of French sources at first sight can be explained (away) with reference to the special French–Algerian bond, such an explanation is itself founded within a specific and contingent discourse. Therefore, I do not employ such prior explanations to justify that it suffices to include French statements only. On the contrary, I have sought to include as many non-French texts as possible, although at times they were in short supply.

A somewhat similar problematic arises in relation to the synchronic analyses. Yet the problem here emerges from a self-conscious analytical choice. Focusing on legitimations of non-intervention and intervention creates some "self-inflicted problems", in that all those voices that did not participate in legitimizing the intervention in Kosovo and the non-intervention in Algeria have not been included. For instance, in the case of Kosovo, what might be designated as respectively realists, pacifists and left-wing intellectuals, very actively spoke against the intervention, albeit from very different grounds, and hence also produced different boundaries and content to the concept of state sovereignty (see, for example, Kissinger, 5 April 1999; Chomsky, 1 March 1999; Said, 1 March 1999; Bourdieu, 31 March 1999; Zizek, 1 March 1999). In Algeria there were equally many contending voices, who did not all participate in legitimizing non-intervention, but rather spoke in favour of intervention.[7] Curiously, it was in fact especially left-wing intellectuals – in contrast to the case of Kosovo – who argued for the necessity of intervention and who questioned the delimitations and meaning of Algerian sovereignty (see, for example, Pierre Vidal-Naquet and Francois Gèze, *Le Monde*, April 1998, 5 March 1998; Robert Fisk, the *Independent*, 5 November 1997; Pierre Bourdieu, *Le Monde*, 3 September1997; Lahourari Addi, *Le Monde*, 1 February 1998).[8] As it will be shown in the diachronic analysis, it was partly due to these voices that politicians and others had to legitimatize why intervention was an absolute impossibility in the first place. Similarly, those who spoke in favour of intervening against the Algerian government – whether in the form of an investigating mission or in the form of a peace-keeping force – did not construct the relationship between government and people and between people and the Islamists in the same manner as those who justified a position of non-intervention. Yet the synchronic analysis will only focus on the latter.

Given this focus, one might argue that the analysis hegemonizes a whole discursive field by only including legitimations of intervention in the case of Kosovo and non-intervention in the case of Algeria. However, the objective of the synchronic analysis is not to describe all discursive positions on intervention/ sovereignty. It does not aim to map a whole discursive field, distinguishing, for instance, between marginal and dominant discourses, as Hansen (1998) and Campbell (1998a) have done in relation to Bosnia. Hence, the claim is not that the intervention/sovereignty construction in each case constituted all it was possible to enounce in relation to Kosovo and Algeria. Moreover, the combination of a diachronic and synchronic strategy in addition to the comparative perspective should compensate for this, in so far as the dual analysis of Algeria and Kosovo exactly seeks to demonstrate that there is always more than one discourse at play; that it is possible to articulate sovereignty in a myriad of ways.

Turning to the second and related question: when has one read enough? The straightforward answer is that one can stop analysing texts when confronted by a continuous repetition of themes and relations; when nothing new is added upon reading new texts (for a similar point see also Milliken 1999; Holm 1999: 47; Neumann 1996: 3). This is of course the ideal situation and a very general answer hinging on Foucault's understanding of discourses as structured fields, which regulate the formations of objects, subjects and concepts, where one ought to follow the references' references, as pointed out earlier. In practice, the reading process and the identification of discourses are, however, less straightforward. New decisions will continuously have to be made on the status of various texts and old decisions will be revised in the light of third or fourth readings of one's material. Or when writing the actual analysis one might realize that further references and texts will be needed. This may, in turn, spur a revision of the existing structure of the discourses in question. In practice, reading, as well as text selection, is therefore an endless process, where one at some point pragmatically decides "enough is enough". This decision must be based on a prior meticulous reading of several piles of material. Yet it will necessarily entail an arbitrary and pragmatic element, which cannot be rationalized or made fully transparent.

To end where the discussion of this chapter began, creating an analytical strategy should not be confused with a promise of complete transparency and rationalization. Hopefully, this chapter has directed the reader's attention to the basic choices and assumptions guiding the empirical analysis, as well as made it possible to ask critical questions. At the end of the day, it is, however, the conclusions and analyses made that are to convince the reader of the soundness and fruitfulness of this study.

3 From object of observation to object of intervention

> After months of diplomacy, after months of dialogue, after months of seeking peace, after witnessing Milosevic's thugs who were massing to unleash an ethnic slaughter once again on the people of Kosovo, we knew that we would not sit on the sidelines of history and remain indifferent to cruelty and the misery being inflicted. We had no choice but to act.
>
> (Secretary Cohen, 26 May 1999)

Endless efforts, so the story goes, were made to persuade President Milosevic to choose negotiations and peace. Every possible means was tried and every diplomatic path was explored in order to hinder this brutal and repressive dictator from committing yet another crime of ethnic cleansing and genocide. But Milosevic preferred violence to peace, hatred to tolerance and therefore in the end left the international community with no choice. A point of no return had been reached. Milosevic and his regime, despite all the international peace proposals, continued and even intensified his campaign of ethnic cleansing. Under such circumstances NATO had no choice but to act; that is, to intervene.

Intervention, hence, became a necessity, and the past was easily written in terms of present needs and concerns. Conclusions could be placed at the beginning. To engage in a military intervention was neither a political decision, nor a situation of choice or alternative possibilities. The mounting genocide demanded action and the only way to act was seemingly to intervene.[1] All other responses were equated with passivity, hence not being articulated as actions at all. This writing of the intervention made it almost impossible to question NATO's bombings: arguing that nothing should be done when what amounted to a genocide was occurring at the outskirts of Europe was obviously unthinkable and since intervention forcefully was made synonymous with action – and all other alternatives with passivity – there seemed to be very few possibilities for resistance and criticism.

The fixation of Kosovo as genocide and the construction of intervention as the only act that could put an end to the intolerable atrocities was of course neither a given fact nor an obvious outcome of a linear process. These crucial fixations were rather a result of continuous discursive battles and selections over the 1990s, which gradually constituted and re-constituted what Kosovo was about and how to respond to it. Starting from the question of how this discursive fixation came into being, the purpose is, as outlined in the former chapter, to trace how it became possible to represent intervention as inevitable; *how Kosovo came to emerge as a situation demanding intervention.*

As previously argued, this question is founded on a specific present *problématique*: a *problématique* that seeks to answer how we got here and yet refrain from the common practice of writing history retrospectively. In Judah's (2000: 84) book on Kosovo it is, for instance, argued that: "In retrospect the human rights question takes on some very interesting dimensions. The first is that many Kosovars successfully convinced many Westerners that the question of Kosovo was really one of human rights. *In fact it was not ... with the benefit of hindsight*, we can see how the question of human rights became another weapon in the arsenal of the Kosovars" (italics added). Instead of writing the past in terms of present givens, instead of determining what Kosovo really was about, although nobody had discovered it at the time, this chapter aims to account for the different and changing ways whereby Kosovo was constituted over time. This also means that, for instance, the extensive monitoring mechanisms, which were set up in Kosovo during the early 1990s, cannot be interpreted a priori as signs that Kosovo was ignored and nothing was done. The important point is exactly, as we will see, that "doing something" was constituted differently over the course of the 1990s.

To trace this process of constitution and selection, I divide the analysis into two stages, which moves from object of observation to object of problematization and finally to object of intervention. The diachronic analysis, in this way, comes to serve as a critical background of the synchronic chapter to come. When reading through the next chapter on the legitimations of the intervention and the constitutions of state sovereignty, the diachronic analysis will hopefully function as one means to counter articulations based on a historical narration of the necessary and unavoidable, as well as highlighting how and in what ways the legitimations of the intervention drew upon prior discursive stabilizations.

The constitution and reproduction of an object of observation

The predicament of the Kosovar Albanians and the precarious role of the Kosovo province were not matters that were hidden and silenced through the 1990s. Nor, as many scholars would have it, was Kosovo a place forgotten prior to the establishment of the Kosova Liberation Army (KLA) and the outbreak of violence in 1997 and 1998 (Judah 2000; Weller 1999b; Ignatieff 2000; Chomsky 1999). Kosovo rather, I will suggest, operated as an object to be watched and a place of concern from the early 1990s. Kosovo was already back then referred to as a potential powder keg and as the most likely place from where violence and ethnic war would commence in Yugoslavia. Only from hindsight – from a perspective of the present – and only by equating the numerous human rights and conflict prevention mechanisms with "not doing something" can the history of Kosovo be looked upon as a place forgotten and ignored.

The following sections will account for this discursive production and reproduction of Kosovo. It will be divided into two large parts: the first section describes how Kosovo was articulated as a question of violations of minority rights, threatening to lead to full-blown ethnic conflict, and therefore needing to be closely watched and assessed. The second section describes the first gradual shifts in how Kosovo was articulated, pointing to the emergence of Kosovo as an international problem.

Bringing transparency

In October 1991 CSCE decided to send the first of what was to become a series of missions to Kosovo. The first mission – a so-called Human Rights Rapporteur Mission – was to survey and assess "the human rights situation, including the rights of minorities", and subsequently deliver a report to the CSCE and the Conference on Yugoslavia (7-CSO/Journal No.2 Annex 2, 22 October 1991). The report was finished in January 1992. It concluded that "in Kosovo there is a highly unsatisfactory human rights situation. So far, neither a dialogue between the Serbian and the Albanian communities nor any mediating efforts take place." It further asked for "immediate consideration and action of the CSCE" to address what was called "the paralysis of public life in Kosovo", recommending that yet another mission should be sent to Kosovo to pursue this end (CSCE Communication, 25 January 1992). Three months later, CSO decided on sending yet another mission to Kosovo, which was followed by a so-called "Fact-Finding and Conflict Prevention Mission" in the summer of 1992.

This third mission also described the Kosovar Albanians' situation as "very grave". The authorities in Belgrade, it was explained, had deprived the Kosovars of their fundamental freedoms and rights as minorities (CSO Statement, 20 May 1991). Yet, in the subsequent report it was stressed: "it is not the military situation but the political situation that is the problem in Kosovo" (Report of the Conflict Prevention Centre Fact-Finding Mission to Kosovo, 5 June 1992). There is "no mounting military tension [between Albanians and Serbs] but the situation is dangerous, and ... conflict is to be avoided" (Report of the Conflict Prevention Centre Fact-Finding Mission to Kosovo, 5 June 1992). The concerns over Kosovo evolving into a violent conflict due to Serbian repression and violation of rights – hence repeating the wars in Bosnia and Croatia – were similarly echoed in the motivation for sending a fourth CSCE mission to Kosovo in September 1992, named The Mission of Long Duration. The Mission of Long Duration was, as the name indicates, a more permanent mission, than the three previous ones, which all had had so-called "exploratory purposes". The permanent mission was to secure a continuous international presence in Kosovo, promoting dialogue among the two communities and collecting information on all aspects relevant to violations of human rights and fundamental freedoms (Decision of CSO, Prague, 13–14 August 1992). At the same time a so-called spillover mission was sent to Macedonia to ensure that tensions did not spread from Kosovo to Macedonia. Kosovo was articulated as a question of human rights and as a site of potential conflict. Ethnic tensions in Kosovo, it was feared, could spread to Macedonia, possibly involving Greece and Turkey (Declaration on Former Yugoslavia, G7 Summit, 7 July 1992). Kosovo was a site of concern and an object to be watched.

The dual concerns with potential ethnic violence and violations of human rights were tightly knitted together. CSCE's surveillance and presence inside Kosovo were presumed to be an effective means of hindering further repression and, in turn, a means to hinder ethnic war. Since the violations of the Kosovar Albanians' rights were presumed to constitute a potential ground for further conflict and violence, improvements of the human rights situation were consequently articulated as means to prevent conflict (see, for example, Dumas, 18 August 1992). It was, in other words, just as much the potential future situation of ethnic war that was to be prevented, as the present situation of human rights violations. In the numerous statements concerning the importance of the Mission of Long Duration it was, for instance, stressed that "The CSCE missions of long duration to Kosovo, Sandjak and Vojvodina remain essential to *prevent expansion of the conflict* which the international community will not tolerate" (italics added; CSO Decision, 28 April 1993; see also CSO Decision, 8 June 1992; Ralph Johnson, US Deputy Secretary of State, 18 November 1992).

> In the view of the Mission, it is necessary to treat the issues involved with partiality, balance, caution, and good background knowledge. Many of the issues will need *observation* ... over a long period of time, *if violence is to be averted*.
>
> (italics added; Report of the Explanatory Mission to Kosovo, 2 August 1992)

Human rights organizations were similarly placing much emphasis on the potential dangers, as on present violations. Amnesty International, for instance, argued that the human rights situation in Kosovo "could lead to the outbreak of ethnic conflict with catastrophic consequences as seen in Bosnia-Herzegovina", and stressed, in a later report, that if the international community again failed to prevent human rights abuses in the former Yugoslavia "it risks seeing simmering tensions, exacerbated by unchecked human rights violations, erupting into open conflict" (Amnesty International Report 2/2–93; Amnesty International Statement of Sec. Gen., September 1993).

Within the UN human rights system, Kosovo was equally taken to need special attention and monitoring. By mid-1992 a Special Rapporteur for Yugoslavia was established and the Thematic Rapporteurs were requested to give special attention to Kosovo (UN Human Rights Commission Resolution 1992/s–1/1, 14 August 1992). Their task was to "investigate first hand ... and to receive credible information ... on a *continuing* basis" (italics added; UN Human Rights Commission Resolution 1992/s–1/1, 14 August 1992). The Human Rights Commission, its subcommissions and the General Assembly were, on the basis of these reports, to make conclusions – in the form of resolutions – on how to respond to the situation in Kosovo. These resolutions continually began by expressing "deep and grave concern about the human rights situation", which – after the first report – came to be concerns over the "*deteriorating* human rights situation" (italics added). Equally, they emphasized their serious concerns about the *dangerous* situation in Kosovo, thereby reproducing human rights violations as essentially being a question of hindering a possible outbreak of ethnic violence (italics added; UN Human Rights Commission Res. 1992/s–2, 1993/7, 1994/72, 1994/76). Kosovo needed to be watched because of a *potential* danger: "We are *watching* and we continue to *watch* Serb action in Kosovo carefully" (italics added; Snyder, State Department Spokesman, 29 December 1992; see also Dumas, 27 August 1992; Bush, 29 December 1992; *Washington Post*, 23 November 1992).

By the end of December 1992 George Bush warned Belgrade – in what was later to become his famous "Christmas warning" – that "in the event of a conflict in the Kosovo caused by Serbian action, the United States will be prepared to employ military force against Serbians" (*Washington Post*, 29 December 1992; see also Judah 2000: 74).[2] Yet for the threat to be enacted, Kosovo had to evolve into something different than it currently was. Threats were formulated hypothetically and in the future tense based on what Kosovo might become. Kosovo was a potentially violent site or powder keg, which easily could spread to Macedonia and further. "And it [the conflict in Bosnia] *could* go into Kosovo, which is next door: it *could* go into Macedonia. It *could* involve the Turks. It *could* involve the Greeks. We *could* have a serious problem" (italics added; Clinton, 10 February 1993; see also Juppé, 28 March 1993). Military action was a possible future response, in the event that Kosovo evolved, as so many were predicting. At present, Kosovo was an issue of concern, needing close observation and reporting, because of the future.

The knowledge of being monitored, transparent and visible was supposed to restrain the behaviour of the FRY, hampering further repressions and violations against the Kosovars, and thereby ethnic war. The presumption was that observations by CSCE, the Special Rapporteur and the UN Human Rights Commission – along with the numerous non-governmental bodies of human rights (for example, Human Rights Watch and Amnesty) – had preventive effects, that the supervision in itself would help to discipline and normalize the conduct of the FRY authorities, and therefore in a second move hinder future open conflict (see also UN General Assembly Resolution 49/204, 1994; UN General Assembly Resolution 50/190, 1995; UN Sub-Commission Resolution 1995/10, 1995).

Yet did FRY "become virtuous by the simple fact of being observed"? (Foucault 1977c: 161). Every new report released by the extensive monitoring machine informed about deteriorating human rights conditions and an overwhelming danger of violence, seemingly paying tribute to Foucault's conclusion that the eighteenth-century prison reformers, as well as present "state reformers", were naïve to believe that a mere gaze reforms. FRY did not normalize despite continuous observation and reporting.

Although the presumption of some causal link between surveillance and righteous/normal behaviour may be naïve, the power and subjection involved in this process by which FRY was singled out for particular monitoring and condemnation should not be overlooked for two reasons. One reason is because the presence of international human rights monitors, and FRY's obligation to comment and report on the findings of the UN Rapporteur and the CSCE missions, produced and reproduced FRY as a "violator" of human rights. FRY became a subject whose actions needed to be internationally constrained and scrutinized.[3] The other reason is because the numerous human rights reports made it possible to document and publicly display how FRY actually was violating basic human rights, justifying the need for continuous surveillance.[4] By way of the seemingly neutral and legal language of the CSCE and UN reports, what was "really" going on inside FRY, and thus in turn whether FRY was normalizing and reforming according to the legal principles and values of the international community and the CSCE, could be established. The extensive human rights monitoring was inscribed with a special capability to provide objective information about the behaviour and nature of the FRY.[5]

Indeed, on the basis of the reports by the CSCE Mission on Serbian atrocities in Bosnia and its human rights record in terms of Kosovo, the CSCE suspended FRY's membership to the organization in July 1992. The question of renewed membership was to be reviewed in light of FRY's compliance with the principles, commitments and provisions of the CSCE, and its acceptance and cooperation with the CSCE Missions to Kosovo (CSO Decision on the Suspension of Participation by the FRY, 7 July 1992).[6] In 1993 FRY was expelled from CSCE, with a general reference to its grave and severe violation of CSCE principles, and with a specific reference to the situation in Bosnia-Herzegovina.[7]

In spite of FRY's temporary expulsion from CSCE, FRY allowed the CSCE Missions and the UN Rapporteurs access to Kosovo and made the human rights reports as demanded by the UN Human Rights Commission. Yet in mid-1993 FRY seemed to change its strategy. In contrast to 1992 where the demanded reports had been made and where official responses continued to express a "sincere will to cooperate fully and freely with any international investigation into human rights violation in the former Republics of Yugoslavia", FRY now objected to being placed under observation and being selected as a particular place of concern, citing the expulsion of membership of the CSCE as the reason for non-cooperation (CSCE Annual Report, 1993; CSCE Letter to the Security Council, August 1992). FRY similarly denied access to the Special Rapporteurs and rejected cooperation with the UN human rights bodies. In June of 1993 the CSCE Mission of Long Duration had to withdraw from Kosovo after FRY had refused to allow it to continue its monitoring activities.[8]

Refusing access seemed, at first glance, to be a powerful move. After all, since FRY was not physically confined and overseen by a possible guard in a Benthamian watchtower, FRY could, in principle, decide when and by whom it wanted to be watched. Denying access, of course, only enhanced the articulation of FRY (Serbia and Montenegro) as a pariah state who had something to hide, but the continual emphasis by CSCE, GA, Security Council and Amnesty International on how access and international presence were crucial – if the human rights conditions in Kosovo were to be improved and conflict hindered – indicated that human rights monitoring and conflict prevention were dependent on FRY's willingness to

From object of observation to object of intervention 51

cooperate (UN General Assembly Resolution 48/153, December 1993). Yet, the monitoring of Kosovo did in fact continue despite FRY's "non-consent". Reports and resolutions continued to condemn the "discriminatory policies, measures and violent actions committed against the ethnic Albanians in Kosovo" and expressed "awareness of the possible escalation of the situation into a violent conflict" (General Assembly Resolution 48/153, 1993). Monitoring had been made more difficult, but CSCE was still able to maintain its observation and reporting through its embassies in Belgrade.[9]

Between 1993 and 1995, Kosovo, in sum, continued to be articulated as a site of concern and future trouble, where human rights violations threatened to evolve into violent conflict. "The single most important international question mark is whether and when there will be an explosion in Kosovo" (CSCE Special Report, Head of Missions, 29 June 1993). The only means to prevent the potential danger and the deteriorating human rights situation seemed to be further observation and assessments. Keeping the situation transparent and accumulating knowledge of events would in itself, it was still presumed, lead to restraint and prevention (see, for example, UN Sub-Commission Resolution 1995/10; see also UN General Assembly Resolution 49/204, December 1994; UN General Assembly Resolution 50/190, December 1995; UN Committee on Elimination of Racial Discrimination Concluding Observations, 15 September 1993). The frequent international answer to concerns over Kosovo was: further observation. In that way assessments and reporting on Kosovo continued to grow. By 1995 even the General Assembly did not seem to be able to follow and oversee all the various monitoring initiatives, and the General Assembly subsequently asked the Secretary-General to provide a yearly report which summarized the evidence of the UN bodies involved in the monitoring and accounted for the extent to which FRY complied with the General Assembly's demands.

The observations and gathering of information resulted in a large number of resolutions and reports of the General Assembly, of the treaty-based committees and of the Commission of Human Rights. These reports and resolutions accounted in detail police brutality, arbitrary arrest and torture. They described the "discriminatory dismissal" of Albanian civil servants, the closings of Albanian schools and the Albanian University, and they highlighted how Albanian political parties and associations were persecuted, and how the Albanian language was sought to be eliminated. The reports continued to call upon the FRY government to permit the entrance of the Special Rapporteur and the CSCE Mission of Long Duration and to resume a dialogue with the Kosovar Albanian community.

The referent – or addressee – of these calls is, however, important. The "urgent calls" to improve the situation were not addressed to "the international community" or to any other subject outside of Yugoslavia, but to the authorities of the Federal Republic of Yugoslavia. In other words, FRY was still taken to be the responsible (and only) subject for solving and alleviating the conditions of the Kosovar Albanians. In so far as the "international community" or various international bodies and organizations were called upon, this was only to declare that further improvements or extensions of the already existing monitoring activities were needed, or to approve the observations that hitherto had been carried out.[10] Kosovo was ultimately for the FRY to solve and for the international community to observe and describe.

The absence of "'international conferences'" or Security Council resolutions on Kosovo further reinforced that Kosovo was not a problem to be handled internationally. Following the Dayton Agreement in November 1995, where the Kosovo issue was not included, Albright, as many other Western leaders, was asked about the possibility for an international conference on Kosovo. The answer once again depicted Kosovo as a concern that could be met only by monitoring and accumulation of knowledge.

> Clearly the issue of Kosovo is very much on everybody's minds. It has been on our minds from the beginning of this tragedy ... and we are now working very hard to make sure that the OSCE monitors can return into Kosovo ... I do not know specifically whether there is thought to be a conference on Kosovo, but I can just say that the issue is very much on our minds.
>
> (Albright, 11 December 1995)

The French Foreign Minister was also asked following the Dayton Accord whether there would be any international conference on Kosovo:

> Another region of tension in the Former Yugoslavia is Kosovo where there are great risks that war will break out too. Will there be another conference in order to resolve all of the other problems of Former Yugoslavia, since there is a war which threatens to spoil everything?
>
> (Hervé de Charette, 9 December 1995)

In his answer Hervé de Charette simply refused to turn Kosovo into an independent international problem, and instead referred to the importance of overall stability in South Eastern Europe to be guaranteed by the Dayton Accord and the Conference in Paris. The positive developments in Bosnia and FRY's signing of the Dayton Accord were taken to be indicative of progress in relation to the human rights conditions in Kosovo too. The agreement was somehow a step in the right direction for Kosovo as well:

> We are determined to continue making progress toward an overall settlement in the Balkans, and Kosovo remains very high on our agenda. Belgrade's desire to rejoin the international community provides strong incentives to bring about positive change in Kosovo. As a result of the Dayton Agreement we are much closer to securing the protection of human rights and respect for the aspirations of the ethnic Albanian majority in Kosovo.
>
> (US State Department, Q & A on Bosnia, 30 November 1995)

By 1996 the UN embargo on FRY was lifted in response to the signing of the Dayton Agreement, and in April 1996 FRY was formally recognized by the EU

(EU Bulletin EU 4–1996, Common Foreign and Security Policy 8/18).[11] FRY was now recognized as a new state composed of Serbia, Montenegro, and Kosovo; Kosovo being a province of Serbia. In the EU Presidency's statement, it was, however, further stressed that: "development of good relations with the FRY and its position within the international community" will depend on its full respect for human and minority rights and the granting of a larger autonomy for Kosovo" (EU Bulletin EU 4–1996, Common Foreign and Security Policy 8/18). In spite of the recognition of FRY and the resumption of diplomatic exchange, it was stressed that FRY was not yet part of the international community. Relations were not fully normalized. FRY's integration into the international community was a process, which would depend on its efforts regarding an enhanced autonomy for Kosovo and respect of the rights of the Kosovars. Kosovo's status was, however, still portrayed as a question to be settled between the two parties themselves. The task of the international community was merely to monitor the situation:

> We believe that Kosovo should have a status that will ensure the respect for the human and political rights. We believe that FRY will never achieve full integration, will never achieve full acceptance into the international community until it reconciles the status of Kosovo ....We like to have a status for them that will recognize those political and civil rights, but it is something which clearly needs to be worked through carefully, between the leaders of the community in Kosovo and the leaders here in Belgrade.
> (Warren Christopher, 5 February 1996)

The international community was to observe the situation in Kosovo, while the status of Kosovo was something to be worked out between the parties themselves: "Right now, we think that the most important action that the United States Government can take is to talk about what is going on there and to basically *shine a spotlight* on what we believe the ruling party has been up to" (italics added; US State Department Briefing, 26 November 1996). By August a so-called USIS Office was opened and Warren Christopher (15 August 1996) emphasized that this office would enable the world to know and assess what exactly was taking place in Kosovo: "The purpose of that facility will basically be to give the United States and the world as a whole a listening post so that we can have better way to *assess* what is going on in Kosovo" (italics added).

By mid-1996 some first sporadic attacks on Serbian police officers were reported by "The Balkan Peace Team". The attacks were carried out, the report stated, by an "alleged organisation" calling itself the Liberation Army of Kosova (Balkan Peace Team, Special Report, April/May 1996). Yet in the report it was also emphasized that Rugova had described the killings of the Serbian police officers as mere provocations by extremist Serbian circles. The report noted furthermore that several theories circulated with regard to "who did it and why": one theory being that it was Serbs who had carried out the killings themselves; another that Albanians were behind the killings, trying to put pressure on Western governments (Balkan Peace Team, Special Report, April/May 1996).

Yet the beginning of the eruption of violence against Serbian officials was to have crucial ramifications for how Kosovo could be known and spoken of. Faced with that very situation which so many had been predicting for years, it became all the more difficult to contend that Kosovo was only to be watched and assessed.

Entering violence: moving from object of observation to object of problematization

By 1997 several journalists had reported on what were described as planned violent attacks on Serbian military installations and Serbian authorities. In January, the Serbian rector of the Pristina University was sought to be assassinated by a car bomb and on 5 March another bomb exploded close to the University. KLA, a group at that time still unknown by the Western media, took responsibility for both bombings (Judah 2000). By autumn, attacks on Serbian police stations were reported on an almost weekly basis and the familiar scenarios of "a new Bosnia" appeared with renewed intensity (see, for example, *Washington Post*, 9 December 1997). Moreover, warnings were now made to two sides, instead of merely to the Serbian government. With reference to the terrorist acts of the KLA, the Kosovar Albanians were warned about not "resorting to violence to press political demands" (Contact Group Statement, 25 September 1997). Terrorism and the so-called "serious risks involved in choosing violence" were condemned, but these condemnations were simultaneously coupled with condemnations of the Serbian government's human rights violations. Thus, the concern with the human rights violations did not disappear. Official statements were attempting to strike a difficult balance between condemnations of the Serbian government and the KLA; a balance that would prove difficult to hold (see, for example, EU Declaration, Luxembourg, 21 December 1997; see also EU Presidency Statement, 31 July 1997; EU Declaration, Brussels, 18 June 1997; Contact Group Statement, 25 September 1997). The international community was not yet given an independent role. It was the so-called parties themselves that were to find a political solution and engage in dialogue without any international participation or mediation. The task of the international community was still portrayed as a matter of "following the situation carefully".

At the same time it was underlined that demands for Kosovo's independence would not be supported (Contact Group Statement, 25 September 1997). Determining and condemning the Kosovo Albanian violence as terrorism and stressing that Kosovo independence could never be endorsed, of course, opened a door for the Serbian authorities to pursue these "terrorists". If terrorism was perpetrated, then surely the Serbian police had a right to end it, including a right to use its legitimate means of violence. At one and the same time, Serbian violence was hence condemned and facilitated. It was simultaneously demanded that Belgrade refrain from violence, and yet references to and condemnations of Albanian terrorism allowed Belgrade to crack down on "the Albanian terrorists", yet exercising so-called "maximum restraint" (Contact Group Statement, 25 September

1997). These fluid distinctions between legitimate and illegitimate violence, state terror versus civilian terror, human rights violations versus terrorism were, as we will see, to haunt the discourse over Kosovo and Western responses for years to come.

Concurrently with the reports on KLA shootings and bombings, there were also outlets of "peaceful demonstrations" in Pristina. The demonstrators protested against the lack of implementation of the so-called Education Agreement brokered by the Vatican in 1996. Peaceful protest, however, turned into violence, when the Serbian police beat and detained several of the student leaders. Again, as so often before, the violence was followed by statements of concern and dismay, and by renewed calls for the need to refrain from violence (Foreign Commonwealth Office Statement by Tony Lloyd, 1 October 1997; Nancy Rubin to the UN Commission of Human Rights, 4 October 1997). Meaningful dialogue between the country's different political movements, it was stressed, could not take place in such an environment, and *the international community could not remain indifferent to this development* (italics added; EU Bulletin EU 7/8–1997, 31 July 1997). Without specifying how the international community now would avoid to "remain indifferent", this statement, however, opened a door for potential international involvement and hence for the enunciation of Kosovo as a problem that did not reside exclusively within FRY.

The stabilization of an international problem

> Why do these commentators on Kosovo believe that these people are a problem we can solve?
>
> (Orford 1999: 709)

By early March 1998 Kosovo was deemed to be an *international* problem. Kosovo now appeared in the headlines on a daily basis, circulating as a problem in its own right, neither derived from Bosnia, nor figuring as a mere potential problem and danger. After two weeks of what was generally described as an excessive Serbian crackdown on the surrounding villages of Pristina, Kosovo was taken to be a problem that called for an urgent international solution. As we will see, what kind of problem the international community faced was, however, very open. It was not in any way given what the problem consisted of, or how it was to be solved. The formulations of solutions and problems changed and shifted rather rapidly through 1998. But one element seemed to have been stabilized: Kosovo was no longer an internal affair of the FRY.

The following sections will focus on how the problematizations of Kosovo shifted and changed over the course of 1998, bringing a gradual closure to the possible ways whereby problems and solutions could be articulated. It will be shown how the content of the problem of Kosovo initially was very open, yet how tensions and contradictions came to spur changes and selections in problems and solutions. It will fall in three parts. The first will spell out how a new boundary was

56 *State sovereignty and intervention*

drawn between international and national, how Serbian state violence and Kosovar Albanian terrorism were established as international problems, and qua that, how the international community was invested with a responsibility for the solution of the conflict, and gradually turned into a third negotiating partner. The second part will point out how tensions between articulations of state violence and terrorism crystallized into two competing representations of ethnic cleansing and ethnic war, whereas the third part will explicate how it became increasingly difficult to combine articulations of negotiations and ethnic cleansing, military strikes and ethnic war.

From national to international: drawing a line in water

By March the Serbian authorities were warned that if they did not end the repression and use of force against the Kosovar Albanians, the economic sanctions against FRY would not be lifted (see, for example, James Rubin, 2 March 1998).[12] But acts of terrorism were condemned as well (Contact Group Statement, 9 March 1998). Gelbard, the US special envoy, stressed: "We condemn very strongly terrorist actions in Kosovo. The UCK is without any question a terrorist group" (Agence France Presse, 23 February 1998, quoted from Judah 2000: 138). Yet if KLA without any doubt was a terrorist group, then how could the Serbian security forces be blamed for illegitimate use of violence? In the representation of the parties involved, a third party however also figured, namely the "innocent civilians". Only Serbian forces were taken to be the perpetrators of the killing of innocent civilians.

As reports came out on increasing numbers of civilian deaths, condemnations and attention were primarily directed towards the FRY government rather than to the "terrorists". Calls were now made for imposing an arms embargo on FRY via the UN Security Council resolution. At the same time, the North Atlantic Council emphasized: "NATO and the international community have a legitimate interest in the developments in Kosovo, inter alia because of their impact on the stability of the whole region" (NATO Press Release, 5 March 1998). Along the same lines the OSCE stressed "the crisis is not solely an internal affair of the FRY because of the violations of the OSCE principles and commitments on human rights, and because it has a significant impact on the security of the region" (OSCE Permanent Council Decision NO 218, 11 March 1998; Cook in House of Commons, 10 March 1998). The War Crimes Tribunal for the Former Yugoslavia issued a statement emphasizing that the investigations would also include the events in Kosovo. The Tribunal's chief prosecutor further added that: "her office would not normally comment on ongoing investigation, but that the recent events in Kosovo were of an *exceptional* circumstance" (italics added; BBC News, 10 March 1998). In other words, the boundary between national and international affairs began to drift. Kosovo was no longer identified as an exclusive affair for the FRY to solve and the international community to watch. It was a legitimate *international* problem.

The escalation of violence seemed to push "the problem of Kosovo" into the international sphere. Yet this was, of course, not just a matter of uttering the word "violence". Violence was related to specific subjects and objects, hereby constituting a certain type of violence. The escalation of violence was described as a legitimate *international* interest, due to the fact that violence was conducted by the state apparatus against innocent civilians. Civilians were distinguished from terrorists and innocence separated civilians from criminals and lawbreakers. Furthermore, the (ab)use of state violence could effectively be related to the knowledge produced over the years by the human rights monitoring machinery. The numerous reports from the 1990s on discrimination, repression and violations of human rights went hand in hand with the constitution of a violent and repressive state and an innocent people. Yet, we were far away from articulations of ethnic cleansing or genocide and the KLA continued to disturb easy dichotomies between state and civilians, guilty and innocent.

It was not merely the Serbian police's violence against innocent Kosovar Albanians that turned Kosovo into an international problem. The intensification of violence was simultaneously positioned as something that had an impact on international security at large; hinging on those spillover scenarios that had circulated for years. State violence was not just illegitimate in so far as it was directed at innocent civilians, but it was also a potential cause of international instability – threatening the security of the whole region. Even Amnesty International seemed to put most emphasis on Kosovo's explosive character and its consequences for the security of the region.

"Amnesty International's challenge to the authorities in the region, the world's governments and international organisations is to dampen the 'powder keg' which Kosovo province represents to FR Yugoslavia and the entire region, and prevent its explosion" (Amnesty International, June 1998 AI-index: EUR 70/032/1998).

The initial solution proposed was to decide on a universal arms embargo. Thus, in late March the Security Council passed its first resolution on Kosovo (1160) imposing the promised embargo on the FRY.[13] This resolution was based on Chapter VII of the Charter, which can be invoked only if the event is conceived as constituting a threat to international peace and security. The resolution did not, however, explicitly define the source of that threat.[14] But the adoption of the resolution within Chapter VII clearly opened the way for referring to Kosovo as an international problem with international repercussions.

The immediate objective of the international community was – as formulated by the Contact Group and the UN resolution – to achieve a so-called "political solution" to the issue of Kosovo through dialogue between the "parties". It was however left rather vague what the political solution to Kosovo was to consist of and how it was to be achieved. No international conferences were set up and the so-called "solution" was frequently phrased in negative terms, as neither independence nor status quo. Alternatively, it was stressed that the territorial integrity and sovereignty of FRY had to be kept intact, while the Kosovar Albanians were to be given "a meaningful autonomy". In effect, dialogue would apparently in itself solve the problem. "We feel that the only way to solve these problems is through serious dialogue and negotiations. That is the most important way to assure that all of the people of this country can live prosperously and peacefully" (Holbrooke

Press Conference in Belgrade, 15 May 1998; Cook in the House of Commons, 30 April 1998).

Who were these so-called parties who had to enter into dialogue and find a solution? On the one hand, Kosovo was still referred to as an internal dispute, where different parties were involved and disagreed. The Kosovars and the Yugoslavian authorities were positioned as equal partakers in a violent conflict, in which they had equal responsibility for reaching an agreement and settling their disputes peacefully. Accordingly, it was stressed that *both sides* had to refuse violence as a legitimate means to solve political disagreements (for example, EU Presidency Statement on Kosovo, 24 April 1998). On the other hand, continuous references to discrimination and repression of the Kosovars constructed a relationship that looked more like one between oppressors and oppressed than between equally guilty parts. "President Milosevic continues to choose violence and repression over dialogue ... it is difficult to have any confidence that the Yugoslavian Army is acting in observance of human rights" (Cook in the Commons, 30 April 1998). Concurrently, references to the KLA began to appear without the prefix of "terrorists", being replaced by terms such as guerrillas, rebels or separatists.

Moreover, Belgrade was apparently not only to negotiate with the Kosovar Albanians but also with the international community. The very articulation of Kosovo as an international problem had turned the international community, and those claiming to speak on its behalf, into a third negotiating party. "The Contact Group is encouraged by the fact that President Milosevic has taken personal responsibility for the start of the dialogue, and now look to him to show that he has made a clear choice *to work with the international community*" (italics added; statement issued by the United Kingdom as Coordinator of the Birmingham Contact Group Meeting, 18 May 1998).

The Serbian authorities, however, vigorously opposed this. Any international attempts to negotiate a settlement would be seen as foreign interference, Milosevic stressed. In April a referendum was held on whether foreign mediators should be allowed to solve the dispute. Unsurprisingly, the result was an overwhelming 95 per cent "No". The boundary between national and international had, however, already moved. Kosovo was deemed an international problem regardless of the Serbian vote.

To sum up, by early 1998 Kosovo had become an international problem. Kosovo was established as an object that demanded an international solution rather than mere observation. The problem of Kosovo was now moved out of the sovereign and exclusive sphere of FRY and into the international realm. Yet what the problem of Kosovo consisted of and how it was to be solved was filled with tensions. These tensions, as we will see, crystallized into two competing representations.

Ethnic cleansing or ethnic war?

Articulating Kosovo as both a matter of violent repression by the Yugoslavian government and as a matter of a violent internal conflict between Serbs and Kosovars entailed a number of tensions and contradictions. First, Kosovo was articulated simultaneously as an internal conflict between the government of FRY and the KLA and as a case of fierce repression by the Yugoslavian government against all Kosovar Albanians. Second, Kosovo was both articulated as an international problem demanding an international solution and as an internal conflict of the FRY, which the so-called parties themselves had to solve. Third, who these two sides were, and who could speak on their behalf, was filled with contradictions: Were the two parties composed of Serbs and Kosovar Albanians, where Milosevic represented the former and Rugova the latter? Or were they composed of the KLA and the Serbian government, or of a repressive regime and an innocent population? Dialogue presumed the presence of only two sides and legitimate representation, yet this presumption was constantly being undermined by the distinctions made between terrorists and Kosovar Albanians, Milosevic and Serbs, Rugova and the KLA. During the summer of 1998 these tensions developed into two competing problematizations of Kosovo.

In the beginning of June, reports from journalists and international humanitarian organizations came out on further escalation of Serbian violence directed not only against KLA members but also against innocent civilians. In particular, emphasis was put on the plight of the ever-increasing numbers of refugees and displaced persons living in poor conditions without food and shelter. The UNHCR estimated in July that 100,000 had been internally displaced and by the end of September the number was estimated to be 200,000 (UNHCR Update, 29 July 1998; UNHCR Update, 30 September 1998). Unarmed civilians were fleeing as a result of Serbian shelling and journalists reported on incidents where civilians were gathered in groups and shot in the back (see, for example, *Washington Post*, 8 June 1998, 15 June 1998, 18 June 1998; BBC News, 5 June 1998, 10 June 1998). The UN Secretary-General, commenting on these events, condemned "the atrocities committed by Serbian military and para-military forces" and stressed that "They must not be allowed to repeat the campaign of ethnic cleansing and indiscriminate attacks that characterized the war in Bosnia" (Kofi Annan, UN Secretary-General, 5 June 1998). Similarly, the US special envoy for the Balkans said, "What we have seen is something that ... sounds an awful lot like an ethnic cleansing" (BBC News, 5 June 1998). The EU stated:

> The reports of widespread house burning and indiscriminate artillery attacks on whole villages indicate a new level of aggression on the part of the Serb security forces. We are disturbed by reports that these new attacks are beginning to constitute a new wave of ethnic cleansing.
> (EU Statement on Kosovo, 11 June 1998)

Several Western leaders also characterized the situation in terms of ethnic cleansing. Madeleine Albright, for instance, stressed: "We believe this is his [Milosevic's] ethnic cleansing and it must stop" (PBS News Hour, 12 June 1998). And Chirac in a similar vein noted "The Serbs' actions represent a desire for ethnic cleansing" (BBC News, 13 June 1998).

In contrast to these enunciations of ethnic cleansing, Tony Blair spoke about different sides in a war, stating that: "The world needs to send the strongest possible signal to the warring parties" (BBC News, 5 June 1998). Also, the NATO ministers of defence issued a statement on Kosovo saying: "We support the international efforts to secure the agreement of the parties to a cessation of violence and engagement and helping to create the conditions for serious negotiations" (NAC Statement, 11 June 1998). In a PBS News Hour (22 June 1998), a researcher from the Brookings Institute explained what she called "the nature of the current conflict", as a war waged by a large majority representing 90 per cent of the population against a tiny ruling minority.[15]

Kosovo was depicted both in terms of ethnic cleansing and in terms of ethnic war. In contrast to the invocations of ethnic cleansing, the invocations of ethnic war were, however, often painted in the excited and vivid language of the war correspondent. An extract from an article in the *New York Times* may serve to illustrate the point. The headline states: "Both sides in the Kosovo conflict seem determined to ignore reality", and it then proceeds:

> War has a choreography that only its participants understand. Fighters locked in embrace, feel out the daily rhythm until the set is shattered by a surge of violence. The old order is then replaced with another, just as ephemeral as the last. Such a dance is under way in Kosovo, where armed peasant farmers and other residents, joined by hundreds of rebels who have picked up weapons and uniforms are facing down 50,000 government soldiers and special police forces.
>
> (*New York Times*, 22 June 1998)

This aestheticization of war – war as a choreographed dance – stood in sharp contrast to the narrations of the plight of the thousands of refugees and the mounting ethnic cleansing, which similarly circulated in the media. Just as political leaders and international organizations, the media was producing two very different problematizations of Kosovo, where each representation struggled for hegemony over what the nature of the conflict consisted of.

In what sense were these two problematizations different and what turned them into competing articulations? Three aspects can be pointed out here. First, the two forms of problematizations can be said to be constituted around different ideals or nodal points. Ideals, as Kjær and Åkerstrøm (1996) have argued, make up the conditions of possibility for the articulation of problems, in that problems only can be articulated as problems because they divert from an articulated ideal. I suggest that the problematization of Kosovo as an ethnic war was constituted around an ideal that inscribed *consensus* as the foundation of domestic communities, echoing the Habermasian conception of consensual inter-subjectivity. Conflict and particularity, it was assumed, could only be resolved through conversation and dialogue. Presumably, consensus would emerge through dialogue, which in turn would guarantee peaceful and harmonious co-existence within FRY. Politics was equated with a process of dialogue. Dialogue was to lead to consensus and agreement about common goals and values, in opposition to violence and combat that were articulated as the very anti-thesis of politics. The numerous calls upon the two parties to find a political solution and refrain from using violent means were based not only on a dichotomy between violence and peace, force and politics, but also on the assumption that disputes should be settled by consensus.

The problematization of ethnic cleansing, however, operated on a different ideal. The conditions of possibility for domestic communities and peaceful coexistence were not attached to the creation of consensus by dialogue free of force, but to the respect of *judicial liberal rights*. If law and rights were observed, it was assumed, differences would be tolerated and equality prevail (for example, Holbrooke, 15 May 1998). The basis for "peace within" was not ethnic homogeneity or sameness, but respect for differences, to be achieved through the respect of law. Dissolution of FRY's territorial integrity was accordingly not a solution. The road to solve the problem in Kosovo was not through independence, or through a redrawing of borders along ethnic lines, but via the safeguarding of the judicial rights of the Kosovo Albanians to coexist and express themselves freely *within* Yugoslavia (see, for example, NAC Meeting Statement, 11 June 1998).

The two problematizations were not only based on two different ideals, they also explicitly referred to one another as opposing representations. Each portrayed the alternative version as misguided and misinformed, as out of touch with the truth and reality of the nature of the events. In a Danish newspaper, a broadside against a newly formed Kosova Committee appeared. The author – a well-known peace researcher – argued that:

> False references are made to Bosnia, [it is argued] that what happened in Bosnia now takes place in Kosova ... they [the Kosova Committee] do not mention that it takes two to wage a war [.] They furthermore lack the courage to acknowledge that what we are dealing with are two militant actors who inflict, very effectively, suffering on civilians and antagonists.
>
> (Jan Øberg in *Politiken*, 29 August 1998)

The Kosova Committee replied a few days later:

> An appeal which has been made to support one of Europe's poorest and most oppressed people – the Albanians in Kosova – has been attacked by a peace researcher. He appears to believe that this is a conflict between two warring parties [...] he believes that we are dealing with two militant actors ... and that the persons responsible for establishing "Aid to Kosova", are ignorant about the background of the conflict.

And the response then goes on to describe the "accurate" background of repression and ethnic cleansing (*Politiken*, 2 September 1998).

As this exchange also demonstrates, the two parties of the conflict were constructed very differently within the two problematizations. By problematizing Kosovo in terms of a war, both sides came to be articulated as equally responsible for the fighting; for not carrying out politics but war. Kosovar Albanians as well as the Serbs were taken to be guilty of killings and atrocities. Each side made use of illegitimate and senseless means to obtain their political goals. As the peace researcher remarked: "it takes two to make a war." The references to ethnic cleansing, however, did make it possible to distinguish between guilty and innocent, victims and perpetrators. The very subjects involved were also articulated differently. The two sides were not composed of two ethnic groups, but of innocent civilians and a brutal and powerful dictator commanding his security forces to commit random extrajudicial killings and expulsions. Small wonder, an editorial in the *Washington Post* argued, that

> Milosevic sees Western threats as empty rhetoric and continues to slaughter Kosovars with impunity ... So far, Milosevic has had four months of free rein in Kosovo, where his henchmen have killed some 300 Kosovar Albanians, created tens of thousands of refugees and displaced persons, and laid hundreds of new land mines to kill and maim for years to come.
>
> (*Washington Post*, 18 June 1998)

It was Milosevic's abuse of power, which was to be stopped: "We are considering ... how we can make sure that President Milosevic is prevented from using the power of his military against the civilian population" (Cook, 8 June 1998).

The incommensurability of dialogue and ethnic cleansing, strikes and ethnic war

The references to ethnic cleansing served to facilitate easy distinctions between guilty and innocent, and effectively invested Milosevic with the sole responsibility for the killings. However, the invocation of ethnic cleansing also made it much more difficult to propose dialogue as a sensible solution. To argue that a people subject to killings, expulsion, or even extinction merely needed to engage in dialogue with their perpetrators seemed absurd. Problematizing Kosovo in terms of an ethnic war equally closed off some solutions. It was much more difficult to argue in favour of military strikes, as long as it was settled that bombings would punish only Milosevic's regime in Belgrade. The emerging threats of force seemed to demand that one part only could be identified as guilty. Moreover, the simultaneous presence of both of these problematizations also made it more difficult to establish how "the problem" of Kosovo was to be responded to. In the absence of a settled problem, solutions were equally difficult to define. As we shall see, these tensions, hinging on articulations of victims and perpetrators, responsibility and innocence, were present right up to the intervention.

Prior to the summer of 1998, Kosovo had already been constructed as an international problem – as accounted for above – but the solution to this problem had predominately been portrayed as a matter that the two parties themselves had to, and could, find through dialogue. Rugova's meeting with Milosevic in mid-May, however, demonstrated the inherent tensions in combining dialogue as a solution with enunciations of ethnic cleansing. A clip of Rugova and Milosevic in close conversation – Rugova laughing and smiling – had been repeated continuously on Serbian television and caused outrage amongst the Kosovar Albanians.

According to Judah (2000: 154), one politician noted: "After all, while Rugova laughs, half of Kosovo is bleeding." And as follow-up talks between the Rugova delegation and Milosevic were about to be arranged, reports were simultaneously coming out on Serbian offensives around Decani. The Rugova delegation henceforth explained that they would not continue talks. Similarly, Cook (28 May 1998), the British Minister of Foreign Affairs, added that he initially had welcomed the dialogue, but now it was being undermined by Milosevic's actions of escalating violence. Instead of dialogue between the two sides, direct international participation in the talks was now proposed (Contact Group Statement, 8 July 1998).

For the first time, attempts were made to achieve an internationally negotiated solution to the problem of Kosovo. The Contact Group, headed by US Ambassador Chris Hill, in cooperation with Richard Holbrooke, started to work out proposals for negotiations through shuttle diplomacy between Western capitals and Belgrade/ Pristina. Yet, while direct international participation in the formulations of a negotiation plan and in the possible future negotiations was the first of its kind in relation to Kosovo, it did not confront the question which Cook himself had posed, namely how could negotiations take place while Milosevic was escalating the violence? And indeed rather than referring to Serbian shelling and ethnic cleansing, the calls for negotiations were followed by condemnations of terrorism and appeals to both sides of showing restraint, engaging in a ceasefire and choosing peace and negotiations (*Le Monde*, 1 July 1998). Amnesty International explicitly condemned KLA's use of force, emphasizing that "the victims are Albanians and Serbs ... the UCK too has deliberately and indiscriminately attacked Albanian and Serbian civilians" (Miller, Director of Amnesty's Mission to Kosovo in *Le Monde*, 1 July 1998).

In early June NATO threatened for the first time with the use of military force. The British Defence Ministry confirmed that: "NATO is considering all options, including the most radical ... We are examining very carefully military options that could and might have to be made available" (BBC, Radio 4, 5 June 1998).[16] The threat of force was followed by a show of force. On 11 June NATO decided to conduct air exercises over Albania and Macedonia in order to demonstrate – as it was put – "NATO's capability to project power rapidly in the region" (NAC Statement, 11 June 1998). A general of the US Air Force explained, we will "see a lot of muscle-flexing ... essentially we could make a lot of noise and make ourselves noticed in Albania" (PBS News Hour, 12 June 1998). Besides these air exercises NATO's military was ordered to draw up plans for a future military intervention. In a press conference in Washington, Solana explained that:

> NATO leaders asked them [the military leaders] to assess and develop a full range of military options, including the use of air power and the deployment of ground forces into Kosovo. *Stopping the Serbian government's systematic campaign of violent repression and expulsion in Kosovo is the immediate goal.*
> (italics added; American Forces Press Service, 17 June 1998)

The threat of force was explicitly targeted against the Serbian government, in contrast to the calls for negotiations, which ritually were followed by condemnations of terrorisms and appeals to both sides to choose the path of peace.

Following the initial air exercise, there was no shortage of statements describing the amount of power that had been displayed and how this display of strength would send a clear signal to Milosevic, stopping what was termed the Serbian crackdown in Kosovo. "If Milosevic does not get the message from today's show of military might ... NATO will start considering, a range of military options" (Cohen, 15 June 1998). Also, the media engaged in lengthy descriptions of the number of flights involved, the degree of planning and organization it took, and the reactions it spurred on the ground: "The roars of high-flying fighter jets rolled over the mountains of Albania today as NATO staged a dramatic, five-hour show of force aimed at ending Serbia's military crackdown in Kosovo. To residents of northern Albania it was the sound of peace" it was curiously noted (*Washington Post*, 16 June 1998). NATO's power and ability to punish was to be clearly visible, it was emphasized. Milosevic was to see and to hear the flights at the border of Kosovo. Milosevic was not only to know, but also to sense, the imbalance of power.

Yet, speaking in the language of compliance and threats of course connoted that it was already settled who needed to comply and whom the threats were directed towards. However, it was far from unequivocally given who was to be blamed, who needed to comply, who were the guilty parties and who were the innocent. While the international negotiations and the UN resolutions still were premised on the idea that the problem of Kosovo involved two responsible parties who both needed to refrain from violence and enter into negotiations, the threat of the use of force was, as noted, explicitly directed against the Serbian government and not against the Kosovars or even the KLA. "The Belgrade authorities, and I think of course of President Milosevic, must respect the terms of the resolution urgently and in their entirety" (Vedrine, 23 September 1998). "That is a very clear and very blunt statement to President Milosevic on the importance of him complying in full with the demands of the international community" (Cook, 13 July 1998).

Hence, the threat of the use of force was, just as the proposals for negotiations, intertwined in the discursive struggle over what the problem of Kosovo consisted of. It was difficult to uphold that Kosovo was a problem where two parties were to blame and to make concessions at the negotiating table, while at the same time claiming that the threats of the use of military force were targeted only against Belgrade. Solutions came in this sense to shape the articulation of problems. To put it simply, if force was the solution to the problem of Kosovo, then the KLA and Belgrade could not be equally responsible.

At the same time, commentaries and media outlets increasingly questioned the effectiveness of diplomacy and negotiations, continually invoking the so-called lessons of Bosnia (*Le Monde*, 7 July 1998). In the same vein, doubts were raised in terms of the credibility of the threats of the use of force. Were not these threats mere sabre rattling? Was the international community once again standing passively by, snared by Milosevic's cynic political play, while a whole population was being slaughtered and hundreds of thousands of refugees were to starve in the coming winter? (*Washington Post*, 4 August 1998, 30 August 1998). The threat of the use of force was to guarantee that yet another Bosnia would not materialize.

> I think that if we use diplomacy and force that threatens, we should be able to succeed ... All of you who have been following the last few months in Kosovo must begin to wonder whether another Bosnia looms on the horizon ... already the shelling, the ethnic cleansing, the indiscriminate attacks on civilians in the name of security are taking place ... all our expressions of determination to never again permit another Bosnia will be cruelly mocked if we allow Kosovo to become another killing field. It is in our hand now.
> (Annan, 15 July 1998 quoted from Knudsen 1999b: 41)

The invocation of Bosnia and the numerous references to ethnic cleansing also made the condemnations of terrorism difficult to sustain. At a French press conference, the French Minister of Foreign Affairs was faced with the difficult task of explaining whose terror the Security Council resolutions actually were condemning and why statements primarily were addressing and reproaching terrorism. How could Kosovar Albanian resistance be determined as terrorism, when Milosevic was bombing, persecuting and driving them out of their homes, it was asked (Press Conference, Vedrine, 23 September 1998).

In the end, Vedrine was probed to condemn the Serbian Army's repression and acts of terrorism, although still evading whether terrorism referred to the KLA or to the Serbian forces. These tensions and the increasing number of references to the "lessons of Bosnia" looked like the emerging hegemony of a problematization of ethnic cleansing and military strikes. Yet in October the problematization of Kosovo shifted once again. The problem, which the international community now seemed to face, was a mounting humanitarian catastrophe. Terror, violence and ethnic cleansing were, for a while, relegated to the margins, while the plights of the refugees, the need for humanitarian organization to get access to Kosovo and the dangers of the coming winter took precedence.

On the verge of a humanitarian catastrophe? A short deviation

The establishment of Kosovo as a humanitarian catastrophe had crucial implications. It vested the problem of Kosovo within a humanitarian realm which seemingly was untouched by politics and partisanship, where the aim and motives of the international community were portrayed as neutral and humanitarian; as a matter of bringing aid and relief, while the subjects to be brought relief were spoken of as refugees and victims of circumstances they had no control over.

In late September the previous French and British attempts to draft yet another UN resolution bore fruits. Although Milosevic had been threatened that such a resolution would include further enforcement measures, the resolution did not come to entail additional sanctions. Notably it lacked a mandate for the use of force. The resolution was, however, again adopted within Chapter VII of the charter, and in contrast to the previous resolution, the source of the threat to international security and stability was now being spelled out as an "impending humanitarian catastrophe" (UN Security Council Resolution 1199). Moreover, the language of the Security Council resolution also slightly changed. Emphasis shifted from "substantive dialogue between the parties" (UN Security Council Resolution 1160) to a "negotiated political solution with international involvement" and from concerns over "excessive use of force and acts of terrorism" to concerns of the "flows of refugees and an impending humanitarian disaster". It also echoed previous demands for direct international involvement. "Calls upon the authorities in the Federal Republic of Yugoslavia and the Kosovo Albanian leadership to enter immediately into a meaningful dialogue without preconditions and with international involvement" (Security Council Resolution 1199).

Within a few days after the adoption of the Security Council Resolution 1199, fresh reports from journalists appeared on yet another massacre of civilians at Gorne Obrinje in Kosovo (BBC, 30 September 1998; Cook, 30 September 1998). The immediate reaction to these reports was to arrange so-called emergency meetings in the Contact Group as well as in the Security Council, and once again reiterate the possibilities of a future military response from NATO. Before these meetings were to commence, the Secretary-General was to issue what was termed his "long-awaited" report on the situation in Kosovo, and on FRY's compliance with Security Council Resolutions 1160 and 1199 (BBC, 5 October 1998). On the basis of the Secretary-General's conclusion NATO was then to determine, it was argued, whether or not air strikes were necessary (Pickering, Under Secretary of State for Political Affairs, 5 October 1998; BBC, 5 October 1998).

The report of the Secretary-General was granted a prominent place. References to the findings of the report came to appear over and over throughout October in official speeches as well as in the media. Kofi Annan was, of course, not the master of his own text, in the sense that he, as any "'author'", could control neither its use, nor its proliferated meanings. Annan's report could be endlessly produced and reproduced, and yet at the same time, he could be used as the original and authoritative voice of these reproductions; as the neutral and authoritative observer who had a particular access to determine the truth of the events in Kosovo. Cook, for instance, argued:

> The other developments of this afternoon are that the text of the report of Kofi Annan has been released. I have studied this report and I am impressed by the extent to which the Secretary-General shares our deep alarm at the worsening situation in Kosovo.
>
> (Cook, 5 October 1998)

With respect to Yugoslavia's compliance with the Security Council resolution it was argued that Annan's report clearly demonstrated that Milosevic was not anywhere near full compliance, whereas others stressed that Annan had argued that he could not make any assessment of compliance since the UN had no direct presence on the ground (Lockhart, White House Press Secretary, 6 October 1998;

Albright, 7 October 1998; Cook, 5 October 1998; BBC, 5 October 1998; *The Guardian,* 6 October 1998). As one journalist noted: "There is something for everyone in this report" (BBC, 5 October 1998). However, two assessments, in particular, came to circulate: first, that the Serbian forces were engaged in disproportionate violence against civilians and that the victims of the current violence predominately were Kosovar Albanians. This was, of course, hardly a new observation, but it could now be affirmed by an "objective authority" that it was civilians – rather than guerrilla or terrorist groups – who were the targets of violence, and furthermore that it was the Kosovar Albanians – rather than Serbs – who were the prime victims of terror and brutality. Second, a new form of problematization also emerged from the circulation of Annan's report. Kosovo was no longer *only* a problem of unproportional repression and violence, Kosovo was also a potential *humanitarian* disaster. If the situation in Kosovo did not change, it was stressed, the current humanitarian crisis would turn into a humanitarian catastrophe, which could only be prevented if Milosevic came into full and immediate compliance with the latest Security Council resolution.

Much emphasis was obviously put on the plight of the refugees and displaced persons, in particular as winter was soon approaching. As Cook concluded on behalf of the Contact Group following its emergency meeting:

> The report of the Secretary General ... has already spelt out the serious humanitarian crisis in Kosovo, particularly among the refugees. Tonight we would reinforce that message by reminding the world of the urgency of obtaining full compliance with Resolution 1199 before winter sets in and turns a humanitarian crisis into a humanitarian catastrophe.
>
> (Cook, 8 October 1998; see also Albright, 7 October 1998; Vedrine, 23 September 1998)

In spite of the warnings put forward by Annan in his report, attention was turned to the problem of how human suffering in Kosovo could be alleviated, rather than, as Annan put it, how a comprehensive political solution could be reached to the problem of Kosovo (Report of the UN Secretary-General, 3 October 1998). Of course, Annan's statement presumed that it was evident what the problem of Kosovo consisted of and that a boundary safely could be drawn between political and humanitarian aspects. However, what Annan did clearly foresee were the effects of articulating Kosovo solely in terms of a humanitarian crisis.

What were the consequences of articulating Kosovo as a humanitarian problem? First, by emphasizing the terrible conditions of the refugees, the difficulties of bringing forward humanitarian assistance and the potential dangers of the harsh winter in the area, politics became relegated to the margins. By casting the problem of Kosovo as a mounting humanitarian disaster, Kosovo came to be presented in the same category as natural catastrophes and famines. The problem, which needed to be dealt with, was how shelter and food could be provided and ultimately how the refugees could return safely to their homes: "As you know, there are tens of thousands of people up in the hills and winter is coming. So there needs to be the ability for humanitarian agencies to deliver food and to let the people go back to their homes" (Albright, 8 October 1998; see also Pickering, 5 October 1998). Second, the articulation of Kosovo as a humanitarian catastrophe also produced a different type of subject from ethnic cleansing or ethnic war. The articulations of a humanitarian catastrophe operated with what one might call anonymous collectivities. It operated with mere victims being described in neutral terms as refugees, displaced persons, people or humans. Third, the detailed descriptions of the character of the humanitarian crisis, of the thousands of refugees stranded in the mountains facing the winter with little shelter, clothing, clean water, sanitation or food served to bring the question of the need to do something beyond question and debate. That is to say, it was impossible to disagree that this was an intolerable situation, which needed to be solved. The international community was faced with a humanitarian rather than a political problem. They were faced with humans who were suffering from harms that they had no control over; harms that they had not inflicted on themselves.

But what was the meaning of "doing something given"? In order to solve the humanitarian problem the twin track strategy of diplomacy and force was once again invoked as a means to obtain obedience from Milosevic. It had, however, become increasingly difficult to articulate force and diplomacy as part of the same package. The international community had to decide whether it wished to continue along the diplomatic route – which, it was widely established, had not achieved any progress – or engage in a military intervention. This zero-sum logic was now forcefully dissolved. Having – presumably – learned the lessons of Bosnia, it was contended that diplomacy could not work alone. It had to be backed by force. "It is extremely significant that the diplomatic efforts that are now being conducted, [... are] backed up, as they are now, with the serious potential of the use of force" (Pickering, 5 October 1998). Milosevic, it was stressed, was only able to understand the brute language of force, and although the Western leaders would prefer other means, they had realized that only force could make diplomacy work. "We would prefer – we would far prefer – to secure President Milosevic's compliance with the will of the international community in a peaceful manner. But NATO must be prepared to act militarily ... to prevent another humanitarian catastrophe in the Balkans" (Clinton, 8 October 1998). Force was, in other words, turned into the condition of possibility for diplomacy. In an almost circular logic it was argued that in order not to use the means of force, one had to make diplomacy work, and that could only work if backed by force.

This was a powerful move. Not only did it serve to undermine the constitution of diplomacy as complacent, it also served to silence – or please – hawks and doves alike. It made it difficult to argue that diplomacy was not pursued, just as it became difficult to argue that the current policy was appeasing. It now appeared obvious that diplomacy was derivative of force. In accordance with this logic, Richard Holbrooke was once again sent to Belgrade, backing his shuttle diplomacy with NATO's use of force. And on 13 October NATO issued its so-called activation order for a phased air campaign, which was to commence within 98 hours, if Milosevic did not reach a deal with Ambassador Holbrooke (Statement by NATO Secretary-General, 13 October 1998).

Legitimizing humanitarian intervention

Whereas no questions seemed to be raised in terms of the necessity of backing diplomacy with force, the legitimacy of a potential NATO intervention without a UNSC mandate indeed gave rise to debate. Faced with questions of how a military intervention could be carried out in the absence of a UN mandate, Western leaders were forced to legitimize intervention, even before it had begun. This was carried out by three crucial moves: first, by invoking the authority of the Security Council and granting the Council a specific will, which only NATO had the ability to represent; second, by constructing a future intervention as an apolitical, neutral and necessary act qua its humanitarian purpose, and third by constructing the possible intervention as an exception. I will go through each of these in turn.

First, the language of the Western leaders echoed that of the Security Council resolutions and the statements of Kofi Annan to an astonishing extent. Often the exact same phrases were used. In this way the authority of the Security Council resolutions and the Secretary's reports were constantly invoked, blurring distinctions between NATO and the UN. Rather than undermining or questioning the authority of the Security Council, NATO was in fact abiding by the will of the Council. NATO's Secretary-General summarized NATO's position on 9 October the following way:

> The FRY has yet not complied with the urgent demands of the International Community, despite UNSC Resolution 1160, followed by Resolution 1199 ... both acting under Chapter VII of the UN Charter.
>
> The very stringent report of the Secretary-General of the United Nations pursuant to both resolutions warned inter alia of the danger of a humanitarian disaster in Kosovo.
>
> The deterioration of the situation in Kosovo and its magnitude constitutes a serious threat to peace and security in the region as explicitly referred to in the UNSC Resolution 1199.
>
> On this basis ... I conclude that in the particular circumstances with respect to the present crisis in Kosovo as described in UNSC Resolution 1199 there are legitimate grounds for NATO to threaten and if necessary to use force.
>
> (quoted from Simma 1999)

By articulating NATO's demands and the demands of the Security Council as equivalent, or rather by refraining from making the distinction between the two in the first place, it was possible to argue that NATO was not pursuing any goals of its own, but merely attempting to enforce compliance with the demands of the UNSC.[17] NATO was, in this way, portrayed as a weather vane or black box. NATO was neutrally mirroring and carrying out the already existing demands of the UNSC. It was seemingly not adding to, interpreting or violating these demands. Drawing on the Security Council's supposed capacity to represent the international community, it could be claimed that NATO was acting in correspondence with the will of the international community. Demands made were often not related to NATO or to the Security Council. Rather it appeared as if it was the international community who spoke and demanded. In a representational logic of three steps, it could be asserted that NATO was acting on behalf of the UN who, in turn, was acting on behalf of the international community. This strategy was, as we will see, to be repeated during the intervention.

Second, as touched upon on above, referring to the potential humanitarian catastrophe served to justify the need of immediate action if crisis was not to evolve into disaster. By problematizing Kosovo as a humanitarian problem, the necessity of "doing something" appeared to be self-evident. "The Secretary-General and I have discussed NATO's role in the crisis. I fully concur with his assessment that the Alliance has the legitimacy to act to stop a humanitarian catastrophe" (Albright, 8 October 1998). The problem of Kosovo was a humanitarian crisis, and those involved and in need of help were no longer portrayed as terrorists, guerrillas, secessionist or warring parties, but as humans. The act of alleviating the suffering of humans was by nature humanitarian.

Moving Kosovo from a political realm to one of humanitarian necessity was closely linked with the third strategy: the positioning of Kosovo and the military intervention as an exceptional act. Kosovo was taken to be a case transgressing the normal field of International Relations. It constituted an exception due to the catastrophic humanitarian conditions and this made it all the easier to justify an abnormal response.

By fixating the exceptional, the normal was simultaneously established. Intervention would *normally* demand a UN mandate, but this particular case transcended the normal. By the construction of the humanitarian situation as belonging to the extraordinary, the ordinary was neither questioned nor resisted but on the contrary affirmed. The humanitarian situation justified, Chirac explained, an exception, and France would therefore not hesitate to intervene in order to help those in danger.

> I have told you that France ... thinks that military action under any given form should be called for and decided by the Security Council. In this particular case we have a resolution, which, indeed, opens the door to the possibility of military action. *I add and repeat that the humanitarian situation constitutes a reason which can justify an exception to a rule* no matter what its strength and firmness. And should it appear that the humanitarian situation demands this then France would not hesitate to join those who would like to help those that are in danger.
> (italics added; Chirac, 6 October 1998)

In a similar vein, Klaus Kinkel (16 October 1998), the German Foreign Minister, argued before the Bundestag that the situation in Kosovo was of such a desperate nature that a humanitarian intervention was justifiable even in the absence of a UNSC authorization. At the same time it was possible to invoke the authority of the Security Council and to argue that the Council's authorization was unnecessary in times of exceptional human suffering.[18]

In October 1998 the battle over the legitimacy of intervention had thus already begun. Yet, it quickly came to a halt, and one may say never really evolved, in that Holbrooke obtained an agreement with Milosevic in mid-October. This agreement was endorsed by the Security Council shortly after. Accordingly, it could now be established that diplomacy worked when backed by the threat of the use of force and that the Security Council had in fact implicitly embraced the use of force by recognizing Holbrooke's settlement (Cook, 14 October 1998; Weller 1999a).[19]

As reports started to come out on a gradual Serbian pullout from Kosovo and as the first stories of refugees returning to their homes and the increasing presence of the Kosovo Verification Mission emerged, Kosovo almost disappeared from the headlines. The general conception was that Milosevic – just as in the case of Bosnia – had bent to the language of force and that the humanitarian catastrophe now was averted (Cook in the *Guardian*, 14 October 1998; UNHCR to BBC, 21 October 1998).

The end of a humanitarian catastrophe and the beginning of war

The problematization of Kosovo as a humanitarian catastrophe had worked to portray the immediate problem to be solved as a matter of alleviating human suffering through the safe return of refugees and access of the humanitarian organizations, applying, if necessary, even exceptional means. The problem had primarily been formulated as one of food and shelter: a problem of basic rather than political needs. During the winter of 1998 previous problematizations were now rearticulated. The humanitarian problem had been solved, it was contended, through the threat of force, but sporadic violence on both sides were still occurring and a political solution had not been reached. Once again it was stressed that terrorism and independence for the Kosovars were unacceptable, just as it was underlined that it was intolerable for the Kosovars to live under Serbian domination and repression. The catch phrase of the summer, "neither independence nor status quo" reappeared. And once again the way to a settlement between the parties was deemed to be an affair of diplomacy.

From November 1998 to January 1999, Ambassador Hill presented three different draft proposals on the future of the status of Kosovo to the parties. In early November a political settlement was still portrayed as only a step away (Hill, 5 November 1998), but by December – after three rejected proposals and no direct talks between the parties – the media started to report on resignation on behalf of the diplomats and both sides were criticized for delaying the peace process (see, for example, BBC, 9 December 1998, 11 December 1998, 12 December 1998). In mid-December Kofi Annan (Press Conference, 14 December 1998) warned that if the efforts to find a political solution were not intensified, an *all-out war* would emerge in Kosovo. The attempts to reach a political settlement had come, it was contended, to yet another dead end, and the cease-fire was broken. Kosovo was on the verge of war. Again appeals were made to both sides to renounce violence and to solve their difference through political means (Cook, 23 December 1998; Solana, 24 December 1998). The peace was shattered, it was stressed, and the international community faced a war where both sides were in breach of the UN resolutions (BBC, 24 December 1998, 26 December 1998; William Walker, US Ambassador,12 January 1999; Cook, 17 January 1999).

Following the disclosure of the Racak killings, the problematization of Kosovo and its possible solutions once again crystallized into the two competing representations of ethnic war and ethnic cleansing. Kosovo was referred to in terms of brutal repression and ethnic cleansing led by a cynical dictator. The killings were widely identified as yet another proof that the West could and should not negotiate with Milosevic. As in the case of Bosnia, the international community had been snared by Milosevic's empty promises and allowed him, unpunished, to continue his policy of ethnic cleansing. Bosnia was again used as a powerful reference point. The West had, it was argued, to learn the lessons of Bosnia. What these lessons consisted of was presumed to be fairly clear. History seemed to constitute a well-defined reservoir of directly accessible knowledge; a guide of the past to the present. Although, it had been established only a few months earlier that NATO had applied the instructive experience of Bosnia – threatening Milosevic into concessions – Bosnia still loomed as an example of failed Western responses and complicity, which taught us what happens when the international community reacts much too late. An editorial in *Le Monde* under the headline of "There will be more Racaks", explained how Racak should not have come as a surprise to anyone. Seen in the light of the massacres in Bosnia and Croatia, Kosovo was foreordained, it was argued. The West's continued attempts to find a solution at the negotiating table, rather than applying force, not only conflated perpetrators and victims, but also tragically assured that there would be other "Racaks", just as in Bosnia and Croatia.

The instructive "lesson" of Bosnia came to serve as yet another prescription for air strikes and as a guide through which the nature of the current conflict could be understood. Milosevic's ethnic cleansing and dreams of a greater Serbia were not a result of ancient hatred among different groups, but of cynical and criminal political leaders. In spite of Milosovic's criminal acts, he had been allowed to reign and had been invited to talks and negotiations, which had legitimized him as a serious leader and negotiating partner. Milosevic, it was stressed by a British Labour MP, had for more than six years been named as a suspected criminal and yet he had not been indicted (*Guardian*, 27 January 1999).

The mainly official representation, however, portrayed Kosovo as an ethnic war, composed of two responsible and extremist parties who were determined to solve their political difference by violence and killings. Within this representation it was continuously emphasized that the KLA was just as responsible for the stalemate in the political negotiations and for the brutal killings, as the government in Belgrade. The killings in Racak were condemned, but at the same time, it was stressed, that the cause of the continued violence rested with both sides, or even primarily with the KLA. "On its part, the KLA has committed more breaches of the cease-fire, and until this weekend was responsible for more deaths, than the security forces" (Cook, 18 January 1999). The suggested solution was to make the parties realize that neither side could win a war and that only a peaceful settlement reached through meaningful negotiations constituted a viable and rational path to settle differences. Nevertheless, doubts were raised on how the two parties, suddenly, were to realize this compelling logic when they had not been able to over the last six months: "The new mass killing is a chill reminder that the warring parties in Kosovo are in no mood to take notice of outside opinion as they pursue their nasty ethnic war" (*Guardian*, 29 January 1999).

Although calls for negotiations appeared rather unconvincing in light of previous failures and continued killings, the only alternative solution seemingly presenting itself was also deemed to be impossible. It was difficult to justify a renewed threat of air strikes as a sensible response to avert full-scale war, when the responsibility for the halt in negotiations and resumption of violence was placed mainly with the KLA. An air campaign was deemed to be a partial and one-sided response, which would punish the government in Belgrade only, and perhaps even fortify the strongholds of the KLA. The West was not to take sides in this ethnic war by air strikes, which in effect would come to serve as a strategic and unintentional air force of the KLA, Solana (22 January 1999) argued. As the *Guardian* similarly argued "Western European countries say air strikes could be effective against Serbian military targets but would be a pointless way to try to punish the KLA which, they argue, is responsible for many of the provocations in recent weeks" (*Guardian*, 28 January 1999).

In sum, a deadlock had emerged. The two well-known representations of events in Kosovo were invoked once again; at the same time the only two solutions, which anyone seemed able to envisage, were paths already travelled. This impasse was further confounded by the fact that the use of force over the years had been articulated as the last and most radical means available; as a solution to be used when everything else had failed. Now the situation was exactly articulated as a case where everything had been tried and failed, and yet force could not be used. Military strikes were constituted as a partisan response, entailing no promise of making the Kosovo Albanians refrain from violence.

Enforced negotiations: the constitution of responsibility

By the end of January, the stalemate was evaded by so-called *enforced negotiations*. On 29 January the Contact Group "summoned" the two warring parties in Kosovo to talks in Rambouillet, and made clear at the same time that it would "hold both sides accountable if they failed to take the opportunity now offered to them" (Contact Group Statement, 29 January 1999). Specifying this statement the next day NATO stressed that the two parties would need to attend peace talks in France and work out a political agreement within twenty-one days, otherwise they would be faced with NATO strikes (NAC Statement, 30 January 1999). Both of the so-called warring parties were taken to constitute potential targets of such threats. The threat of military strikes was to compel both parties to find a political solution and was supposedly aimed at both sides (Pardew, US Ambassador, 3 February 1999; Clinton, 4 February 1999; Cook to the House of Commons, 1 February 1999; *Guardian*, 31 January 1999). While the notion of equal responsibility was combined with the threat of force, no specifications were made, however, of how this threat was to induce both sides to make peace or how potential strikes would avoid constituting a strategic help for the KLA.

Enforcing negotiations on both parts and holding them equally responsible for current violence – as well as for the success or failure of negotiations – were taken to be effective means of peace, and tokens of international neutrality and balance: "We are not taking sides here", Rubin (11 February 1999) emphasized. "The unanimous international community has mobilized itself. Its action isn't direct against anyone" (Chirac, 6 February 1999).

The Rambouillet talks were in this way opened with a strong emphasis on the responsibility of the two parties. The road to peace was to be facilitated by international presence, but ultimately war could be ended only if the two sides realized their own responsibilities. "To the representatives of the two parties, Serbs and Albanians of Kosovo, I say that peace is in your hands. I appeal to your responsibilities" (Chirac, 6 February 1999). Yet, if reaching peace was entirely in the hands of Serbs and Kosovars – being their sole responsibility – this would, of course, by definition rule out the need for international involvement in the talks, as well as in that implementation or monitoring phase, which had to follow a peace accord.[20] Yet, as Albright (5 February 1999) added: "We cannot succeed if the parties refuse to live up to their own responsibilities. But we would not be meeting our own responsibility to them or to ourselves if we do not do what we could to lead the way." "We", in other words, equally had a responsibility to make these talks work. Failing to live up to "our" responsibility would not only connote a wrongdoing in terms of the Serbs and the Kosovars, but also in terms of "ourselves". Staying outside the conflict would harm our very own identity. Kosovo was also our problem and our future (Clinton, 16 February 1999; Albright, 5 February 1999).

The negotiations at Rambouillet were portrayed foremost as a question of peace or war. References to repression, ethnic cleansing or crimes against humanity seemed virtually to disappear. Rambouillet was conveyed as one last attempt to hinder full-scale ethnic war, if each warring party was willing to compromise in order to achieve the goal of peace. Rambouillet was referred to as *peace talks* and the continued violence in Kosovo as a simmering war. If either side failed to sign the accord it would indicate unwillingness to peace and NATO strikes would consequently follow.

By the end of February, the logic of equal responsibility and equal punishment, however, started to crumble. The deadline of the Rambouillet talks had been expanded twice and no agreement had yet been signed. Simultaneously, media reports were coming out on increasing levels of violence in Kosovo and now questions started to be raised whether NATO would still intervene in case neither side signed an agreement. Although it was stressed that "both sides are to blame for the current violence", it was argued that NATO would apply the means of force *only* if the Serbian delegation did not sign! (Vedrine and Cook, Joint Press Meeting, 23

February 1999). "In order to move towards military action, it has to be clear that the Serbs were responsible", it was stressed (Rubin, 21 February 1999). "Whether NATO bombs or not that depends on the Serbs" Clinton (23 February 1999) equally explained.

Talks resumed in Paris on 15 March. Two weeks were allotted for the delegations to convince the Kosovar Albanians and the Serbs respectively that the agreement needed to be signed. No attempts were made to hide that the Kosovars had to sign, if NATO was to bomb Belgrade. If the Kosovars agreed, then Belgrade could be held responsible (Pardew, 4 March 1999; Cook and Vedrine, 5 March 1999; Cook, 15 March 1999). The signatures were to deliver a NATO intervention rather than a peace agreement.

On 18 March the Kosovo Albanian delegation signed the Rambouillet agreement and it could be accordingly determined that the Serbs were responsible for the failure of the talks as well as for NATO's bombings. In fact, the decision to intervene did not reside with NATO, but with Milosevic; he had inflicted the bombings on himself. NATO merely reacted to a situation created by others. One journalist asked whether they [the Rambouillet negotiators] all agreed that the Serbians were responsible and Petritsch answered as if this was only evident: "Of course, the Kosovo Albanian delegation is ready to sign the agreement in its entirety" (Contact Group Negotiators Press Conference, 18 March 1999).

In what was portrayed as one last attempt to persuade Milosevic to sign, Richard Holbrooke once again flew to Belgrade. Concurrently, efforts were made to explain the goal of the pending NATO bombings. The strikes, it was emphasized, were to hinder ethnic cleansing against innocent civilians and prevent a humanitarian catastrophe. One journalist, noting the shift in the forms of justifications, argued:

> NATO's mission has subtly changed in recent days. The mission is now to prevent an impending humanitarian disaster in Kosovo, and to prevent Milosevic from taking advantage of the OSCE withdrawal to resume brutal offensives against innocent civilians, bombarding villages and forcing people to leave, a NATO spokesman said last night.
>
> (*Guardian*, 22 March 1999)

Now with a clear positioning of responsibility for the continued violence and unwillingness to peace, it could be established that this was a matter of hindering Milosevic from massacring civilians. While Holbrooke was on his way to Belgrade it was stressed: "President Milosevic is leaving us no option but military action" and "We regret the fact that we are having to take action, but the alternative to action is a humanitarian disaster in Kosovo, thousands of people being displaced and killed" (Cook in the *Guardian*, 22 March 1999; Tony Blair, 23 March 1999). This was to be repeated many times in the months to come. NATO had in fact no choice. If "we" did not want to stand idle, if "we" wanted to act, "we" had to intervene.

A short conclusion: the constitution of an object of intervention

This chapter has analysed how the articulations on Kosovo moved through a gradual process of selection – where some articulations were closed off and others made possible. The analysis has shown how state violence and terrorism in late 1996 and early 1997 crucially moved Kosovo from an issue of human rights to be observed, assessed and reported, to an international problem needing to be solved; from an internal affair of Yugoslavia to an international problem demanding international involvement. What the problem consisted of, and how it could and should be solved, however, shifted and changed rather rapidly through 1997–1999. Tensions in the way the problem of Kosovo was articulated – for example, between terrorism and state violence – and in the way problems and solutions were combined – for example, dialogue and ethnic cleansing – changed articulations of problems and solutions. However, these shifts, and the gradual closure of possible responses, did not follow any pre-given path or moved towards a necessary telos of intervention. The enunciations of a humanitarian catastrophe over the fall of 1998, for instance, marked a curious detour, just as the articulations of proper solutions over 1998 did not simply follow a stepwise escalation from diplomacy, to negotiations, to sanctions and intervention.

Yet, one of the defining events of 1998 was, of course, the battle over ethnic cleansing versus ethnic war based on the two different ideals. These competing representations, I argued, also shaped the articulations of possible solutions and responses. By referring to Kosovo as either ethnic cleansing or ethnic war, crucial decisions were made in terms of whom the international community needed to pressure and sanction, or help and support. Solutions, however, also shaped the articulation of problems. With the emerging articulations of the use of force as the last and most radical means available, and the gradual perception that diplomacy and sanctions had been exhausted and proven ineffective, a clear division of responsibility was needed. The invocation of ethnic cleansing and the lessons of Bosnia evidently rendered this easier. This lesson – always appearing in singularity – could powerfully be invoked to call for the need of acting and using force before it was too late.

But the positioning of force as synonymous with "doing something", depended itself, I argued, on a certain narration of prior events, on the establishment that all other means already had been tried. This is an important point to stress, since "action" and "doing" commonly are rendered synonymous with intervention.

In short, the equation of intervention and doing something, and the positioning of Rambouillet as the end of a long process of failed attempts, where every peaceful means had been tried and exhausted, constituted a powerful combination. Hereby, it became extremely difficult to question the "need to intervene". These crucial stabilizations were to play important parts in the legitimations of the intervention, as we are to see in the next chapter.

4 Sovereignty and intervention

Intervention had been constituted as the only way to act; as being synonymous with action. To argue that NATO should not intervene could therefore be inscribed as passivity and indifference at times of ethnic cleansing and mounting genocide. This obviously made it very difficult to question the legitimacy of the intervention.

Yet, reading through the legitimations of the intervention one becomes struck by two apparently competing and contradictory claims: one holding that NATO was not intervening in the internal affairs of Yugoslavia, the other holding that NATO indeed was carrying out an intervention. These two claims did not appear as contradictious; neither did they seem to compete in terms of "true representation", but rather seemed to complement one another.

How could these contradicting claims live side by side? How could it be that these conflicting assertions never were confronted as being inconsistent or paradoxical? I will show that this was possible because these claims were based on, and reproduced, two very familiar perspectives on state sovereignty. The apparent contradiction is part of sovereignty's own powerful and uneasy double-role that at one and the same time differentiates and links the international and national realm, yet constituting the very condition of possibility for both (Bartelson 1995). This enables, as spelled out in Chapter 1, state sovereignty to be articulated both as an internal relationship between ruler and ruled – where sovereignty denotes a hierarchical concentration of state power and authority inside – and as an external relationship between independent political communities, where sovereignty denotes the antithesis, in the form of anarchy and the absence of power and authority concentration.

This duality of sovereignty allows for different perspectives and furnishes a seemingly natural division between inside and outside. This chapter will show how the two contradictory claims were predicated on these familiar perspectives of inside and outside. It will show how it was possible to argue that NATO was not violating the principle of sovereignty by articulating sovereignty solely as a relationship between people and state, and conversely how it was possible to argue that NATO was violating the principle of sovereignty by viewing sovereignty solely as a relationship between different states. Each perspective enabled problems, tensions and differences of the other to be silenced and treated as resolved. Hereby, as we will see, it became possible to simultaneously contend that NATO was, and was not, engaged in an intervention.

How were the inside and outside differentiated and given content through legitimations? This is shown by the help of the three analytical questions outlined in Chapter 2. I will begin by asking: (1) How is violation represented? How is sovereignty violated and who is violating it? (2) Which potential community is constituted through that representation? (3) What are the conditions of possibilities for that community? These three questions will be put to each of the two perspectives.

Speaking from the inside: this is not an intervention

Already by the summer of 1998 it had been established that the so-called extrajudicial killings committed by Milosevic's security forces did not constitute an internal matter. This contention was further elaborated and reinforced in the legitimations of how NATO's action did in fact not constitute an intervention. As the sections to come will conclude, sovereign power was exclusively placed with Milosevic. He had used his power outside of the confines of law, thereby violating his right to rule. By drawing a distinction between state and people, solely problematizing the exercise of power, the responsibility of violence and ultimately of genocide was placed with Milosevic. The people(s) of Yugoslavia were turned into passive victims of Milosevic's repressive state apparatus and they were constituted as *one* potential community, which had become torn by Milosevic's skilful manipulation and his ability to repress freedom and truth. The peoples of FRY were not inherently driven by ethnic hatred. On the contrary, the latent wish of the peoples of FRY was to live in a community marked by rights, pluralism, tolerance and coexistence.

How sovereignty was violated by Milosevic

Let us proceed first by analysing the claim that NATO was not intervening in the internal affairs of the FRY. This claim was foremost based on a differentiation between, and an ideal conversion of, the right to rule and the power to rule between state and people. Milosevic, it was assumed, had transgressed and abused his sovereign power by violating the rights of his people, and he thereby lost the right to exercise power. As Robin Cook (19 April 1999) explained: "no government should be able to take away the rights of people by force simply by claiming it has the sovereign power to do so." Lionel Jospin, the French Prime Minister at the time, similarly installed a limit to sovereign power by a reference to rights and used this limit as a basis to assert that "we" were not intervening in the internal affairs of the FRY.

> Are we by engaging ourselves in this conflict of Kosovo about to interfere in the domestic matters of the Federal Republic of Yugoslavia? I do not think so ... We should recall to all European leaders that sovereignty, at least in the democratic Europe, does not give the *right* to leaders to terrorize their own citizens.
>
> (italics added; Jospin, 27 April 1999)

These articulations were not only based on a distinction between state and people, leaders and citizens, but also on an ideal about how this relationship was to be regulated. Within states, power could not be allowed to reign undisputed, it had to be limited, and the proper limits to power were to be defined through liberal-judicial rights. It was through the respect of rights that legitimacy was conferred to sovereign power. When power took the form of law, freedom and autonomy were made possible within.

Although the people was invested with rights and appeared as the foundation of Milosevic's rights, they were seldom if ever granted a status as acting subjects. The people appeared as a mere passive object. One either spoke of what Milosevic had a right to do and not to do, or of those rights of the people that Milosevic had violated. However, whether one referred to the rights of Milosevic or to the rights of the people seemed to amount to the same thing: in either case, it was Milosevic who was invested with the capability to act, and his acts which seemingly needed to be restricted. There was already instituted a hierarchical relationship between Milosevic and the people, where power only resided with Milosevic, operating from top to bottom. The power of government was taken to reside entirely with one man. Milosevic had captured the state. He personalized the state, and Milosevic, regime, and government could therefore be taken to converge into the same thing. In speech after speech it was in this way possible to refer to "Milosevic's military machine", "his tanks", his "repressive police apparatus", "his brutal and corrupt dictatorship" (for these phrases, see Cook and Albright, 17 May 1999; Blair, 17 May 1999).

By portraying Milosevic as the all-powerful head of state and a manipulating dictator, the people of Yugoslavia emerged as a passive body, which had no voice and no possibilities of resistance or evaluation: a society who had been blinded and muted by the excesses of power. On the cover of *Newsweek* from April 1999 Milosevic's visage, for instance, appeared framed by raging hell fires and was accordingly identified as "The Face of Evil". Inside the issue the corresponding article ran under the headline: "The man behind the agony" depicting Milosevic as equivalent to Hitler and Stalin. Milosevic was a political leader who was neither interested in ideology nor in the well-being of his people, but only in keeping his all-embracing power, it was explained (*Newsweek*, vol. 134, 1999). Milosevic was a ruthless dictator who merely was interested in vesting and expanding his power base, who was even willing to turn against his own people in order to serve that purpose: "We are fighting for a world where dictators are no longer to be able to visit horrific punishments on their own peoples in order to stay in power" (Blair in *Newsweek*, issue 16, 1999). This demonization of Milosevic and victimization of the people also had crucial consequences for the constitution of a domestic community, as will be spelled out in the next section.

Thus, by drawing on a discourse of rights, a boundary to sovereign power was made. Milosevic had transgressed his sovereign power by operating outside of the realm of rights as codified in law. Rights, Albright (26 May 1999) stressed, were people's protection against repressive governments; a protection against the misuse of state power. When the basic rights of the ruled were violated by the ruler, when the state no longer applied its power according to the confines of rights, the outside could not stand by (Blair, 17 May 1999). In Serbia, Cook argued: "the law is merely the dictator's tool, truth is a means of control, and rights can be taken away and freedom extinguished" (*Guardian*, 5 May 1999). Milosevic had subjected law to force.

Milosevic's rule was in this way constituted as comparable to an absolutist monarchy of the past. He was represented as an all-powerful dictator, who resided above the law, and who until now had succeeded in exercising his power without limitations or restrictions. Law was accordingly not only installed as that code which rule ideally was to obey, but also as that yardstick by which Milosevic's power could be criticized and judged. Speaking in the name of law and rights seemed in that way unproblematic because it reproduced our familiar notions of how sovereign rule is to be exercised – and criticized – drawing on both the historical narrative of progression from absolutism to constitutionalism, and on distinctions between dictatorship and democracy.

Yet, deriving rule from rights allowed the power involved in the specification of a boundary to sovereign power to be concealed. Law was portrayed as an institution outside of, and unblemished by, power; a privileged point, from where the use of (state) power could be accurately judged. The code of law was that code which power needed to obey. In that way it seemed as if there were no subjects and no power involved in the evaluation of Milosevic's rule, only voices that spoke through law. At the same time, law was, however, represented as something that could be manipulated and overtaken by power, always potentially open to contamination and abuse. Milosevic, it was argued, had used and twisted the law for his own purpose, hence illustrating how law can turn into a mere mouthpiece of power. Law simultaneously appeared as an instrument of power and an instrument outside of power. The law by which Milosevic's rule was assessed, was seemingly able to resist the workings of power, whereas the law, which Milosevic applied, had been corrupted by power.

So which privileged law was invoked when Milosevic's power was judged? The answer to this question remained mostly implicit. Albright (26 May 1999), for instance, spoke of the need to "enforce *our* rule of law" or of Yugoslavia as an "outlaw regime" (italics added). Hence, it was not specified whether the law invoked was the "original law" of Yugoslavia – pre-Milosevic and pre- the abolishing of Kosovo's autonomy – some form of natural law, or international law. I will, however argue that this – the issue of which privileged law – never really emerged as a problem. By the invocation of genocide it could be established that Milosevic clearly had violated his sovereign power. In other words, genocide functioned as that clear marker and legal basis upon which a limit to sovereign power could be safely drawn, leaving no doubt that power had been horrendously abused and the most basic rights violated. Milosevic had failed the primary task of sovereign power, by using the means of violence to kill and persecute his own people, rather than using this power to guarantee the people their continued existence and well-being. Milosevic was exercising his sovereign power with the intention

Sovereignty and intervention 81

of eliminating rather than protecting the lives of his people. As Tony Blair (13 May 1999) put it "There are literally thousands of Kosovar Albanians [being] brutally massacred as an act of deliberate policy by Milosevic."

Genocide served to make it obvious that Milosevic had transgressed his sovereign power; that he had infringed on the most basic rights of his people. The point is not, however, that genocide did not take place in Kosovo; neither is it the claim that the invocation of genocide was part of a conscious and cynical plan of political leaders that they employed in order to avoid hard questions of boundary drawing. Rather, I wish to emphasize genocide's depoliticizing effects. "Genocide's power" to construct the obvious implied that the question at stake, rather than being one of whether, and in what way, Milosevic had violated his power, became one of representational truth. Or to put it differently, there was no need to establish that genocide constituted a transgression of sovereign power, that power was unlawfully exercised. Genocide is the very incarnation of unlimited power, symbolizing the horrific potentials of modern state power. This was not a fuzzy or grey area of disputed boundaries. A ruler who systematically kills and terrorizes his own citizens had per definition to be illegitimate in the eyes of everyone. Instead, it needed to be shown that Milosevic indeed was carrying out genocide; that genocide corresponded to the actual events on the ground. The issue at stake became one of verifying the truth and in order to verify the truth evidence needed to be collected. In the words of the Blair citation above; it had to be proven that "*literally thousands*" had been "*massacred*", as an act of "*deliberate policy*" by "*Milosevic*" (Blair, 13 May 1999).

A battle over truth

As we saw in the previous chapter, it was widely held that Milosevic's forces were engaged in ethnic cleansing prior to the intervention. Although the use of violence continued to be referred to as ethnic cleansing, genocide was simultaneously used to denote the character of the violence committed by Milosevic's security forces (see, for example, Cook, 19 April 1999; Blair, 23 April 1999; Albright, 6 April 1999; Lieberman, US Senator, 28 March 1999; James Rubin, 7 April 1999; Chirac, 6 May 1999; Charles Josselin, 30 April 1999). Genocide is however – in contrast to ethnic cleansing – a legal category and closely associated with the Holocaust. As noted above, this grants genocide great discursive power, but also implies that there are very strict rules guiding its enunciation (see also Malmvig 2001b). In terms of its legal confines: to characterize the acts of Milosevic's forces as genocide, it had to be shown (or rather proven) that violence and repression was planned and intentional and that it was directed against a specific ethnic group with the intent to destroy it. Hence, the object of Milosevic's power and repression had to shift from the encompassing category of "people" or "peoples" to the Kosovar Albanians. When references were made to Milosevic's unlawful rule and excessive power, it was possible to refer to "all of the peoples of FRY" as objects of Milosevic repression. But speaking in terms of genocide demanded that a specific ethnic group could be pointed out. This also meant that a crackdown against the

KLA or any other socio-political group within FRY could not qualify as genocide. Neither could so-called sporadic and spontaneous acts of violence against Kosovar Albanians qualify as such. It had to be systematic and well planned. Repeatedly it was emphasized that what we were witnessing was a result not of idiosyncratic actions by individual Serbs, but of a well-thought out plan emanating from Belgrade: "What we have witnessed in Kosovo has not been spontaneous emotional anger by random servicemen; what we are witnessing has been a deliberate coordinated program of deportation" (Cook in Foreign Affairs Committee, Fourth Report, 1999: 96).

But genocide is not merely confined by its legal definition; its linkages with the Holocaust have further delimited its meaning. Although the genocide convention does not mention scale or systematic, the Holocaust experience seems to demand that only massive state-led campaigns of extinction and destruction can count as genocide (see Campbell 1998a:100–1). This of course resonates well with the representation of Milosevic as the all-powerful dictator who had captured the state and subjected it to his whims and will. Yet the status of the Holocaust as a unique historical event, incarnating evil and being incomparable with other massacres and persecutions, at the same time necessitates that genocide is distinguished from the Holocaust. Comparing current atrocities or historical massacres with the Holocaust is per definition equal to questioning the unique character of the Holocaust and to relativize its evilness (see also Zizek 2001). To invoke genocide is thus to engage in a complicated game where one both needs to compare and separate the event from the Holocaust. The French Foreign Minister was, for instance, at pains to emphasize that the atrocities in Kosovo were outrageous in themselves, needing no comparison with the horrors of 1941–45: "Let us recall which incomparable abominations, committed between 1941 and 1945 this term 'genocide' refers to. It is not necessary, in order to denounce the horrors committed in Yugoslavia, to lose the sense of proportion and assign a term hereto" (Vedrine, 21 May 1999). Although Clinton did not refrain from identifying Milosevic's abuse of power as genocide, similar to Vedrine, he positioned the Holocaust within a special realm: the atrocities in Kosovo, he noted, were "not the same as the ethnic extermination of the Holocaust" (Clinton, 14 May 1999). Also, Tony Blair, in a speech in Germany invoked the Holocaust, emphasizing that it was the most evil form of genocide. But Kosovo ranked just beneath it: NATO was acting "against the most evil form of genocide since my father's generation defeated the Nazis" (Blair, 13 May 1999).

Yet, it was not sufficient both to invoke and detach Milosevic's actions from Hitler's and the Holocaust. Evidence and documentation also needed to be collected. In this struggle over truth, there were, as we will see, only certain types of subjects who were allowed to claim objectivity and truth and only a certain way by which knowledge could be gathered and granted the status as truth.

Critics claimed that NATO had not proved that there was a well-thought plan of ethnic extinction behind Milosevic's acts and orders. Rather, the mass expulsion was a result of NATO's bombings, it was asserted. The numbers of dead and missing persons were exaggerated and unaccounted for. Genocide was not an accurate term, but a mere propaganda trick. The *Boston Globe*, for instance, featured an article in which so-called experts in surveillance photography and wartime propaganda rebutted the figures of missing persons proposed by official sources. The State Department reports of 100,000–500,000 unaccounted-for Albanian men are "just ludicrous ... NATO is running a propaganda campaign, there's no question about that" (*Boston Globe*, 21 April 1999). The *New York Times* similarly ran an article questioning the Clinton administration's portrayal of the events:

> The Clinton Administration officials have been deliberate in their language, using words like genocide combined with blurry photographs suggestive of mass graves to conjure up the Holocaust, even when they were not explicitly invoking it. As a result, Americans are getting a view of what is going on in the Balkans that, accurate or not, is stage managed and subjective.
>
> (*New York Times*, 18 April 1999)

The problem for the media seemed to be that politicians could not be regarded as objective, they were prone to misrepresent reality. Conversely, the problem for the politicians was that they were always already articulated as subjective, having to prove that they were speaking the truth. Both, however, shared a quest for neutral representation where language must correspond to reality, signifier to signified. In addition, as we will see, whether engaged in the task of assessing representation or with representation, both articulated truth as a matter of being able to see for oneself. Many journalists, for instance, complained that since they were not given access to the combat zone in Kosovo and since they were not present on the ground, they were being prevented from seeing events with their own eyes. They were therefore unable to "sift through competing and often contradictory accounts" (*New York Times*, 18 April 1999). Being left with statements and imagery by NATO spin doctors, it was extremely difficult to verify the number of killed and ultimately to detect the truth (see also the *Guardian*, 15 May 1999). A media analyst was quoted for saying: "You have a situation where you don't have any access to make a determination about truth. The ability for each side to create its own reality is almost unlimited" (*New York Times*, 18 April 1999). Another journalist similarly confronted the French Foreign Minister Vedrine with the question of truth during wartime:

> It has been said that truth is the first victim of war. Can you affirm that we are not dealing with spontaneous vengeance by the Serbs in Kosovo, but rather systematic ethnic cleansing, planned ahead in Belgrade? Which proofs of Serbian exactions have you put forward?
>
> (Vedrine, 12 May 1999)

Thus, there was an ever-present demand for distinguishing propaganda from truth, for knowing that official speech was not mere exacerbations and wartime distortions. Mass expulsions, deportations, and systematic massacres were, everybody knew, powerful forms of legitimations. And since politicians and state officials could not be regarded as speakers of truth, genocide had to be documented and proved by external sources. In order to be true, statements could not be "contradicting, competing or subjective". They had to be based on thorough, consistent and neutral documentation.

And documentation was indeed provided in meticulous detail. In spite of the fact that Milosevic had hindered the access of journalists, UN bodies and human rights organizations to Kosovo, a multitude of "data" were collected and reported on systematic Serbian massacres, burning and looting of villages, collective rapes and mass expulsion of Kosovar Albanians based on interviews with refugees, eyewitness accounts, aerial pictures and imagery, films and photos smuggled out of Kosovo. Common for each of these "means of documentation" were their claim to accurate representation qua their vision and sight. Whether it was photos or refugee accounts, they could apparently claim the truth because they had actually seen it (see, for example, Scheffer, US Ambassador, 24 May 1999; UNFPA Report, 26 May 1999; Human Rights Watch, Human Rights Flash #24, 8 April 1999; BBC, 30 March 1999; BBC, 4 April 1999; Parismatch photo series "How the Serbs have 'cleansed' Pristina", *New York Times*, 29 May 1999). On a weekly basis the United States' Information Agency prepared a so-called "update on atrocities in Kosovo" in which what was termed as "the latest violations of humanitarian law" were meticulously described. In mid-May these accounts were gathered into a complete report by the State Department and named "Erasing history". The title was carefully chosen an official explained: "The last six weeks we have been witnesses not just to history, but the erasing of history. We know that unprecedented brutality has occurred in Kosovo, but most of it has occurred out of *our sight*." Milosevic had tried to prevent the truth from coming out, to erase his crimes, by denying access to Kosovo. This report would, however, allow the American public to know that: "mass killings, rapes, and abductions of Kosovar Albanians were taking place, although they [the American public] had been prevented from *seeing* it" (italics added; USIA, 13 May 1999).

Refugee and eyewitness accounts played a dominant role in the US State Department report, as well as in newspaper articles and broadcasting. The Kosovar Albanian refugees were the ones who had seen and experienced the atrocities. Because they had seen the killings, facts could now be known, in spite of Milosevic's attempts to bring the atrocities out of sight. At a press conference and before the US Senate two Kosovar Albanians refugees were, for instance, used to testify to the extent of the atrocities and to verify that the ethnic cleansing had begun months before NATO's bombings.

> The idea that attacks on civilians began only after NATO began bombing is untrue ... the cases of ethnic cleansing were growing very rapidly in the months before the NATO attack began ... NATO bombs did not force me from my home. Serbian forces did.
>
> (USIA, 15 April 1999)

Adding to the reports that Kosovo constituted the largest forced deportation since the Second World War, the Kosovar Albanian women asked the Senate Panel not to describe them as refugees: "We are deportees. We have been forced to leave our homes" (USIA, 15 April 1999). The combination of eyewitness accounts and imagery allowed us to know what was going on, as if we had actually seen it.

In addition to the documentation of actual genocide, which the refugees' testimonies and the aerial imagery of mass graves were to prove, came the indictment of Milosevic by the International Criminal Tribunal for the Former Yugoslavia (ICTY) in May. At the day of the indictment Albright explained:

> The fact that the Tribunal has provided evidence about the atrocities simply underlines, reinforces the case we have been making from day one ... I believe that the indictment is a very important step in terms of really emphasizing ... that this is not some figment of the imagination of NATO.

In other words, the indictment proved that NATO had been right all along, that genocide indeed was taking place orchestrated from Belgrade. Milosevic had attempted to shield the truth by preventing us from seeing it. If somebody still were to doubt the accuracy of the evidence, the ICTY were now validating, as Albright noted, NATO's representation of the truth (Albright, 26 May 1999).

The indictment also seemed to verify that it was Milosevic who was entirely responsible for and behind the acts of genocide; that it was Milosevic who brutally had abused his power: "There is no question that Milosevic is personally responsible for directing the ruthless massacres of thousands of innocent civilians ... our goal must be to remove Slobodan Milosevic from power; this indictment underscores and reinforces that point" (Senator Helmes, 27 May 1999). "The bottom line is here that we have no fight with the Serbian people and it has now been made very clear that their leadership is, or the indictment says responsible for these heinous crimes" (Albright, 26 May 1999).

The constitution of a Yugoslavian community

Hand in hand with the representation of Milosevic as the sole acting subject who possessed and exercised unlimited power, and who seemed to hold the ultimate responsibility for the genocidal acts, went the constitution of an object of this ominous violent power. This object was, in other words, given meaning through the very articulation of repression and genocide. Yet, these articulations of the objects of Milosevic's repressions had to rely on the presumption that the identity of this object already was given and pre-existing: that making such references was an innocent political practice, which merely mirrored prior identities (Malmvig 2001b).

References were, as we have seen, made to people, peoples, civilians and refugees in general, but also specifically to Kosovar Albanians. Whereas the objects of Milosevic's illegal rule and coercion often were referred to as the people of Serbia (Serbs as well as Kosovars), it was only possible to refer to the Kosovar Albanians as objects of genocide and ethnic cleansing. Even though Serbs and Kosovars in this way were reproduced as distinct ethnic groups and as objects of different forms of repression, they were not portrayed as mutually excluding identities.

Differences, tensions and conflicts among Serbs and Kosovars were vigorously erased and downplayed. They were turned into a mere result of Milosevic's skilful manipulation. In effect, Serbs and Kosovars were articulated as one multi-ethnic community moved by a common predicament and aspiration. The problem of Serbia/FRY did not reside on the horizontal or societal level, but on the hierarchical, between Milosevic and his peoples.

Thus, the shifts in referent objects partly hinged on whether it was repression in general or genocide and ethnic cleansing that was referred to. Yet, genocide and repression could be articulated simultaneously. There was no contradiction in arguing that the people(s) of Serbia were repressed, while also arguing that the Kosovar Albanians were victims of genocide.

This was made possible, I will argue, by two interrelated moves, which in conjunction constituted and gave meaning to *one* harmonious community of Serbs and Kosovars. I will go through each of these moves in turn. The first move places the source of ethnic cleansing and the problems of Serbia with Milosevic. The second move invests Serbs and Kosovars with a common identity made possible by the constitution of Milosevic as the sole source of conflict and the bearer of responsibility.

Genocide and repression, in contrast to ethnic or civil war, institutes a hierarchical relationship between a perpetrator and a victim, a subject and an object. It was, as noted, Milosevic who was inscribed as the all-powerful dictator who stood behind the ruthless massacres and persecutions, while the Kosovars and Serbs were presented as victims of his pursuit of ever-more power. Repeatedly, it was emphasized that NATO had no quarrels with the Serbian people. They were just as innocent as the Kosovar Albanians: "It is important to remember that we have no quarrels with the Serbian people ... In a sense they are victims of this tragedy too" (Clinton, 15 April 1999). "NATO's objective is not to harm innocent Serbs, but to stop the attacks in Kosovo" (Albright, 25 March 1999).

> You may have heard me say some tough things about Serbia in the last few years, but what I have said is directed against one man, and it is directed against this man for what he has done to you as well as for what he has done to others. I cannot stand to see what Milosevic has done to a country and people that I still love. You deserve better than this.
>
> (Eagleburger, 21 May 1999)

Milosevic's repression turned Serbs "into victims of this tragedy too". Since Serbs, so the logic went, were not free but repressed, they did not have access to the truth. And conversely since they did not have access to the truth, they were not free. Milosevic had eliminated the independent media and any form of freedom of expression and representation and hence the conditions of truth. He had created an alternative reality for the Serbs: a reality of lies and manipulations, which consequently released the Serbs from responsibility and dissolved Milosevic's claim to speak on their behalf. As Tony Blair (5 April 1999) noted: "The Serb people don't know what is being done in their name. Milosevic ruthlessly controls the TV and newspapers in his own country." Albright similarly questioned that Milosevic was representing the Serbian people and that his acts corresponded to the wishes of the Serbs. Having detached Milosevic's will from that of the Serbs, Albright (11 May 1999) could firmly express how the Serbs "really would feel" if they knew what Milosevic was doing on their behalf: "When this conflict is over good and decent Serbs will be appalled at what has been done in your name." The absence of an independent media in conjunction with Milosevic's overwhelming power established the Serbs as innocent, manipulated and without actual representation. As Clinton explained:

> Since I'm here I cannot help noting that one of the truly striking aspects of this moment is the dark contrast it illuminates between a free society with a free press and a closed society where the press is used to manipulate people by suppressing or distorting the truth ... The government-run press has constructed an alternative reality for the Serbian people in which the atrocities their soldiers are committing in Kosovo simply does not exist.
> (Clinton, 15 April 1999)

Also, Eagleburger, being a former US Ambassador to Yugoslavia and therefore seemingly holding a special knowledge of the Serbian people, conveyed the Serbian people as civilized just as "us" – the rest of the civilized world. It was the absence of truth which prevented them from condemning the horrors:

> I cannot believe that the many Serbs I knew if they knew the truth about what is going on in Kosovo would be any less horrified than the rest of the civilized world ... I am also deeply sorry for the increasing suffering of the Serb people. It is time for Milosevic to begin thinking about them and allow the conflict to end.
> (Lawrence Eagleburger, 21 May 1999)

Freedom, truth, representation and responsibility were turned into necessary conditions for one another. And since each of these elements was absent in Serbia, it was possible both to grant the Serbs a status as innocent victims, and thereafter to interpret their true will. Having first established that the Serbs did not have access to accurate knowledge within Serbia, it could then be established, in a second move, which opinions and feelings they really had.

However, to represent the Serbs as innocent it was also necessary to wrest free of earlier discourses on Balkan barbarity and previous references to the Serbian people as particularly nationalistic and aggressive. Much effort was devoted to turn around former discourses on the Balkan wars (for these see, for example, Hansen 1998, 2006; Campbell 1998a) by emphasizing how the knowledge of the Balkan people had improved since the early 1990s. The representations back then of the Balkan people and their history had been false and simplistic, it was stressed. Clinton (14 May 1999) even confessed – it seemed – that he himself had spoken of the Balkans in terms of inherent ethnic characteristics, but now he had read the real history of the Balkans. Ethnic cleansing, it was made clear, was not a result of ancient hatred or primordial enmity. It was not the peoples of Yugoslavia who were inherently barbaric or unable to live together:

> And we do no favours to ourselves ... when we justify looking away from this kind of slaughter by oversimplifying and conveniently, in our own way, demonizing the whole of Balkans by saying that these people are simply incapable of civilized behaviour with one another.
> (Clinton, 14 May 1999)

As Eagleburger also emphasized in the quotation above, when he in the past had said some tough things about Serbia it was not really Serbia he had meant, but Milosevic. Serbs were not essentially evil, the responsibility for the genocide rested with Milosevic and not with the Serbs. Clinton further elaborated with reference to the Holocaust:

> The villain [in] Yugoslavia is Milosevic not the Serb people ... political leaders do this kind of thing. Do you think the Germans would have perpetrated the Holocaust on their own without Hitler? Was there something in the history of the German race that made them do this? No. We've got to get straight about this; this is something political leaders do.
> (Summary of Clinton's Address to National Defence University in *Washington Post*, 14 May 1999; see also Albright, 20 April 1999)

In accordance with this representation of responsibility, Lionel Jospin, as many others, placed the responsibility with Belgrade and emphasized how the Serbs were not the targets of NATO's action:

> We are not fighting a war against the Serbian people. We are not enemies of the Serbian nation. But it is necessary to state, today, that the Belgrade authorities are solely responsible for the present crisis. It is not a people which is targeted, but a repressive and militaristic apparatus. It is not a nation which is proscribed, but a regime.
> (Jospin, 26 March 1999; see also Albright, 21 May 1999; Solana and Blair, 20 April 1999; Cook, 25 March 1999)

The demonization of the peoples of the Balkans, so present in the early 1990s, was thus substituted with a demonization of Milosevic. In contrast to the early 1990s, the source of the conflict in Kosovo was rarely understood via an analysis of the "national psyche" of Serbs and Kosovars, nor through an engagement with their so-called "complicated Balkan history". Nationalism was seen as a mere smoke screen and an instrument of political leaders to expand their power on the altar of the well-being of the peoples of Yugoslavia (see, for example, Vickers 2000). Therefore, it was the behaviour of Milosevic and his cronies that needed to be explained. Characteristic of this impetus to explain Kosovo from what was driving Milosevic, Judah wrote:

Everything he has done would appear to indicate that the only thing he cares about is power and that, while brilliant at manoeuvring on a day to day basis and week to week basis, he has no long term vision. Milosevic [merely] realized that the issue of the Kosovo Serbs was one, which he could use.

(Judah 2000: 56)

Mccgwire (2000: 3) similarly contended in *International Affairs*: "By all accounts, Milosevic is a callous, ruthless, politically adept, power-hugging man. He can be socially engaging, but must never be trusted." This form of analysis was also echoed by Western politicians and officials: Milosevic was portrayed as a man who in fact did not even care about the Serbian cause, but only used it as an instrument for keeping and expanding his power (see, for example, Clinton, 14 May 1999).

Obviously what I am suggesting is not that the demonization of Milosevic should be replaced with one of Serbs or of Kosovars, or that the roots of the conflict should be explained through ethnic characteristics or through a specific Balkan tradition and history of violence. Rather I wish to emphasize that the demonization of Milosevic went hand in hand with the victimization of Serbs and Kosovars. This allowed, as noted above, for a construction of a passive body under the sway of Milosevic's power. The peoples of Serbia (FRY) became an open identity with "no eyes and no voice". It thereby became possible to grant and invest them with any form of Western wills, values and characteristics. This also meant that precarious questions of border revisions or of Kosovar Albanian demands to self-determination or independence could be eschewed, since the problem did not reside in the relationship between Kosovars and Serbs, but with Milosevic. Prior to Milosevic, Serbs and Kosovars had been able to live together. Kosovar Albanians' claim of independence could, in this way, be read as a mere symptom of Milosevic's repression, rather than as a genuine political wish. By identifying Milosevic as the problem and source of a decade of repression, the natural solution was not an independent Kosovo, nor a separation of Kosovars and Serbs, but a removal of Milosevic and a change of regime.

On the basis of the identification of Milosevic as the problem of Serbia and the identification of Serbs and Kosovars as victims of his repression, Serbs and Kosovars could be invested with an "open identity". In a second move, it could be claimed that Serbs and Kosovars shared a common history, destiny and aspiration. They in fact constituted *one* multi-ethnic community. They were both objects of Milosevic's repression and power that latently – underneath Milosevic's suppression and manipulation – shared a wish for a democratic Serbia marked by pluralism, tolerance and coexistence. But this potential multi-cultural community had not been able to flourish and be given expression yet. If not for Milosevic, Clinton argued, Serbs and Kosovars would have realized a multi-ethnic democracy just as Macedonia, Bulgaria and Romania had before them (Clinton, 15 April 1999). They would have become part of modern Europe which, learning from its past, had come to know that diversity is a source of prosperity, of cultural strength rather than weakness (see also Cook, 5 May 1999).

To grant Kosovars full independence would therefore only be to pay tribute to Milosevic's vision of ethnic purity; a vision of the past. Creating homogeneous states along ethnic lines would run counter to progress and modern European values and, hence, also conflict with the interests of the peoples of FRY (Clinton, 15 April 1999; Cook, 5 May 1999). Again and again it was emphasized that the territorial borders and sovereign integrity of FRY had to be kept intact (see, for example, Vedrine, 4 April 1999; Cook, 1 April 1999; Albright, 11 May 1999). Kosovo was not to gain independence. FRY was to be a common home for all, regardless of ethnic identity. As the US Deputy Secretary of State also spelled out, the foundation of a truly modern state is tolerance and inclusion in contrast to "Milosevicism" which is based on ethnicity and exclusion.

> An acceptable outcome from the current crisis is one, which will leave the map intact, which will not result in the creation of new states or the redrawing of boundaries. It is very, very important for the principle of a viable modern state, tolerant, inclusive and including ethnic and all forms of minorities, to prevail over the principle that might be described as Milosevicism. And what Milosevicism means is using pressure and violence to build states on the basis of ethnicity.
> (Strobe Talbott, US Deputy Secretary of State, 5 April 1999)

Linking border revisions and independence for Kosovo with Milosevic's ethnic cleansing effectively delegitimized articulations of independence. It was extremely difficult to raise the question of an independent state for Kosovo, since suggestions of independence were positioned alongside Milosevic's project of clean ethnic states. Since it was nearly impossible to suggest that Kosovars would endorse an ideology similar to Milosevic's, the real interest of the Kosovars could in effect be placed in opposition to independence.

> The real question today is not whether Kosovo will be part of Serbia. The real question is whether Serbia and the other states in the region will be part of the new Europe. The best solution ... for all the countries of South East Europe is not the endless re-jiggering of their borders, but greater integration into a Europe in which sovereignty matters, but in which borders are becoming more and more open ... It is to affirm the principle that Milosevic has done so much to undermine – that successful modern states make a virtue, not a blood feud, out of ethnic and religious diversity. That is the solution that Western Europe accepted not too long ago.
> (Clinton, 15 April 1999)

Thus, even though Talbot spoke of multiple identities and of an all-inclusive Yugoslavian community, this identity inscription just brought another form of closure and essentialism than articulations of ethnic homogeneity. What it might mean to be Serbian or Kosovar Albanian was in effect narrowed down to one thing. The only self, which Serbs and Kosovars had the ability to become, what they in fact already latently were, were mirror images of Western and in particular of

European states. The West and now also states such as Romania and Bulgaria had founded their states on multi-ethnicity and tolerance, "fighting against the idea that statehood must be based entirely on ethnicity" (Clinton, 15 April 1999). It was therefore the West, in Clinton's (15 April 1999) words, who "was to provide the model for the people of Yugoslavia". The (potential) Yugoslavian community was to become like Western communities.

Yet, as we will see below, it was only through the aid and support of the West that this community could be expressed and realized.[1]

The conditions of a Yugoslavian community

> I think the best way is to become the 51st state of US.
> Excellent. But how do we do that?
> We declare war on the US.
> And then?
> Then, they take us seriously; they invade us; they occupy us; they set us straight.
> Brilliant. And what if we win?
> (A joke recycled in some East European countries, quoted from Todorova 2000: 159)

It was, as we have seen, possible to refer to a multi-ethnic, tolerant and pluralistic community of Serbian and Kosovar Albanian coexistence by articulating this community as a latent and slumbering possibility. Instead of advancing the rather difficult claim that Serbs and Kosovars already were accepting and embracing diversity and pluralism, it was claimed that they were not inherently nationalistic, intolerant and discriminating. Absence was thus turned into presence. The absence of nationalism and ethnic hatred was taken to denote the (potential) presence of multi-ethnicity and tolerance.

But if this community only was potentially present, if it was not already here, it had to lack something in order to be fulfilled and come to life. This section will describe which elements were articulated as necessary for the realization of a multi-ethnic Yugoslavian community, or in other words, which conditions of possibility were enounced for realizing this community.

Democracy was given a vital role as the condition of a Yugoslavian community. If only democracy was instigated then there would be no need for an independent Kosovo and the multi-ethnic, tolerant and plural identity could be realized. Democracy would enable Serbs as well as Kosovars to be represented at the same time, hereby creating a common community in which minorities and differences were respected and could flourish. One of the daily NATO briefings spelled out how democracy would facilitate pluralism:

> It is clear that when a people have been badly oppressed within their own country they probably see that the only solution is independence, but if

Serbia were to be a democratic Serbia, a Serbia based on pluralism, a Serbia that would give rights to its ethnic groups like most other European countries do ... then I think the situation would look very different, and it is true that autonomy generally works only in democratic societies because democratic societies are willing to make the sort of compromises to make this work.

(NATO Briefing, 18 May 1999)

In other words, what the potential Yugoslavian community was lacking in order to become fully constituted was democratic representation. Democracy would make independence claims superfluous, since these claims essentially were results of oppression. As Rudolf Scharping (24 May 1999) also pointed out, if Serbia developed into a democratic state – which would demand a removal of Milosevic – then the problems of Kosovo could be solved. The refugees, everybody, Sharping emphasized, wished for a peaceful and democratic Kosovo. Responding to a question of recent reports about attempts to destabilize Milosevic's regime, Scharping again answered with reference to democracy:

It is very important in a long term perspective to see both things together, first of all to solve the problems within Kosovo to make the refugees able to go back home under secure conditions; and on the other side the democratic development within Serbia, because we are not fighting against the Serbian people, we are fighting against the last dictatorship in Europe. I think it is necessary to make clear to the Serbian people: you have a chance to come to Europe but without Milosevic.

(Scharping, 24 May 1999)

It was, thus, not a matter of arguing that the conditions for multi-ethnic and tolerant community were not present. The only actual barrier to the realization of this community was Milosevic. Yet it was democracy, which was installed as the creator and facilitator of a community of tolerance pluralism, safety and harmony, rather than these elements being the conditions of democracy. Democracy did not demand any prior unity, consensus or endorsement of common values; democracy would produce such values. That community which democracy supposedly was to represent did not exist prior to representation, but only through representation. The community was already there. Yet, it could not be actualized in the absence of democracy. Democracy could not be realized from within the community itself because it was not a proper self prior to the installation of democracy.

In order to remove Milosevic and bring democracy about, Serbs and Kosovars needed help from outside. NATO's *campaign*, as it was often put, was to produce: "An alternate vision to Milosevic's campaign of terror, tyranny and vicious intolerance. We are united in urging Belgrade to choose a future of integration not destruction, we will do all we can to make that future a reality" (Burleigh, US Ambassador to the UN, 17 May 1999). It was NATO who was to create a future Yugoslavian community through democracy. Yet, it was supposedly the Yugoslavian peoples' wishes and interests that NATO was defending, in spite of the fact that this community only was articulated as a potential community. NATO was not imposing its own values, but simply giving expression to and facilitating the interest of the people (NATO Briefing, 12 May 1999).

The peoples of Yugoslavia were in this way again presumed to be a passive mass, which potentially could prosper and become a proper subject, but for now were unable to act on their own. As Clinton argues below it was time for leaders – in effect for the leaders of NATO – to take them down the road of the future:

> Already the region's democracies are responding to the pull of integration by sticking with their reforms, taking in refugees and supporting NATO's campaign. A democratic Serbia that respects the rights of its people and its neighbours can and should join them. We will help to restore it to its rightful place as a European state in the Balkans, not a Balkanized state at the periphery of Europe. The Balkans are not fated to be the heart of European darkness, a region of bombed mosques, men and boys shut in the back, young women raped, all traces of group and individual history rewritten or erased. Just as leaders took their people down that road, leaders must take them back that road; leaders must take them back to a better tomorrow. Ultimately, we and our allies can make this happen, if we stick with NATO's campaign.
> (Clinton, 23 May 1999)

Clinton's statement displays a certain tension in the depiction of the identity of the "peoples of Serbia". They were potentially like "us", Americans in disguise as Zizek noted, but they were not quite like us. By constructing and differentiating between several communities or regions of Europe, Clinton installed a boundary between "Europe proper", Central Europe and South Eastern Europe. The full chain consisted in the order of increasing distance to "Europe" where one moves from Europe to central Europe to South Eastern Europe to the Balkans (Hansen 1998: 141). In this chain, South Eastern Europe is portrayed as moving closer and closer to Europe – "responding to the pull of integration by sticking with their reforms, taking in refugees and supporting NATO's campaign" – whereas Serbia is located at the border of South Eastern Europe and the Balkans, only potentially becoming part of South Eastern Europe (see also Vedby Rasmussen 2000). Therefore, without NATO's campaign, Clinton emphasized, they would risk remaining in their dark Balkan periphery.

Summing up, in a twofold logic, the pre-conditions of a tolerant, multi-ethnic and pluralistic Yugoslavian community were formulated as the installation of democracy and the help from NATO. On the one hand, there was not articulated any intrinsic barriers to democracy emerging from within. Democracy seemed only to need that the Yugoslavian peoples were *not* inherently barbaric, nationalistic and discriminating, hereby enabling democracy to create a multi-ethnic community in which minority rights were respected and tolerance reigned. On the other hand, the installation of democracy – and hence the realization of a multi-ethnic community – could not emerge as long as Milosevic prevailed. Only with

94 *State sovereignty and intervention*

NATO's help and campaign against Milosevic and Milosevicism could democracy come true. Democracy could not emerge from within the community itself because the community could not become a proper self, before democracy was installed, which in turn could only be installed by NATO's campaign.

Sovereignty from inside – a summary

As suggested in the beginning of this chapter, on the basis of the internal perspective it could be claimed that NATO was not carrying out an intervention. In three steps, it was argued that NATO was not violating sovereignty since: (1) Milosevic had already transgressed his sovereign power and authority to rule with his brutal repression and ultimately by committing the act of genocide; (2) NATO was targeting Milosevic, not the peoples of Yugoslavia; and (3) NATO was giving expression to, and helping, a Yugoslavian multi-ethnic community to come to life through accurate democratic representation.

Moving from the first part to the second part of this chapter, the perspective changes. Whereas the claim that NATO was not intervening in FRY was based on an internal perspective, where the plight of the Yugoslavian people took a central place, the claim that NATO indeed was carrying out an intervention rested on an outside perspective. The community to be built, the centre of articulations, was no longer the Yugoslavian community but the global community. To put it simply, the intervention did not seem to be about the relationship between Milosevic and his people, but about "all of us"; about the relationships between states and the possibilities of creating a safer and better international community of the future. The external perspective engages with questions of international law, national interest and the legitimacy of force without a UN mandate, questions which had been excluded from the internal perspective. Yet, the external perspective silences, as we will see, questions of responsibility and innocence, truth and freedom, and turned people, state, and regime into one.

Speaking from the outside: this is an intervention, but ...

In the external perspective sovereignty was articulated as a horizontal relationship between states and other states in an international community. Here, Yugoslavia was articulated as one indivisible subject. It was identified as a rogue state that had continually defied the will of the international community. This implied, as we shall see, that the intervention was inscribed as a crucial test for the future relationship between states; as a defining event that would decide on the future of the international community as a whole.

According to the three questions outlined in the Introduction, the first part of this section will describe how and who was violating sovereignty. The second part will spell out which community was constituted through that violation and the third part will depict the conditions that were articulated as necessary for the realization of this community.

How NATO violated the sovereignty of FRY

Speaking from the external perspective, there were few denials of the fact that NATO was engaged in an intervention. The alliance was violating the sovereignty of FRY. Yet this was neither articulated as a violation of the basic norms and rules of the international community nor as a breach of the UN Charter. How could that be? In order to answer that we will have to look into how the violation of sovereignty was represented and which characteristics and intentions NATO was inscribed with.

There was no denunciation of the fact that NATO had not obtained a Security Council mandate; that NATO was carrying out an intervention against a sovereign state. It was therefore difficult to suggest that the intervention was legal and the intervention was in fact seldom justified legally.[2] Rather than trying to justify the intervention on its legal merits, it was argued that law did not constitute a necessary factor for claiming the legitimacy of the intervention. By drawing a distinction between legitimacy and legality, it was possible to contend that legitimacy was not simply a derivative function of law. Moreover, legitimacy and legality were not only articulated as separate realms, the latter also tended to be portrayed as subordinate to the former. Seen in the light of moral and political necessity, legal rules appeared as formalities and technicalities. Law was important, it was stressed. But when faced with a tragedy it appeared formalistic and conservative if one acted strictly according to law. Intervention could be legitimate, in spite of it being illegal.[3]

Law, it seemed, needed to correspond to morality rather than the other way around. An editorial in *The Economist*, for instance, argued that even though Kosovo was part of a sovereign country, this should not restrain the Alliance from intervening:

> The more *conservative* sort of international lawyer has been shocked by this. The law is the law he argues even if it does not square with what is pretty *obviously right*. There is a good case for saying that this bit of law needs bringing up to date.
>
> (italics added; *The Economist*, 31 July 1999)

Simply evaluating the intervention from a legalistic platform was, *The Economist* argued, absurdly legalistic when something akin to genocide was taking place (*The Economist*, 4 July 1999). Or as another scholar put it, "Criticizing NATO's decision on legal grounds ... seems beside the point. This author for one believes that the Alliance's military action was necessary on moral and political grounds" (Guichard 1999).

Even international lawyers did not consider NATO's intervention solely on legal grounds. Having established the illegality of the intervention, they swiftly moved on to emphasize that from a moral perspective, the intervention was legitimate; thereby echoing the claim that current law did not fit with what was ethically right: "Having made these points, I cannot but add, however that any person deeply alert to and concerned with human rights must perforce see that important moral values militated for the NATO military action ... from an ethical viewpoint, resort to armed force was justified" (Ambos 1999). In a special issue of the *American Journal of International Law* (1999) several international lawyers similarly – and perhaps somewhat surprisingly given that they were lawyers – argue that the intervention could not be justified legally. As Shinoda (2000: 8) also puts it, "Surprisingly or not ... the international lawyers pointed out the defects of law, rather than condemned the intervening states."

In short, in contrast to the evaluation of Milosevic's exercise of sovereign power, where power needed to correspond to law, where legitimacy was derived from the respect of legal rights and law was the yardstick by which power should be judged, the evaluation of NATO's use of force could and should not take place on a legal basis alone.

NATO, it was established, had violated a legal rule but it had not infringed on the *basic* values and rules of the international community. The intervention did not constitute a breach of the UN Charter. The intervention was rather giving expression to and enforcing the values of the Charter (Henderson, 22 April 1999). How could this be asserted, given the overall consensus that NATO's action was not legal or mandated by the Security Council? It was possible, I will argue, by two interrelated claims: first, by reference to the very logic and intentions of the Security Council and second by reference to Yugoslavia's record of non-compliance. The NATO countries, Solana (25 March 1999) explained: "think that this action is perfectly legitimate and it is within the logic of the UN Security Council". NATO was merely enforcing the numerous Security Council resolutions against FRY and hence the will of the international community as stipulated in the three Security Council resolutions of 1998 (Vedrine, 20 April 1999; Henderson, 22 April 1999). Yugoslavia was a disobedient and aggressive state that had inflicted on the norms and workings of the international community numerous times. The international community and its various human rights bodies had condemned the actions and human rights record of FRY for years, but Belgrade had ignored all of these calls. The UNSC and the Contact Group, in particular, had worked for a peaceful and diplomatic solution since 1998 but to no avail. All diplomatic avenues had been exhausted and all alternatives employed. But Yugoslavia had continued to disrespect the Security Council resolutions and the various diplomatic efforts. Belgrade: "had chosen to defy repeatedly the will of the international community" and intervention had therefore in the end become the only available option (Jospin, 26 March 1999; Cohen, 26 March 1999).

Recalling the diachronic analysis we can see how the writing of the international community's past engagement with FRY constituted a powerful form of legitimation. The intervention could be inscribed as the only available action through the writing of the history of the 1990s as a continuous effort by the international community to find a diplomatic and peaceful solution to the problems of Yugoslavia. The international community had applied every peaceful means available until the intervention in the end – that end, of course, being a construction in itself – stood out as the only means left. Moreover, by depicting Yugoslavia as an uncooperative and rogue state, which had continually challenged the will of the international community, it was possible to assert that NATO's intervention against this state, in fact, was in full concurrence with the will and intentions of the Security Council.

Yugoslavia, it was even suggested, could not claim the protection of state sovereignty and non-intervention. States such as Yugoslavia could not be allowed to hide behind the principle of sovereignty, merely using sovereignty as a protective shield. As one scholar argued: "It is difficult to respect the territorial integrity and sovereignty of a state that has shown such disregard for the integrity and sovereignty of others" (Ignatieff, 4 May 1999). A professor from Colombia University similarly argued at the US State Department's website: "Rogue states such as Yugoslavia cannot hide behind the United Nations Charter" (Phillips, USIA, 19 May 1999). And in commentaries and editorials it was proposed that: "President Milosevic is abusing Serbia's sovereignty by attacking his own citizens ... dictators whose soldiers target women and children in the name of national sovereignty deserve little legal protection" (*The Record*, 30 March 1999). "Ideally there should have been a UN Security Council Vote endorsing the military action ... Happily most of the Council agreed that ethnic cleansing was not something that could be shielded behind a dubious claim of national sovereignty" (*The Nation*, 26 April 1999). Sovereignty, it was argued, should not be allowed to function as a protective shield behind which dictators could hide and continue to defy the international community's norms and rules. Yet, by articulating sovereignty as a shield; as that principle which divides the national from the international and one state from other states, while at the same time making references to Milosevic, these statements came to display a crucial tension in terms of who sovereignty supposedly resided with, and who it was protecting: on the one hand, references were made to the sovereignty of Yugoslavia, vesting the right to protection with the Yugoslavian state as a whole. On the other hand, it seemed to be Milosevic and "dictators" who were hiding behind the shield of sovereignty. It was not clear, in other words, whether it was Milosevic's or Yugoslavia's right to protect the inside from the outside, which was questioned, or whether the two in fact were synonymous. When Albright addressed what she called the "questions of sovereignty" the same tensions emerged:

> There obviously are questions of sovereignty. I think the whole issue of sovereignty is one that is complicated by the fact that when somebody like Milosevic has been an aggressor in other places, he is in some ways giving up his rights in terms of protecting what goes on inside his country. He has transgressed, in the most serious way, on the fabric of how the international community operates.
>
> (Albright, 6 April 1999)

Albright thus questioned Milosevic's right to sovereignty in respect of the international community, but at the same time she referred to that right as a matter of protecting the inside; of "protecting what goes on inside his country". Sovereignty both seemed to reside with Milosevic and with the country as a whole. Contrary to the internal perspective, Albright did not argue that Milosevic had lost his right to protect his country, due to his behaviour towards his own people, but qua his behaviour towards the international community!

By identifying Milosevic as an "aggressor", portraying him as a new Saddam Hussein, images of Iraq's invasion of Kuwait could be invoked (see also Blair, 23 May 1999). The intervention could hereby once again be represented as an act, which the international community in fact was carrying out, in order to enforce its will against a state that was not complying with the community's established rules and norms. Just as Iraq had failed to comply with the Security Council resolution(s) of August 1990, and hence faced an allied intervention, so was Yugoslavia seemingly facing an intervention due to its "serious transgression on the fabric of how the international community operates" (Albright, 6 April 1999). By making a comparison with an already established interpretation of an event – Saddam Hussein's aggression on Kuwait and his violation of international law – the intervention in Yugoslavia could be granted further legitimacy simply by equating the two events.

In sum, the references to the *logic* of the Security Council resolution and the portrayal of Yugoslavia as a unruly state, who for over a decade had disobeyed the will of the international community and for this very reason could not be allowed to hide behind the shield of sovereignty, made it possible to claim that it was Yugoslavia that was violating international norms rather than NATO. It was NATO who – through the intervention – was helping to enforce rather than undermine these norms.

In concurrence with the claim that NATO was in fact implementing the "logic of the Security Council resolutions" merely enforcing its will against a non-compliant state, it also was continually emphasized that the intervention was not based on particular values, ulterior motives or self-interest. NATO was engaged, as Cohen explained, in a moral war: "No one wanted territory, No one wanted booty. No one even wanted to impose an ideology" (Cohen, *Washington Post*, 14 May 1999). Havel similarly denied any reference to "particular interest". This was not about national interest but principles and values. Kosovo had no oil fields and the nations of the alliance had no territorial demands on Kosovo. Neither was the territorial integrity of any of the member states threatened (Havel, 29 April 1999). Echoing Cohen and Havel, Blair also derived justness and legitimacy from the intentions behind the act. If the intervention was carried out in order to topple specific regimes or for territorial gains it would be illegitimate. Yet, if it was based on common humanitarian values – on "the doctrine of international community" – legitimacy could be assured (Blair, 23 April 1999). As Cohen (26 May 1999) explained: "The conflict in Kosovo is not one about territory, money or market but about the future shape of our society." Hence, a crucial and well-known distinction between "the right intentions" and "the wrong intentions" was a key element in deciding the legitimacy of the intervention. The right form of intentions were defined as those intentions that were commonly shared in opposition to the wrong form of intentions based on particularistic values and national self-interest.

Repeatedly it was stressed how NATO was moved by moral and altruistic motives, thereby seemingly countering claims to the opposite. NATO's emphasis on the importance of intentions – which was also played out in much of the academic literature, however, opened up the possibility for criticizing NATO's intervention exactly on the basis of intentions. For how could it ever be decided which motives or intention really guided the act? How could any state or alliance wrest itself free of accusation of abuse; of cloaking national interest in universal language? (See, for example, Guichard 1999; Weller 1999a; Chomsky 1999.)

The emphasis on the right form of intentions in that way came to open a door for a *hermeneutics of suspicion*; that door which these statements were to close in the first place. By basing the legitimacy of the intervention on the intervening actors' intentions and purposes, NATO came to validate and make possible a particular form of evaluation; an evaluation which is based on an interpretation of intentions. Proponents of the intervention could seemingly assess the legitimacy of the intervention by merely establishing whether or not NATO really meant what it was saying.[4] But critics of the intervention could equally question the legitimacy of the intervention only by proposing that NATO in fact was moved by some hidden interest: in spite of what it said, NATO meant something entirely different. In reality, NATO sought to expand its sphere of influence acting on the basis of strategic self-interest alone.[5] This type of criticism became one of the dominant ways of questioning the intervention (see, for example, Chomsky 1999; Fisk 1999; Mccgwire 2000; Said 1999).[6]

The constitution of an international community

The intervention was articulated as an act that should be judged on more than mere appearance; on more than the "act in itself". There was much more at stake, it was argued, than whether one was pro or contra this particular intervention. NATO's campaign was about the "future shape of our society" (Cohen, 26 May 1999). It connoted a defining moment, which would decide on those values, norms and rules that were to guide state action in the future. Through a representation of two starkly opposed versions of international life structured around a series of binary oppositions – which were positioned as respectively belonging to the past and the potential future – the intervention was inscribed as a crucial test that would decide on which of these two versions was to prevail.

> With just seven months left of the 20th century. Kosovo is a crucial test. Can we strengthen a global community grounded in cooperation and tolerance, rooted in common humanity? Or will repression and brutality, rooted in ethnic racial and religious hatreds dominate the agenda for the new century and the new millennium?
>
> (Clinton, 14 May 1999)

> I will ask all of you to ask yourselves how you view the history of the last 50 years and how you imagine the next 50 years unfolding ... Now at the end

of the 20th century we face a great battle between the forces of integration and the forces of disintegration, the forces of globalism versus the forces of tribalism, of oppression against empowerment ... That is why we are in Kosovo. The Balkan war that began in Kosovo ten years ago must end in Kosovo. It should be the last conflict of the 20th century. It should not be the defining conflict of the 21st century.

(Clinton, 15 May 1999)

In this sense subject and objects disappeared. It was no longer NATO, or even the international community, which intervened in Yugoslavia. It was a battle between civilization and barbarity, democracy and tyranny, cooperation and self-interest, tolerance and hatred, between the *forces* of light and the *forces* of darkness, between two competing versions of the future (Cook, 5 May 1999; Blair, 23 April 1999; Jospin, 10 April 1999; Clinton, 14 May 1999, 15 April 1999).

Yet these binary oppositions only became meaningful by referring to and thus constituting a specific community. Similar to the logic of the "internal perspective" these articulations produced a potential community; a community on the verge of becoming. As Blair explained, although the international community had changed in a fundamental way since the Cold War, this improved and strengthened community was still in a process of becoming. It was yet volatile and open to setbacks and obstructions. The decision to intervene in Kosovo, however, connoted one more step in the right direction: "Twenty years ago we would not have been fighting in Kosovo. We would have turned our backs on it" (Blair, 23 April 1999). The fact that we had not turned our backs on Kosovo was an indication of how the international community was evolving and progressing. We were now: "witnessing the beginning of a new doctrine of international community" (Blair, 23 April 1999). According to this doctrine, state action would no longer be guided by self-interest and power, but by values and cooperation. This doctrine would also entail rules of cooperation and engagement between states. Until now, these rules had tended to be ad hoc, and it was therefore necessary to work towards a set of more coherent rules. These rules were to be formulated on the basis of those values of partnership and cooperation, which had been realized in domestic communities. The values of domestic communities needed "to find their *international echo*" (italics added; Blair, 23 April 1999).

In this respect, Blair emphasized, one of the most difficult rules to formulate was when to intervene:

The most pressing foreign policy problem we face is to identify the circumstances in which we should get actively involved in other people's conflicts. Non-interference has long been considered an important principle of international order, and it is not one we would want to jettison too readily. But the principle of non-intervention must be qualified in important respects ... genocide can never be an internal affair.

(Blair, 23 April 1999)

Sovereignty and intervention 101

The question of when to intervene was only an element in a much larger vision of how the new rules and values could guide state action in the future and hence create an international community of tolerance and cooperation; an international community that would mirror the national community. As Kouchner similarly noted:

> Can we dream of a 21st century where the horrors of the 20th will not be repeated? Where Auschwitz or the mass exterminations that took place in … Kosovo cannot happen again? The answer is a hopeful yes – if as part of the emergent world order, a new morality can be codified in the right to intervention against abuses of national sovereignty.
>
> (Kouchner 1999: 4)

Thus, the new international community was not completely realized yet. This gave rise to tensions between universalism and particularism; between the values of all states and the values of certain states. On the one side, the British prime minister portrayed the values and forms of coexistence within domestic communities as that ideal model that ought to be transferred to the international community, hereby allowing for progress and improvements. In this sense, all states were taken to be based on similar ideals of tolerance, cooperation and partnership within. On the other side, it was exactly the presence of intolerance, hatred, tyranny and nationalism *within* some states, which threatened the volatile international community in the making. It was only the values and workings of particular kinds of domestic communities that would create an enhanced international community. Clinton characteristically noted:

> The central irony of the time, is that *most of us* have a vision of the 21st century world with the triumph of peace and prosperity and personal freedom; with respect for the integrity of ethnic, racial, and religious minorities; within a framework of shared values, shared power, and shared plenty.
>
> (italics added; Clinton, 15 April 1999)

Blair was even more explicit in spelling out who "the most of us" were:

> NATO's success in Kosovo will be the biggest deterrent to tyrants the world over; and the biggest rallying call for democracy. That is why whatever it takes we must succeed; this is the struggle for the future. Milosevic is the past. *We, the Democrats, are the future, it is our common destiny.*
>
> (italics added; Tony Blair, 23 April 1999)

The "common destiny", the "we" and the "most of us" were evidently identified as democracies; as those types of communities in which the values of tolerance, pluralism, freedom and respect prevailed.

This tension between the universal and the particular directs us to the third question; which conditions that were represented as necessary for the realization

The conditions of the international community

In this emerging international community, states would act according to values, not according to interest. In fact, interest and values would blend and merge. States would, as individuals in democratic communities, be guided by morals and values of freedom, tolerance and human rights (Tony Blair, 23 April 1999). The nature of the future international community was defined by those values which states' actions would be shaped by. If states in their relations with one another were moved by values of tolerance and cooperation; if their behaviour were reflecting those values guiding relations within their domestic communities, then an international community would be created in which relations equally were guided by values of cooperation and tolerance. But, of course, this also meant that if some states were not marked by these values on the inside, then they would not be able to act according to these values on the outside.

By way of this second image logic, the source – as well as the cure – of the current international community's imperfection was placed with the nature of states (Waltz 1954). Only democratic states founded on ideals of freedom, tolerance and diversity, would act accordingly. And since the future international community was defined by the way states would act, it had ultimately to be composed of democratic states. In order to be fully realized, and fulfil the promise of cooperation and shared values among states, it was necessary that all states, in the end, became democratic. Risking oversimplification, it may, however, be argued that the new doctrine of international community rested on a "second image" assumption. The creation of good states – that is democracies founded on values of tolerance and cooperation – would lead to states that were engaged in good relations with other states, and this in turn would create the foundation for a good international community. If all states became democratic, clashes of interest would be substituted by a convergence of interest. State action was, in this sense, not seen as a function of the structure of the international community, rather the international community was seen as a function of the structure of states. Therefore, to transform the international community one had to transform the nature of states.

Although it appeared as though the world automatically was moving and progressing towards the realization of democratic states – as Blair noted, "we the democrats are the future" – that did not mean that we – the democrats – "should sit on the sidelines of history" (Cohen, 26 May 1999). Democracies should spread their values (Blair, 23 May 1999). The intervention could therefore be inscribed as history in the making; a history that seemingly could only be made by democratic states. It served the progress of the international community in a double-sense: the intervention was articulated as yet another proof that democratic states act according to values rather than self-interest and power; that NATO, as an alliance of democratic states, had moved on from the rationales of the Cold War (Blair, 23 May 1999). Also, the intervention was taken to signify a concrete effort to support the installation of democracy in Yugoslavia. By building a democratic Yugoslavian state, marked by values of pluralism and tolerance, the international community would collectively move in the right direction towards the spread of democracy. As a first step the ethnic cleansing needed to be reversed, but the necessary long-term goal had to be the instigation of democracy (see, for example, Blair, 17 May 1999; Clinton, 23 May 1999; Albright, 25 May 1999). The realization of this future community both seemed to be an automatic outcome of history, the way history inevitably moved forward, and to be the result of a conscious creation by the already existing democracies. The future dictated, on the one hand, that this was the way the international community necessarily was moving. On the other hand, NATO needed to intervene in Kosovo in order to create this community; to hinder the past from becoming the future.

To realize the international community of the future was in this way not a matter of transcending state sovereignty or overthrowing the state system. The obstacles and hindrances to be passed did not seem to rest with the fact that the international community was composed of sovereign states. The subjects of the future international community were states. Yet, it was to be a certain kind of states which, as an effect of their internal structure and ideals, were guided in their actions with one another by values rather than interest. By changing the nature of states, one would, it was assumed, change the nature of the international community.

A preliminary conclusion

Moving in one direction, from intervention to sovereignty, this chapter has shown how sovereignty was assured and given content through the very practice of intervention, and hence how sovereignty, in this sense, was dependent on intervention. Moving in the other direction this chapter has, however, also demonstrated how intervention was dependent on the way sovereignty was articulated, how the identification of an intervention relied on the manner in which sovereignty was conceptualized. This gives intervention, as described in Chapter 2, a paradoxical character. Intervention is both one of those practices that confirms and reproduces the importance of sovereignty, and yet at the same time intervention is taken to be a violation of sovereignty.

Whether NATO's campaign was inscribed as an intervention or not depended on the way sovereignty was articulated and related to other concepts; on whether sovereignty was represented as an internal or external relation. It was claimed that NATO was not intervening in the internal affairs of Yugoslavia by reproducing sovereignty as a relationship between ruler and ruled, where the former was invested with the power to govern and represent the latter in so far as the ruler operated within the confines of law and rights. Sovereignty was articulated as sovereign power, however, a power that had to obey the principles of law. And yet it was also claimed that NATO indeed was intervening in Yugoslavia by portraying state sovereignty as a legal rule (non-intervention) that regulates the relationship between already constituted states. Sovereignty was represented as a hard shield which differentiates the domestic sphere from the international sphere; protecting the inside from the outside.

104 *State sovereignty and intervention*

The two claims did not seem to contradict one another, in so far as they were related to and predicated on a differentiation between an international and national sphere, marked by very different concerns and problems. From the inside, it could be safely claimed that: "the Kosovar people and their plight are the reason for the NATO campaign ... The question, which takes precedence is what will serve the interest of the people of Kosovo and, in a more indirect way, the people of Serbia (*The Guardian*, 23 March 1999). From the outside, however, NATO's intervention could be articulated as a matter of "strengthening a global community grounded in cooperation and tolerance". From the outside, Yugoslavia was seemingly a unitary state, an indivisible subject that was acting in a community of other states. From the inside, however, distinctions were drawn between territory, regime and people, between Kosovars, Serbs and Milosevic. Viewed from the international sphere tensions between state and people, power and law, democracy and dictatorship were silenced and treated as resolved. The state was, to put it simply, turned into a black box. From the external perspective it was possible to eschew those very questions that had been problematized in the internal perspective. Conversely, speaking from the external perspective it was possible to treat the international sphere as a given background. Distinctions could be drawn between different subjects and wills within, and the inside could be characterized by a plurality of voices, since it was assumed that the state already was demarcated territorially from other states and recognized by these as an independent unit. From the inside, questions of how the sovereignty of states are upheld or violated, or how states can or should engage with one another in the absence of an overarching authority could be avoided. The status of international law, of reconciling interest and values, particularism with universalism could be treated as given and resolved, exactly by speaking from the inside. The inside was installed as the foundation of the outside and conversely the outside was installed as the foundation of the inside. But the two perspectives could never meet. It was therefore possible to assert that NATO both was engaged in an intervention and that NATO was not engaged in an intervention.

In Algeria, however, a very different logic prevailed. As we will see, here it had to be justified why the international community should not intervene. Here it had to be answered how come human rights abuses, massacres and government repression constituted the "internal affairs of Algeria", which Algeria had a legitimate right to solve on its own?

5 From object of concern to object of non-intervention

The Algerian people had been tormented. Husbands and fathers had disappeared, mothers had had their babies killed, or their throats cut, and whole villages had been massacred in a senseless and incomprehensible war, which had left up to 80,000 killed. Civilians were caught between terrorists and regime, between unspeakable brutality committed by unknown perpetrators and extrajudicial killings, torture and disappearances by the security forces. This was a war without a name; without a signifier. A war filled with uncertainties, where nobody knew the identity of the killers, where no one could find a rationale or political motivation behind the brutal acts.

This brutality had to be condemned and solidarity with the victims expressed. The whole world, politicians explained, was suffering with the Algerian people and sympathizing with their plight. But due to the uncertainties involved, due to the lack of clear denominators, it was extremely difficult for the outside to do anything: Who are we to fight, Western government leaders asked? It is impossible for the outside to intervene in this murky conflict, it was explained, since intervention demands a clear delimitation of responsibility.

Yet "we" are not indifferent, it was simultaneously asserted. But it has to be recognized that Algeria is a sovereign and independent state. This means that the outside cannot tell the Algerians, how they are to solve their own problems, how they are to regulate their own society. We cannot intervene and act as if sovereignty does not exist! Intervention was, thus, inscribed as impossible, and yet this impossibility seemingly had to be legitimized. The suffering of the Algerian people was taken to demand international action, placing a moral responsibility on the outside, and yet it was answered that given the realities, the outside was incapable of "doing something".

As in the case of Kosovo, I will analyse the constitution of non-intervention as a result of continuous discursive battles and selections, which gradually constituted and reconstituted what Algeria was about and how to respond to it. The purpose of this chapter is, in short, to trace how Algeria became this object of non-intervention, demanding legitimations.

In contrast to much of the literature on Algeria, which tends to write the history of international responses to Algeria from a perspective of a conscious international suppression and silencing of the truth of the Algerian conflict that in the end had to be revealed, I will argue that this precise writing came to serve as a powerful point of reference in 1997 and 1998, which in itself participated in constituting Algeria as something which the international community had to do something about (see, for example, Stora 2001; Roberts 1995; Spencer 1998). Instead of determining or trying to illuminate what was really going on in Algeria despite the conscious attempts to silence the truth or the murkiness of the conflict in itself, this chapter will trace the different ways whereby Algeria and possible responses to Algeria were constituted and re-constituted over time.

To trace this process of constitution and selection I will, as in the case of Kosovo, divide the analysis into three stages here called: *object of concern*, *object of problematization*, and *object of non-intervention*. Again it must be emphasized that these three headings are analytical constructions. The three categories are used to structure the historical narrative and highlight those shifts that the discursive articulations on Algeria went through. This chapter also sets the conditions of possibility for the next chapter, in that it studies those very processes of discursive selections and productions, which gradually came to render Algeria in terms of an international problem that could not be ignored and which demanded that politicians and officials justified why intervention could not be undertaken.

Algeria as an object of concern: from democracy to Islamic terrorism

From 1992 to late 1994 Algeria can be seen as what I have termed an object of concern. The "situation" in Algeria was portrayed as something which the West, and in particular France, had to follow carefully; a situation which caused concern. Why was Algeria a concern? This was closely related to articulations of Islamic fundamentalism and terrorism as international threats, and to what was portrayed as the central schism involved in the annulment of the second round of parliamentary elections; namely the prospects of an Islamic state versus the prospect for democracy. The concern was in this way primarily based on fears about the future, rather than on the present situation. By projecting the future into the present, the present emerged as a concern (see also Vedby Rasmussen 2003).

In this first phase, the conflict in Algeria came to be very powerfully represented in terms of a rigid dichotomy between state and Islamic terrorists. The latter was portrayed as the antithesis of democracy and Western values, and since there apparently only existed two subjects and two forces, it became almost impossible to raise a critique of the regime or to voice concern over the conditions of democracy and human rights in Algeria. It became obvious who one was against, although less obvious who one was siding with. In a difficult balancing act it was asserted that the West, and in particular France, was not supporting the regime, and yet economic aid was necessary in order to alleviate those socio-economic problems that had caused the Algerians to vote for FIS (Islamic Salvation Front), thereby hindering that Algeria *became* an Islamic state, which would turn against the West.

This first phase from 1992 to 1994 will be divided into four main sections. First, it will spell out how the dilemma of democracy was framed. How the takeover by the army could both be inscribed as a democratic and an anti-democratic move. Second, it will be shown how the question of democracy was turned into a question of Islamic fundamentalism. The third part will look at how the "situation in Algeria" was closely coupled with events in France. How the boundary between domestic and foreign, Algeria's sovereignty and France's sovereignty constantly moved and shifted over the course of 1993 and 1994. Finally, the fourth part will show how it became increasingly difficult to inscribe economic aid alone as a proper response to the Algerian crisis.

The democratic dilemma: a move towards or away from democracy?

On 11 January 1992 the second round of parliamentary elections was annulled in Algeria and President Chadli Benjedid, who had ruled Algeria ever since 1978, resigned. Shortly afterward, a so-called [The] High Committee of the State (HCE), headed by the former war veteran Boudiaf, was set up by the army.[1] As demonstrations and violent clashes between the opposition and the army escalated, a state of emergency was declared, FIS members, religious leaders and several journalists were arrested and detained in camps in Sahara, and FIS was outlawed. However, while the army began its crackdown on Islamic groups, scholars, journalists and commentators were debating whether the foreseeable victory of FIS justified the army's annulment of the elections and its subsequent coup.

Whereas few official statements, as we will see, were made in the aftermath of the events in January and throughout 1992, commentaries and editorials abounded on the annulment's implications for democracy. The positions were, perhaps unsurprisingly, divided in two, resting on two different conceptions of democracy. This made it possible for each position to portray the annulment as respectively anti-democratic and democratic.

One position argued that in spite of some of the FIS leaders' anti-democratic statements, the party should be allowed to be put to the test. One could not a priori dismiss FIS or evaluate its democratic credentials when it was not allowed to govern in the first place. When in office, FIS might turn out to be democratic, not least in the light of the considerable Algerian bureaucracy and Algeria's relatively well-founded civil society, it was contended. Both would, it was argued, function as restraints on any "revolutionary government" and grant the process a certain inertia. Moreover, echoing the "co-option argument" (see, for example, Esposito and Piscatori 1991; Esposito 1998), it was also put forward that experiences in other Islamic countries had shown that Islamic extremism and violence only could be avoided if Islamic parties were invited (co-opted) into the political system. Only hereby could Islamic movements be made accountable towards their peoples and this would also serve to moderate their more extremist tendencies (*Le Monde*, 14 January 1992; *Daily Telegraph*, 14 January 1992; *The Economist*, 18 January 1992; *Washington Post*, 13 January 1992). Islamic parties would, hence, not bring instability and violence, as the regime and some commentators argued. On the contrary, only because of the cancellation of the second round of election, would Algeria now "face an indefinite period of civil strife" (*The Economist*, 18 January

1992). In line with the democratic dilemma, it was equally argued that the heart – but also the paradox – of any democratic system rested on the fact that democracy must allow even anti-democratic parties to be elected into government, whether their ideology is approved of or not. To overrule an electoral result only because "the wrong people had won", as *The Economist* (18 January 1992) put it was to violate the very core of democracy. Giscard d'Estaing in the same vein argued "The interruption of the electoral process reveals an antidemocratic and dangerous character. It is an error to interrupt an ongoing electoral consultation because the results are not convenient to you" (*Le Monde*, 15 January 1992). Non-democrats alone, *The Economist* (18 January 1992) concluded, would cheer (see also *Washington Post*, 13 January 1992).

The competing position, however, argued that democracy could not allow its own eradication. FIS would, as soon as it was elected into office, eliminate the very electoral process that had brought it to power (*Washington Post*, 19 January 1992). If democracy, in this way, were to support its own abolition, this would constitute a contradiction in terms and possibly lead to catastrophic results: the Nazi party's victory in Germany in 1932 being one tragic example (*Le Monde*, 22 February 1992). The Algerian army had merely, one commentator noted, acted preventively (*Le Monde*, 15 January 1992). It had, in fact, saved the democracy of Algeria "Even if it seems contrarian to democratic principles this decision is real; a last chance for Algeria to save democracy and eschew the fatality of a totalitarian *intégrisme*" (*Le Monde*, 14 January 1992). Another commentator similarly noted: "Just like in Turkey and Egypt the army can sometimes help the progress towards democracy" (*Le Monde*, 22 February 1992). These arguments, moreover, advanced the point that a certain number of pre-conditions needed to be fulfilled in order for a society to be characterized as mature enough for democracy and prepared for potential "subversive" results at the ballot box. Democracy entails more than the ritual of four-year elections, it also requires a certain culture and stability which Algeria lacked; it was argued. It was, hence, far too premature to allow FIS to experiment with democracy. Before this "democratic culture" was properly rooted in the Algerian society, and the right dispositions achieved, extremist views and parties were too likely to take root, constituting a danger for stability as well as democracy (Michel Rocard in *Le Monde*, 23 March 1992; *The Guardian*, 14 January 1992; *Washington Post*, 14 January 1992; *Le Monde*, 22 February 1992).[2]

Each side, hence, portrayed its own position as being moved by the imperative of safeguarding democracy and stability. The former – democracy as machinery – articulated a recognition of FIS's probable victory as a necessity of democracy, and hence positioned the annulment and the takeover by the army as *undemocratic*. The latter – democracy as values – portrayed a possible victory of FIS as an equivalent to an abolition of democracy, and hence inscribed the takeover by the army as, if not being *democratic*, then at least being carried out in the defence and to the advantage of democracy in the longer run. It was accordingly possible for both positions to inscribe the annulment and the takeover by the army as respectively anti-democratic and democratic. The fact that the two positions were founded in two different conceptions of democracy – very similar to what is also known as *procedural* and *substantive* democratic (see, for example, Cohen 1996)[3] machinery or values – made it possible to advance two opposing claims on the state of democracy in Algeria.

As we are to see below, however, the debate on the content and future of democracy was, very shortly after it began, circumvented, and turned into a "question" of Islamic fundamentalism and terrorism.

Westerns officials did seldom explicitly engage in this debate over the content of democracy and its possible dilemmas, and very few official comments were in fact made on the halt of the elections and the subsequent coup. The *Washington Post* and *Le Monde* reported that France, Italy and Spain had sought to say as little as possible about the situation in Algeria and that the Bush administration had thought it wise to follow the European course (*Washington Post*, 15 January 1992; *Le Monde*, 16 January 1992; *Washington Post*, 6 February 1992). Probed directly by a French journalist on how France reacted to the coup d'état, Mitterand (14 January 1992) described "it" as an interruption of an election: "What I think about this is that the present process of the Algerian elections has been interrupted, and that this represents at the least an abnormal act." Mitterand, thereby crucially avoided terming "it" a coup and instead framed the event as an interruption of a democratic process, spurred by a constitutional crisis in the aftermath of President Chadli's resignation; a resignation, which – according to Mitterand (14 January 1992) – had demanded that the authorities improvise a proper response. Since the democratic process only was temporarily suspended, what Algeria needed was to proceed down the democratic path, as countries all over the world in these years were doing. This was also reiterated by the EU, which equally depicted Algeria as being in a process of democratization. The EU expressed its full support to the Algerian authorities in helping them towards democracy and providing economic aid to redress its difficult economic situation (EU Declaration, 17 February 1992).

Yet, as was to become a ritualized remark in the years to come, Mitterand (14 January 1992) also stressed: "I really do not pretend to be the judge of what has happened in Algeria ... a Frenchman ought not to insert himself into the internal Algerian political debate." This was an internal affair of Algeria, which it was not for outsiders to judge. The Bush administration also engaged in a difficult balancing act between the need for public comments and the apparent imperative of not mingling in what was termed as Algeria's domestic politics: at first the "military coup" was deemed to be in accordance with the constitution of 1989. This, however, led to several accusations of Washington being too overt in its support for the military regime (*Washington Post*, 15 January 1992, 6 February 1992). Two days later the administration hence merely stressed that the path of democracy should be followed, while emphasizing that the United States would not take sides in Algeria's *internal politics* (*Washington Post*, 14 January 1992; *International Herald Tribune*, 16 January 1992). "Outsiders have no business trying to dictate the outcome in Algeria", the *Washington Post* (14 January 1992), similarly noted.

In spite of the relative lack of comments or reservations regarding how the new regime had come to power, the so-called "situation in Algeria" was portrayed as something that needed to be followed closely. It was a cause of concern, something of immense preoccupation, it was stressed (see, for example, EU Declaration, 17 March 1992; Daniel Bernard, Spokesperson of the Ministry of Foreign Affairs, 14 January 1992; Marchandt, French Minster of the Interior, 14 January 1992; Bush, 13 January 1992). But what was it that these official statements were concerned about? What did the "it" refer to? This was seldom specified. By only formulating a general concern about the situation in Algeria – "France should be attentive to what happens in Algeria", "France is very closely following the evolution of the situation" – it was left open to interpretation whether it was the faith of democracy and human rights violations or Islamists coming to power in a former Western minded and secular state, which worried Western politicians and called for close attention (Marchand in *Le Monde*, 14 January 1992; Bernard, 14 January 1992).

The Islamic threat: a dangerous cocktail of terrorism and fundamentalism

As reports intensified on violent attacks against police officers and army barracks presumably carried out by FIS clandestine groups, fear was increasingly voiced that FIS militants by the use of force would take that power which they had been denied at the ballot box. What would such a potential violent Islamic takeover imply for Algeria, and not at least for the West, it was asked? (for example, *Le Monde*, 30 April 1992, 6 October 1992).

The "real issue" to be debated in relation to Algeria hence started to move from democracy to "the threat and dangers of Islam(ic movements)". Editorial pages and expert in-depth interviews mainly revolved around explorations of the "nature of Islam" as a political phenomenon which was sweeping the Islamic world and which the West needed to find a proper response to and understanding of. Was this a "new evil empire" or a phenomenon to be accommodated and lived with? (See, for example, *Washington Post*, 6 February 1992; *Le Monde*, 5 May 1992, 16 February 1992, 23 March 1992, 30 April 1992.)

Debating the "nature of Islam" rather than the "nature of democracy" came to have crucial consequences. The situation in Algeria came to be inscribed as a battle only between Islamic fundamentalists and the regime, where the former was portrayed as a threat to Algeria, to the region and to the West. This made it difficult to raise any form of critique against the regime, since this easily could be read as a support of Islamic terrorists. Also, by portraying Islamism as a "protest movement" as a mere symptom of socio-economic problems, the Algerian people could be referred to as being socially discontent rather than genuinely in favour of FIS. I will go through these elements in turn, first spelling out how FIS was projected into the much larger debate on political Islam and fundamentalism.

By solely referring to FIS in conjunction with the "global phenomenon" of political Islam, FIS was rarely inscribed as an actor or subject per se, to be evaluated or assessed on "its own terms". Instead, FIS was spoken of as part of, or synonymous with, the general movement of radical Islam prospering in the Islamic world and the immigrant communities in the West. This also meant that the so-called "situation in Algeria" was projected into a much larger debate on Islam, with all its curious sub-themes, ranging from the Salman Rushdie case, to the revolution in Iran, to the debate over the veil in France and the difficulties of integrating Muslim immigrants in Western capitals. In the initial debate on democracy "the nature of Islam" had of course been present, but it had mainly been a derivative theme related to the question of democracy. Now democracy only seemed to emerge as a matter of absence in relation to Islamic movements, where these movements were being portrayed as democracy's antithesis. Islamists – and hence also FIS – could be referred to en bloc as anti-western, anti-secular and anti-democratic. As one professor at the American University noted in the *Washington Post*: "Is Islam, fundamentalist or otherwise, compatible with liberal, human-rights oriented Western style representative democracy? The answer is an emphatic no ... In Algeria or in Egypt, the modern Islamic movement is authoritarian, anti-democratic, and anti-secular" (*Washington Post*, 19 January 1992; see also *Washington Post*, 6 February 1992; *Le Monde*, 22 February 1992, 30 April 1992). In *Le Monde* (27 June 1992), FIS's apparent resort to violence could in the same vein be inscribed as just one more movement in the Islamic world being on the verge of calling for Islamic jihad.

The prospects of FIS encouraging further violence – turning the fight against the regime into a holy war and taking over the state – was not only debated within the general frame of Islamic resurgence, but FIS was, in this respect, commonly referred to as fundamentalists or "intégristes".[4] Even many of the critics of the annulment of the electoral process, or those who advocated a more multi-faceted stand towards Islamists, warning of not turning political Islam into a new "evil empire", rendered FIS synonymous with fundamentalists. The *Washington Post*, apparently only describing the context of the Algerian crisis, noted: "The fundamentalists were about to take control over Algeria's Parliament through flawed but essentially democratic elections. In a victory of process over values, democratic practices brought anti-democratic forces to the threshold of power (*Washington Post*, 6 February 1992) and "The Algerian experiments effectively ended Jan. 11 when Algeria's army intervened to halt the country's first free parliamentary election, which Islamic fundamentalists were poised to win" (*Washington Post*, 1 February 1992). FIS was not only equated with fundamentalists, but very often FIS disappeared as a proper subject, being substituted with fundamentalists proper.

To invoke fundamentalism is, however, hardly an innocent practice. The very term may in fact in itself serve to securitize (Laustsen and Wæver 2000: 720). The "fundamentalists" (FIS) were in this respect not only articulated as a threat to the secular Algerian state and its secular and Western-minded middle class, but also, and most predominately to the West. This articulation of fundamentalism in Algeria as a threat and danger took three forms. First, FIS was described as a threat to the "welfare and livelihood of millions of middle class secularized Algerians", especially to women, intellectuals, the Berber community and the French-speaking elite (*Washington Post*, 6 February 1992; *Le Monde*, 22 February 1992). Middle-class Algerians believed *The Economist* (8 February 1992) report that FIS would ruin the country and were relieved that the army-backed council took over. If FIS were to come to power, this would threaten the livelihood of those many Algerians who were secular and "just like us". Second, exactly this threat against the secular classes of Algeria was articulated as giving rise to yet another, in the form of a mass exodus of boat people and refugees emigrating to Europe, and in particular to France, in order to escape Islamic fundamentalism and violence. Hence, parallels were often made to the Algerian war of independence, threatening to repeat itself, in terms of waves of refugees and terrorist attacks; possibly moving the conflict to French soil (*Le Monde*, 30 April 1992, 6 October 1992, 17 February 1992; *Washington Post*, 1 February 1992). Third, FIS was in a well-known domino-scenario, inscribed as a "green virus" – green being the colour of Islam – which would spread to neighbouring countries in the Middle East and seek to export its Islamic revolution, as Iran had attempted before it. It was similarly alleged that FIS militants were receiving aid and training from Sudan and Afghanistan (*Le Monde*, 27 June 1992). The *Washington Post* reported that US officials

> fear that fundamentalist rule in Algeria will spill across borders to cause upheavals in other countries. From there, some US officials say, there is a danger of Muslim fundamentalism spreading through the region and creating anti-Western regimes in countries such as Jordan, which is of major strategic and political importance to US policy in the region.
>
> (*Washington Post*, 14 January 1992)

How was this threat to be combated and what was its source? These two questions were, as I will spell out shortly, already in 1992 articulated as closely intertwined. In the wake of several attacks on foreigners, terrorism and fundamentalism were positioned as inseparable terms; only economic aid could help Algeria confront the dual malice of fundamentalist terrorism and guarantee that the path of democracy was followed.

Speaking about the situation in Algeria was not merely a matter of spelling out the different types of threats that fundamentalism posed, but just as much to find the source and explanation of the Islamic revival in Algeria and FIS's overwhelming success. Economic and social distress was, in this respect, a repetitive form of explanation in newspaper articles by experts on Islamism, as well as in official statements. It was the economic stagnation that had turned many Algerian towards fundamentalist parties, the *Washington Post* (14 January 1992) characteristically explained (see also *Le Monde*, 15 January 1992, 14 March 1992; *The Economist*, 8 February 1992). The vote for FIS was essentially a protest vote founded in Algeria's collapsing economy (USIA, 24 April 1992). The population growth which had resulted in 70 per cent of Algerians being under 30 years old, the drastic drop in the prices of Algeria's vital export of petrol, and the world-wide recession were all factors that had spurred an immense rate of unemployment and very poor housing conditions. In conjunction, these social and economic problems had caused the highly deprived and dissatisfied population to embrace Islamic fundamentalism. Therefore, only international aid would "solve the economic and social problems on which religious fundamentalism breeds" the *Washington Post*

(1 February 1992) concluded. In order for the current Algerian government to regain support from the people: "the support from abroad is indispensable" (*Le Monde*, 9 June 1992). In February the French Prime Minister Dumas announced that France had provided significant new loans to Algeria and persuaded the EU to adopt a new financial plan to aid Algeria. France had – "ever since a new team came to power" – continually expressed its sincere will to support Algeria:

> I would like at this moment to express to the Algerian authorities the French will to continue to help Algeria and the Algerian people in this difficult phase which ... only can be overcome if an effort is mounted: a consistent effort to support the economy of this country.
>
> (Dumas, 4 February 1992)

This predominant socio-economic analysis of the source of the fundamentalist resurgence in Algeria, described above, was based on the premise that the cause of FIS's success also entailed its own cure and remedy. Since FIS's strong support was rooted in Algeria's difficult economic and social conditions, the solution also appeared to be evident: to provide economic aid through loans and rescheduling of debt. In this way, articulations moved from the universal to the particular. When FIS was spoken of in terms of a threat, it was not distinguished from other Islamic "fundamentalists", nor seen as a particular Algerian movement, but was instead rendered as part of an overall threat of "radical Islam". Yet, when the causes of FIS success were to be explained, FIS emerged as a particular Algerian phenomenon, to be explained according to particular Algerian circumstances.

The socio-economic analysis also entailed an assumption about the true, yet hidden, nature of the vote and wishes of the Algerians. By depicting the votes for FIS as protest votes, merely cast as a result of economic and social distress, these votes and voices could be inscribed as not "really" being votes in favour of an Islamist party. The Algerians were not Islamists calling for an Islamic state but merely economically and socially deprived, longing for a new solution to severe economic problems. This explanation was to have crucial ramifications in the years to come. It did, of course, not only exclude other possible forms of explanations, for instance, that large parts of the population were dissatisfied with the army and the FLN state, with repression and corruption, or alternatively that the votes in fact signified a genuine wish to put an Islamist party into government, but it also enabled economic support to be articulated as a natural and evident response. Economic aid – and hence development – was a necessary prerequisite for democracy. When the economy was sound, and the living conditions of the people improved, Algerians would vote differently. The socio-economic explanation served to legitimize the provision of economic support to "Algeria" as we are to see, for years to come.

Following a meeting between Dumas and the members of the Algerian HCE in January 1993, Dumas (9 September 1993) declared once again that France stood on the side of the Algerians and would provide as much help as possible. But which side was the Algerian side and which side was it against? This was not specified. In June, six billion francs were sent to Algeria, and Juppé emphasized that France and the EU supported: "the fight against blind terrorism" and that "France has nothing good to expect from *intégrisme*." In a battle which increasingly was shaped as one between the Algerian state and fundamentalist terrorists, it was obvious whom one was against, although less obvious whom one sided with.

The combination of terrorism and fundamentalism hardly left room for critique of the Algerian regime and the rigid opposition between state and Islamic terrorists was exacerbated by the increasing number of attacks against Algerian intellectuals and foreigners within Algeria. At a US subcommittee of Near Eastern affairs debate on Algeria, the Secretary had to spell out – after he had encouraged the Algerian regime to implement democratic and economic reforms – that he was against terrorism and extremism in any form:

> Let me be clear: The United States Government in no way condones violence or political extremism from any quarter or under any guise ... We deplore the continuing assassinations of Algerian Government officials and members of the security forces by those in opposition to the government. We also deplore attempts to justify such violence.
> (US Secretary for Near East Affairs, 22 May 1993)

But why was it necessary at all to emphasize that the US did not condone political violence? To put it simply, by the representation of the conflict in Algeria as a conflict only involving the Algerian state and fundamentalist terrorists, any criticism of the regime was easily rendered as equivalent to a support of fundamentalists. Since there were two parties and two sides, where one of these sides was composed of Islamist terrorists, it became almost impossible to criticize the regime or to voice concern over the prospects of democracy. By the end of 1993, as we will see, the French Interior Minister could, in fact, claim that there was no third party, no moderate fundamentalists and no third way.

Between domestic and foreign, Algeria and France

By the fall of 1993 it became increasingly difficult to identify where French domestic policy stopped and French foreign policy began. The terrorist attacks and kidnapping of French citizens and other foreigners in Algeria were followed by mass arrests of presumed FIS sympathizers in France. During these months of late 1993, the French Interior Minister Charles Pasqua became one of the most dominant speakers on the situation in Algeria. A frequently asked question by journalists and commentators was therefore whether it was the Quai d'Orsay or Place Beauvau (the interior ministry) that defined French foreign policy towards Algeria. The reverse, however, also seemed to be true. Juppé, the Foreign Minister, was continually probed about the government's reaction to the presence of Islamic *intégristes* and potential terrorists in France. And just as Pasqua seemed to justify domestic policy measures with foreign policy, so did Juppé justify foreign policy with domestic measures.

In the French media this was predominantly interpreted as a fight between two ministers over power and ministerial resorts, where Pasqua presumably was attempting to take the role of foreign minister. Yet, this interpretation of course assumed that ministerial resorts always already are clearly distinguishable. I will, therefore, rather suggest that this should be analysed as a discursive battle over the boundaries and content of domestic and foreign policy and a fight over the linkages and boundaries between France and Algeria; a struggle that quickly evolved into a matter of whether France openly supported the "*éradicateurs*" in the Algerian government or merely pursued a legitimate domestic policy.

In a French parliamentary debate in late October, the French Foreign Minister Juppé was asked for the first time, what the French government intended to do with respect to those groups of "intégristes" present on French soil, who were using French territory as a base for directing insurrection in Algeria? France had become, it was argued, a virtual sanctuary for Muslim *intégristes* who were plotting to install an Islamic republic in Algeria. Therefore, it was asked "How does the French government intend to stem the *intégriste* movement's embrace of the French Muslim community?" (three news questions in the National Assembly, 27 October 1993). Since the assassinations in Algeria no longer were an internal affair of Algeria, it was asserted, but a serious problem between Algeria and France, how would the French government act? (Three news questions in the National Assembly, 27 October 1993.) Answering these questions, Juppé attempted to keep the (foreign) relations with Algeria separate from those steps that already had been and were to be taken against extremist groups *within* France. Yet, as the question already reflected, terrorism in Algeria and "intégrisme" in France were presented as two sides of the same coin and Juppé accordingly gave the same answer to both questions: France, Juppé explained, would show no complaisance towards terrorism and religious extremism.

A few weeks later the French police arrested eighty-eight individuals presumably closely affiliated with FIS. Charles Pasqua declared that this operation was taken "in order to disclose any complicity or relations with those in Algeria who have carried out actions that are contrary to the interests of France" (*Le Monde*, 12 November 1993). However, in a later interview Pasqua explained that the police operations against Muslim "intégristes" in France did not belong "to the shared realm of foreign policy, but to that of internal security" (Pasqua in *Le Monde*, 17 November 1993). Yet, in the very same interview, he also stressed that the operation was closely linked to the situation in Algeria. It could "be considered, in this case, as connected to the situation in Algeria". Conversely, when Juppé in December was to explain France's foreign policy towards Algeria, he immediately, and as the first point, stressed that France refused to become a safe haven for terrorists. The primary component of French foreign policy to Algeria was apparently to contain and pursue presumed terrorists on French territory:

> I would like briefly to recapitulate what the government's policy concerning Algeria is. First, it has a component dealing with domestic politics: the government has decided to no longer let France be slowly transformed into a

safe haven for international terrorism. This is why the Prime Minister, with the Minister of the Interior, myself, and all the concerned Ministers; this is why we have created the initiative – that you know – with regard to those who use French territory to organize themselves for terrorist or violent purposes. Measures have been taken against Islamic leaders who do other things than preach the good word and who organize terrorist networks ... We will continue in this direction because it is the responsibility and the honour of France not to lend a hand to movements that will end up turning against her.

(Juppé, 5 December 1993)

Hence, in this foreign policy outline, no references to Algeria or to relations between Algeria and France were made. Instead, France was constructed as the ultimate point of reference: terrorists and extremists within France were to be eradicated because they were against France. It was, in other words, difficult to discern whether the French crackdown on "intégristes" belonged to the realm of foreign policy or domestic policy. The French police's pursuance of possible FIS sympathizers could both be legitimized with reference to the situation in Algeria and with reference to the situation in France. When Pasqua was legitimizing the government's domestic policies, this could be done with reference to the situation in Algeria and "France's national interest". When Juppé was delineating the content of French foreign policy, this could be carried out with reference to the French government's pursuance of FIS sympathizers within France. The events within Algeria and the events in France were coupled and decoupled depending on whether one spoke from a "foreign policy perspective" or from a "domestic perspective". The police operations against "intégristes" in France were simultaneously portrayed as unrelated to the crisis in Algeria – as an act of strict domestic policy – and yet this same pursuit was portrayed as a French foreign policy response to the situation in Algeria. My point here is not that French foreign policy was domesticated, as many journalists were accusing, but rather that it was never clear where foreign policy began and domestic policy ended; where France stopped and Algeria started. The two seemed to be able to substitute one another in an endless game of mirrors.

Commentators and journalists, however, increasingly coupled Pasqua's hard-line against "extremists" in France with the events in Algeria. The pursuit of FIS members was read through the foreign policy perspective alone; being articulated as a response to the events in Algeria, rather than to problems within France. There was, critics argued, a direct parallel between the French police operation and the Algerian regime's severe onslaught on terrorists in Algeria. This was a coordinated effort to eliminate Islamic terrorism and to secure the Algerian regime's hold on power. Here it was the goal in itself which was not questioned – eliminating terrorism – but rather the unintended consequences for France of pursuing this aim: it was predicted that the overt support and cooperation with the Algerian government would loop back and possibly threaten the security of France. Algerian militant groups, and GIA in particular,[5] would conceivably take terrorism to French soil with reference to the French government's feebly covered attempt to maintain the power of the regime in Algeria.[6] GIA had already warned that those who were cooperating with the regime would be viewed as accomplices in the crimes committed by the Algerian authorities, and hence constitute potential targets (*Le Monde*, 17 November 1993). France therefore risked GIA reprisals as long as it was pursuing FIS members and Islamists in France. France's attack on Islamic fundamentalists had created an unholy and dangerous alliance with the Algerian regime (*Le Monde*, 10 December 1993, 17 November 1993; *Washington Post*, 17 December 1993).

This analysis and line of critique of course rendered it increasingly problematic for the French government to speak simultaneously from the Algerian and the French, the domestic and the foreign, perspectives; to speak as if these converged and amounted to the same thing. Politicians needed to explain why the combat against Islamic terrorists within France did not equate a support of the government in Algeria. Juppé accordingly attempted to explain that the French government was solely engaged in a battle against terrorists and *intégristes*; in a fight against those who were against France, not in an endeavour to support "this or that government". To do otherwise would be masochistic, Juppé clarified to a journalist at France 2:

> I have always maintained that one should not be complacent towards those who employ violence and terrorism, and who promote anti-French ideas. There is no need to be a masochist! We are not going to help those who fight us. But I have also maintained that it is necessary that things progress in Algeria. We support not this or that government; we support the Algerian people.
>
> (Juppé, 5 November 1993)

In an interview with *Jeune Afrique*, Balladur, the Prime Minister, similarly asserted that the two events were not linked in any way. The crisis in Algeria was an internal affair of Algeria, which it was for the Algerians and their government alone to solve (Balladur, 23 December 1993). The police operation in France was a domestic affair undertaken in order to protect the fundamental values of France "France, however, cannot accept the development, under the cover of religious practices, movements of a political character which aim to produce disorder and strike out against the fundamental principles of the Republic" (Balladur, 23 December 1993). The security and identity of France was at stake. The French government was defending the core values of the République – in particularly "secularity"– not a particular government, it was asserted.

Tensions and contradictions: insolvable dichotomies and hopeless alternatives

Although the crackdown on and later house arrest of FIS members in France was sought to be decoupled from French foreign policy and from the events in Algeria, this did not bring closure to the question of whether or not France – and the West in general – supported the Algerian regime. Attention was in particular directed to the economic aid and rescheduling of debt that the IMF, the EU and France were providing for Algeria,[7] and to the ever-increasing reports on widespread human rights violation, torture and repression.[8] These two were, in conjunction, read as an indication of Western indifference to the Algerian regime's appalling human rights record, and as yet another sign that the West, in effect, was backing the present regime.

This placed politicians and government officials in a difficult situation from where it seemed almost impossible to speak about the Algerian crisis without being accused of taking the wrong course or supporting the wrong side. On the one hand, Western governments had to demonstrate that they indeed were concerned by the Algerian crisis, with the lack of democratic reform and with the reports on the regime's excessive pursuit of the fundamentalists. On the other hand, they had simultaneously to prove that when addressing this concern, they were neither taking the side of the Algerian government nor that of the "intégristes". This difficulty, of course, hinged on the fact, as I will spell out below, that the Algerian conflict continued to be depicted in terms of a struggle between two parties only. Trying to strike a balance between contradictory imperatives only reproduced well-established dilemmas and thereby marked articulations with tensions and impossible combinations.

Turning to the first dilemma: Algeria's crisis, it continued to be emphasized, was an internal affair of Algeria, which it was not for outsiders to judge or solve (for example, Juppé, 14 September 1994, 15 September 1994; Mitterand, 9 September 1994). France was not responsible for the Algerian problems neither for their solutions: "Sometimes I hear people say: but what does France do? When will she act? We have no intention at all of acting in Algeria. The problem belongs to the Algerians" (Juppé, 11 August 1994). Yet, to contend that the escalating violence and the widespread reports of gross violations of human rights merely were a concern of the Algerians alone, of course, easily gave way to, and reinforced, accusations of French and Western indifference. Thus, having stressed the domestic character of Algeria's problems once more, Juppé (24 August 1993) hastily assured that this not was to be seen as an indication of French passivity and inaction (see also Juppé, 11 August 1994, 11 October 1994; Mitterand, 16 July 1994). It was, however, not only the French government who was caught by this double-imperative of, on the one hand, arguing that the Algerian crisis reached beyond Algeria and touched all of us and, on the other hand, emphasizing that this was a crisis to be solved by the Algerians themselves. The League for Human Rights and the International Committee in Support of Algerian Intellectuals, for instance, issued a joint appeal in which it was stated: "Concerning the crisis which Algeria experiences today only the Algerians can find political solutions. Yet this cannot be born in isolation in the country" (reprinted in Derrida 2002: 301).[9] In other words, those who spoke in the name of universal human rights and criticized the French government – and the West at large – for turning a blind eye to violence and the Algerian government's extrajudicial activities, also seemed compelled to underscore that it, of course, was the Algerians only who could find a solution to *their* problems.

This attempt to create an uneasy position between intervention and indifference was further complicated by the fact that the provision of economic aid and loans increasingly was taken to signify that the West, and France in particular, was supporting the Algerian regime in spite of its continued violations of human rights and its lack of democratic reform (for example, *Le Monde*, 20 August 1994; French Parliamentary Debate, 11 October 1994). The French government responded by arguing that the political crisis had to be kept separate from that of the economic crisis (see, for example, Juppé,14 September 1994; Mitterand, 14 July 1994; Juppé, 24 August 1994, 15 September 1994, 28 September 1994). Algeria's crisis entailed a political and an economic component. These two were not to be conflated, but were to be addressed according to the two separate logics of politics and economics. The years of socialist policies and inefficiency, the burden of foreign debt, world market recession and the drastic drop in prices on gas and petrol had brought the Algerian economy on the verge of collapse, it was explained. Providing loans, rescheduling debt and orienting the country to a liberal market economy was therefore an independent matter, which did not touch on the political situation of the country. Having spelled out, in meticulous detail, the difficulties which confronted the Algerian economy, it could always in the same neutral and economic language be described which new loans or rescheduling needed to be provided or were about to be initiated (for example, Juppé, 30 September 1994; see also Juppé, 15 September 1994, 28 September 1994).

Yet, when spelling out who was being helped and supported by the economic aid and loans, politics sneaked in through the backdoor. The question of economic support seemed impossible to separate from what was termed the fight against terrorism; just as it never appeared as really clear whether it was the Algerian government or the people who was the referent object of support, or whether the two converged into the same thing. Clinton (7 June 1994), for instance, explained: "We have tried to support the current [Algerian] government in working with France to reschedule their debt." "The French are very concerned about Algeria, as we are. And we indicated the importance of supporting the current government" (Warren Christopher, US Secretary of State, 7 June 1994; see also Clinton, 8 July 1994). Yet, in the next sentence, Clinton stressed that the United States stood on the side of the Algerian people in its fight "against terrorism and destructive fundamentalism" (Clinton, 7 June 1994). Mitterand similarly argued that France supported the Algerian government in its efforts to limit terrorism. "What we are looking for in Algeria is to support a process which would permit the government to govern successfully and to restrain terrorism" (Mitterand, 16 July 1994). Yet, when Juppé (11 October 1994) in a parliamentary debate asked "Who do we help? The powers that be or the people?" he unequivocally answered that France was supporting the Algerian people rather than the regime.

These conflicting assertions hinged on two closely related *problématiques* that, in conjunction, carved out a central dilemma. First, it had become increasingly difficult to refer to the Algerian government; the Algerian regime had shown no will of moving forward with democratic reforms, it was argued, neither had it called for new elections. Combined with the many reports on torture, arbitrary arrests, killings and repression made it extremely difficult for any Western government to take the side of the Algerian regime and too readily assume that the Algerian government and the Algerian people amounted to the same thing. Second, the Algerian regime and the Islamist terrorists, however, continued to be articulated as the only acting, purposeful and speaking subjects within Algeria. Politicians were in this way faced with the old dilemma from 1992, and this dilemma was now only more clear in light of the ever-increasing number of reports on the Algerian regime's acts of gross violations of human rights and its uncompromising policy of eradication. Although support could not unambiguously be given to the Algerian regime, neither could Western governments too strongly dismiss the regime. Discharging or condemning the Algerian leaders appeared as an equivalent to letting the terrorists take over the Algerian state. As Pasqua explained: "Everyone knows that the present regime is not a model of democracy, but we know for certain that the idea of a moderate Islamic regime is pure bunkum" (*The Times*, 6 August 1994).[10] Juppé (24 August 1994) equally argued: "It is in France's interest to have a regime in Algeria which is not hostile to her. But an Islamic state would be anti-French, anti-European, anti-western."

Balancing between these equally hopeless alternatives, it was also emphasized that the Algerian government ought to pursue a different course from mere eradication of the terrorists. Democratic reforms should be initiated and dialogue between the Algerian opposition and the regime begun "We wish for a dialogue between the different political movements in Algeria; we do not support a government or a party, we support democracy" (Juppé, 21 December 1994; see also Pelletreau, US Assistant Secretary of State, 3 October 1994; Juppé, 11 October 1994). Dialogue ought to be initiated since the Algerian government could not solve Algeria's crisis through repression and "security measures" alone. The regime's excessive hunt of presumed terrorists should be combined with efforts of reconciliation, dialogue and democratic reform (Juppé, 30 September 1994). Trying to steer free of the Algerian government as well as the "intégristes", it was argued that France had not issued, and would not issue, a carte blanche to the Algerian government (Juppé, 20 January 1994).

But who were to be partners in this dialogue? All agreed that terrorists could not be negotiated with. Those who used violence to obtain their goals and who did not renounce violence publicly could never constitute legitimate partners in a dialogue, it was stressed. They could never be allowed to enter a political process (Juppé, 14 September 1994, 15 September 1994; EU Declaration, 23 September 1994).

The well-established notion that terrorists – in contrast to political parties and movements – cannot be negotiated with, led to a crucial battle over which Islamist "parties" should be determined as terrorists. A repetitive theme was, in particular, whether or not FIS should be described as a terrorist organization (Mitterand, 10 July 1994; Ministry of Foreign Affairs, Spokesperson's Statements, 8 August 1994, 10 August 1994; Balladur, 14 August 1994). Asked if the Algerian authorities ought to initiate dialogue with Algerian *intégristes*, Juppé confirmed, without naming names:

I have a precise rule: as long as this or that movement has not renounced violence; as long as the daggers and Kalashnikovs have not been deposed in the cloakroom, then dialogue is not possible. If one wants to talk, one must stop killing. That's how it is.

(Juppé, 14 October 1994)

The continual reproduction of Islamist parties and groups as terrorist movements founded on ideas of hatred and extremism of course deprived them of any status as genuine political parties; having legitimate political projects and ideologies. It effectively excluded them from being potential partners in dialogue. In practice, there appeared to be no opposition movements or parties with whom the Algerian authorities could talk or include in a process of reconciliation. Pasqua hence explicitly announced that there were no moderate Islamists and no third way (*Le Figaro*, 4 August 1994). Between the terrorists and the army he argued, "There was nothing." There was no other alternative than eradicating Islamic terrorists or supporting them. There was no third option (*Le Monde*, 24 August 1994). Although Pasqua was portrayed as the incarnation of what was referred to as the "eradicators", the so-called "reconciliators" similarly had difficulties identifying a third pole. The democratic pole to negotiate with the government was not readily apparent. When asked, "What are these democratic forces with whom the dialogue is being called for in Algeria?" Mitterand (10 July 1994) accordingly answered: "I have asked myself that question ... by that you mean that it is difficult to engage in a dialogue, a negotiation with people whose tactic is to kill." Although the Algerian regime was neither articulated as democratic nor as a legitimate representative of the people, there were apparently no (political) organizations or parties who were able to represent the people in the government's place. As long as the Algerian crisis continued to be depicted only in terms of two subjects, regime and fundamentalist terrorists,[11] encouragements could endlessly be made of the regime's need to engage in an open dialogue with all democratic parties of the Algerian society, but no such democratic parties could be identified.

In sum, 1994 was flawed with dilemmas and difficult combinations; between neither endorsing fundamentalist terrorism nor dictatorship; of neither becoming involved nor being indifferent; of supporting dialogue, democracy and the Algerian people and yet not being able to identify who the democratic front was who could speak on behalf of the people, and who could legitimately engage in dialogue with the regime. In other words, although the increasing appeals to dialogue and democratic reform marked a difference from previous articulations, the reproduction of the Algerian conflict as a struggle between two equally undemocratic subjects, in practice, rendered dialogue meaningless. This is not to indicate that Western governments merely paid lip service to the need for democracy and dialogue – as critics increasingly were to contend in 1995 – but that politicians (as well as their critics) were caught by these presumptions and unsolvable dilemmas. The so-called third front and third solution, which commentators so often referred to, but never identified, did not yet exist (see, for example, *Le Monde*, 6 August 1994).

State sovereignty and intervention

By 1995, which I will turn to below, the dichotomy between fundamentalists and regime was, however, gradually to dissolve. As we will see, however, representations and policies do not operate as cause and effect. It did in fact not become any easier to respond to the Algerian crisis or to argue for international involvement. Instead, many of the dilemmas and schisms that I have described in this section were now explicitly spelled out by politicians and commentators; now being directly employed as legitimations and explanations of why Western governments, and France in particular, had such problems of articulating any consistent and coherent policy towards Algeria.

On the verge of civil war

> We are being called on to choose sides.
> (*Le Monde*, 11 October 1995)

In the wake of secret talks in Rome, it became increasingly difficult to suggest that there were no moderate Islamists and that the Algerian conflict simply could be described in terms of a dichotomized battle between fundamentalist terrorists and a "not-so-democratic-regime". The multiple actors – who now were taken to be involved in the conflict – and the so-called diffusion of violence that had caused the death of 50,000 were read as indications of an emerging civil war and renewed comparisons with the Algerian War of Independence now appeared. Headlines referred to "The second Algerian war", as would the titles of future books (*Le Monde*, 10 June 1995; see, for example, Martinez 2000; Provost 1996). How to respond to such a complex and difficult situation of quasi-civil war was a real puzzle, a so-called "*casse-tête*" because it was impossible to choose between the warring sides. This was only further compounded by a shift in the articulations of France's role in relation to Algeria. Where France previously had been described as the most active, competent and concerned actor with respect to Algerian affairs – as the one to define the West's policies towards Algeria – now it was continually emphasized that France was the least able to react to the Algerian crisis. I will go through each of these shifts and reproductions in turn beginning with the dissolution of the rigid opposition between regime and terrorists.

The emergence of a third front and the dissolution of a dichotomy

> The United States treats Algeria as if it is a European problem, Europe treats it as if it is a French problem, and the French cannot make up their minds.
> (Hastings in US House of Representatives Hearing, 5 February 1998)

In mid-January a secret meeting between various Algerian opposition parties and movements was held under the auspices of Sant Egidio in Rome.[12] This meeting resulted in a so-called "National Pact" signed by all of the participants including

FIS. The Pact renounced the use of violence, called for a peaceful resolution to the crisis and vowed its support to democracy, pluralism and a multi-party system.

The Rome platform was largely interpreted as an indication that so-called moderate Islamists indeed existed, thereby making it possible to assert that "a third pole" now was present in Algeria. If the Algerian regime seriously wished to engage in dialogue and negotiations there were no obstacles hindering such a process. The third pole, it was argued, was no longer just a small fraction of secular and socialist parties but, in fact, represented at least 80 per cent of the Algerian population, based on the votes from the election in 1991. To imagine democratization in Algeria without Islamists was therefore completely illusionary, one professor argued in *Le Monde* (Addi Lahouari, 12 January 1995). Another article in *Le Monde* (16 January 1995) equally explained "The argument of the advocates of eradication, who estimate that any dialogue with the Islamist is impossible or even harmful, has suddenly lost a lot of its weight."

Just a week prior to the publication of the Rome platform, FIS had already publicly rejected the use of violence and condemned GIA's terrorist attacks against foreigners. FIS emphasized, *Le Monde* (7 January 1995) reported, that they did not view the conflict in Algeria as a holy war between Muslim and other religions, but as a confrontation between a military dictatorship and its people. FIS's denunciations of violence and terrorism, and the many references to the differences between FIS and GIA, were taken to illustrate not only the difficulties of depicting FIS as a mere terrorist organization but also that the Algerian "Islamists" did not constitute a singular and coherent movement with a common strategy, purpose and ideology. The Algerian conflict involved several actors, fractions and different fronts. This was not a mere battle between Islamic terrorists and the regime. The Islamists were divided among themselves and had splintered into several groups and fractions (GIA, MIA, AIS, FIS, MEI, FIDA, LIDD).[13] They were fighting for different goals, employing different means and warring with one another over control of territory and resources. Just as the regime was torn between "réconciliateurs" and "éradicateurs", between the army and the government, so were the Islamists composed of several groups and military wings.

In the middle of all these fronts the "innocent civilians" emerged as the sole victims of violence, being targeted from all sides (Clinton, 31 January 1995; *The Economist*, 13 January 1995). *Le Monde*'s correspondent in Algeria reported – under the headline of "The dirty war in Algeria" – about schoolgirls who had their throats cut and women who were raped and mutilated. In this war, the victims were no longer from one camp or another, but innocent civilians. "Evidently, it must repeatedly be pointed out that all these victims belong to just one side: the innocent civilians, targets of 'barbaric fundamentalism'" (*Le Monde*, 15 March 1995).

Several Western journalists and intellectuals, with reference to the Rome platform, now argued that the international community had to renew its approach to Algeria when such a large part of the Algerian society had proved themselves willing to solve the conflict politically and peacefully (see, for example, *The Economist*, 14 January 1995, 11 February 1995; *Le Monde*, 16 January 1995). At an EU press conference in early February, Mitterand for the first time recognized that the provision of economic aid was insufficient in terms of solving the Algerian crisis and that the EU might play an important role by organizing a European conference based on the ideas of the Rome platform:

> It seems to me that the European Union can contribute to a recovery of the situation. The difficulty is that the administration of aid is done by the government, a fact we do not challenge and that we agree not to take sides in this conflict. So if the European Union would be able to organize a conference in Europe, which would let itself be inspired by the various ideas which have been put forward lately, especially after the conferences of the opposition in Rome ... then there might be a better chance to see these projects be acknowledged by the parties which now oppose them.
> (Mitterand, 6 February 1995)

However, this attempt to turn neutrality into a basis of an internationally negotiated solution, rather than a basis of "not getting involved", was immediately rejected by the French government (see, for example, *Le Monde*, 8 February 1995; *The Economist*, 11 February 1995). Mitterand had, *Le Monde* (6 February 1995) noted, sought and yet failed to formulate a position between indifference and intervention. The British and American administrations refrained from commenting on Mitterand's proposal at all,[14] merely repeating that they viewed the Rome platform as an interesting and serious step toward a non-violent solution.[15] The EU restated the importance of continuing economic support and appealed for dialogue and reconciliation without mentioning the Rome platform. Instead, statements emphasized once again that the Algerians themselves were to solve their problems: "The European Union is following the situation with much attention and concern. It reaffirms that it is for the Algerian people to find a solution to the crisis which is afflicting their country" (EU Declaration, 23 January 1995).[16]

Whereas Mitterand's proposal was ignored or openly rejected, one element was picked up by commentators and politicians: France was the worst suited to do something about Algeria. "If there is a country an initiative should not come from, it is France", *Le Monde* (7 February 1995) reported. Why, Juppé rhetorically asked? "Because the past of France and Algeria is such that we are the worst candidates to meddle in order to organize things" (Juppé, 7 February 1995). France's colonial past and traumatic war of independence made it impossible for France to act; in fact, even to have an Algerian policy. "Does France have an Algerian policy? True, the question is badly formulated. It would be more correct to ask: can France have an Algerian policy? The thing is, France, a former colonial power, is not in a position to point its finger at Algeria" (*Le Monde*, 6 September 1995; see also *Le Monde*, 23 August 1995; *The Economist*, 11 February 1995). Those historical and cultural ties between France and Algeria, which previously had been invoked to qualify that France was the most competent and knowledgeable in terms of Algeria, were now articulated as an obstacle and barrier, blocking and paralysing France from speaking and acting. The "shared history" no longer gave France a privileged access to define the situation in Algeria, but rather emerged as a source of caution and schizophrenia.[17]

While the Rome platform did not result in an international conference, it did, however, disturb the rigid dichotomy between terrorists and regime that had made it possible to suggest that there was no alternative to the present Algerian regime. Previously, it had been difficult to identify "the democratic opposition" since "the alternative pole" only appeared to be composed of fundamentalist terrorism. Terrorism was obviously still condemned – not least in the light of the first bomb attacks on French soil – but the multiplication of subjects and the apparent willingness of FIS to embrace democracy and pluralism – combined with the Algerian government's open rejection of the Rome platform – had effectively dissolved any easy dichotomization and turned the Algerian government into a "party" of a civil war.[18]

How to respond to Algeria was, however, still very difficult to answer; first, because France was "the worst suited" to react towards Algeria, and second because the emerging contours of a civil war made it difficult and unwanted to choose sides. How to approach the Algerian conflict was a headache and puzzle for the politicians themselves; Juppé (7 April 1995) continually explained: "If I encourage dialogue, then it is interpreted as a sign of support to the Islamists and an alienation of the rights of women and democracy, if I do not call for dialogue then it is interpreted as a sign of support to a controversial government" (see also Juppé, 20 April 1995). "The situation is a true puzzle" (Juppé, 20 April 1995). Journalists and intellectuals only seemed to reinforce this picture of a confused and complex crisis which no policies could alleviate or solve. Although criticizing the West – and France in particular – for its wavering and inconsistent policies, it was simultaneously argued that the Algerian conflict gave rise to more questions than answers. The complexities of the conflict itself seemed to explain why policies were incoherent and difficult to formulate (see, for example, Spencer 1996: 139; see also *Le Monde*, 23 August 1995, 11 October 1995; *The Economist*, 7 January 1995).

Thus, although the dichotomy between Islamic terrorists and the regime had been dissolved, the emphasis on civil war and quasi-civil war did not make it easier to reformulate current policies. Asked whether there was anything new that France could do vis-à-vis Algeria in light of the recent events, Juppé (20 April 1995) merely answered, "I search I search ....". The emergence of civil war only appeared to give further credit to the idea that that there was no room for international action or initiatives. The so-called parties, it was still proposed, needed to embark on a process of dialogue and reconciliation and find a negotiated solution. But this was to be created by themselves and for themselves. Who were to participate in such dialogue, or how it was to be arranged, were not matters that "outsiders" were to comment upon or define (for example, Welch, Assistant Secretary for Near Eastern Affairs, 11 October 1995). The new French foreign minister similarly repeated that France was in favour of dialogue and democracy between those who rejected violence. Yet when asked whether FIS, according to Charette himself, had renounced violence or not, Charette (23 October 1995) answered that we should let the Algerians themselves discuss who belonged to one side or the other.

However, in contrast to 1994, several specialists and scholars on Algerian affairs started to question whether the Algerians in fact were able to plan, decide and carry out such forms of negotiations themselves. Merely encouraging the Algerians to embark on dialogue was not sufficient and did hardly constitute a response or policy, since nobody would be able to disagree over the sensibility of dialogue. A well-known scholar on Algeria asked:

> What does dialogue mean? The answer is that it means whatever you want it to mean. That is to say it means nothing in particular. What politician would ever say that he was against it? And if no one can be against it, how can anyone be for it to any purpose?
>
> (Roberts 1995: 255)

The calls for dialogue were hiding that the West in reality was supporting the Algerian government. The image of neutrality was false, another French scholar on Algeria argued (Stora 1995). The concept of non-involvement had been stretched "to degrees of elasticity hitherto unseen by a programme of massive economic assistance, carefully dosed arms sales and tacit political support for the Zeroual regime which only just stopped short of outright advocacy" (Howorth 1996: 158; see also Chenal 1995; Roberts 1995; Provost 1996: 98).

Faced with this type of criticism, Juppé (11 October 1995) tried to explain once again why France could not become involved: "One demands of us to choose sides, and this is exactly what cannot be done. We do not meddle in internal Algerian affairs; we have state to state relations with the Algerian government without passing judgment." The provision of economic aid was taken to be a necessity given Algeria's failed economy and its effects on the population's political views (see, for example, US Assistant Secretary of Near Eastern Affairs, 11 October 1995). Providing economic aid was not similar to taking the side of the Algerian government. Rather, Charette argued, if aid was conditioned or trade and cooperation restricted, then this would in fact constitute an intervention in Algeria's internal matters (Hervé de Charette, 3 September 1995). Charette in this way turned the criticism on its head. Or rather the foreign minister invested neutrality with a different meaning. Ending the economic assistance to Algeria would amount to an economic boycott and therefore constitute a partisan and interventionary act. In order to stay neutral, refraining from punishing only one party and thereby taking sides, aid had to be continued. Economic aid could, in other words, both be inscribed as a neutral and as a biased act. Conversely, stopping this aid could be articulated as respectively biased and neutral. Both positions could be portrayed as abiding by the unquestioned imperative of neutrality.

Following the presidential elections in Algeria in November 1995, it now became, as we are to see, much easier to choose a "side" while still clinging to the presumed virtue of neutrality and non-intervention.

A step towards democracy and peace?

The Algerians have shown strong preference for ballots over bullets.
(Pelletreau, US Assistant Secretary of State, 15 April 1996)

At the end of 1995, and throughout most of 1996, most agreed that the Algerian situation had improved remarkably. The result of the Algerian presidential election – and the very fact that elections had been held – was in itself taken to be a significant move towards democracy and a cause of great optimism. The election did not only signify that Algeria was progressing towards democracy, but also towards peace. The Algerian regime, and the Algerian people as a whole, had come to acknowledge that the use of violence could not solve their problems (EU Declaration, 20 November 1995; Juppé, 19 November 1995; Charette, 21 November 1995; Chirac, 3 December 1995; Pelletreau, 15 April 1996). The popular vote for President Zeroual and his reform initiatives were very encouraging, since they were the first steps toward stability and peace (Charette, 1 April 1996; Pelletreau, 24 June 1996). Contrasting ballots and bullets while causally linking elections and peace, it was possible to argue that Algeria now was near a peaceful solution.

The elections also granted the Algerian authorities a renewed legitimacy. "The president, who has been elected, is re-legitimized by the first true universal election" (Juppé, 19 November 1995). Zeroual was now the legitimate president recognized as such both internationally and by the Algerian people (Charette, 27 March 1996). The electoral process, it was emphasized, had run smoothly and the large turnout at the ballot box signified that those parties who had boycotted the elections had been wrong. President Zeroual had demonstrated that he was on the side of democracy (Pelletreau, 15 April 1996; Schifter, US National Security Advisor, 18 June 1996). Asked in the immediate aftermath of the election whether Chirac now would consider meeting Zeroual, Chirac (3 December 1995) answered "President Zeroual is the legitimate president of Algeria. This does not constitute any problem for me." And, indeed, in December the President of the National Assembly met with Zeroual in Algiers, as did Charette in July 1996 and the US Assistant Secretary of State in March 1996. The latter reported to the Sub-Committee on Near Eastern Affairs that he was much impressed with Zeroual's commitment to strengthen democratic pluralism in Algeria (US Assistant Secretary of State, 24 June 1996). Zeroual was now one with whom Western officials could shake hands without this being interpreted as a controversial support of dictatorship (*Le Monde*, 31 July 1996).

The result of the elections was not only articulated as a sign that the Algerian authorities were embracing democratic reform, but also as a sign that the Algerian *people* were in favour of democracy and peace (Pelletreau, 15 April 1996; EU Declaration, 20 November 1995). The Algerian people were neither extremist or fundamentalist, but moderates who aspired for peace and development.

I do not think that the Algerian community, which is a moderate community, would actually be tempted by some form of fundamentalist or Islamist adventure. These are good Muslims. These are moderate people who aspire first of all, and I emphasize this, to peace and development.

(Chirac, 3 December 1995)

The dispositions and wishes of the Algerian authorities and the Algerian people were in this way constituted as identical. They were both pursuing democracy and peace. They had both – through the election – proven that they wished to end the conflict by political means. There were no longer, it seemed, different sides between whom international observers and actors needed to choose. There was only one side: the side of democracy. Support of democracy could accordingly be expressed without being inscribed as either a support of or condemnation of either "camp". Encouraging the process of democratization was in fact a balanced act. "Outside actors" were merely giving expression to what the Algerian authorities and the people already themselves wanted. How the Algerians would "move forward in the direction of broader democracy and pluralism" was, however, for the Algerians to decide. "It is not for us to set specifics in advance of discussion among Algerian political leaders [we will only] continue to watch the situation in Algeria closely" (US Assistant Secretary of State, 24 June 1996; see also Charette, 31 July 96, 1 April 1996). Outside governments and institutions were neither to be partners in possible dialogue nor parties in the conflict.

In sum, supporting democratization had previously been inscribed as a political and partisan act, but could now be placed within a neutral and consensual realm. The Algerian people, the Algerian authorities and foreign governments were all united in the common goal of democracy. Their wishes for the future were presumably corresponding.

The emergence of an international problem

The equation of democracy and peace and the positioning of the regime and the people on the side of democracy, however, began to be questioned by the end of 1996. As the numbers of civilian killings steadily increased, the former writing of a "democratic spring" in Algeria was challenged. In November and December there were almost daily reports of new massacres of civilians in villages south of Algiers; of women and children who had their throats cut and "disappearances" of persons who had been questioned by the Algerian Security Forces. In a report released by Amnesty in mid-November, it was estimated – in contrast to the dominant writing of past events – that the situation in Algeria had deteriorated significantly over the last *two years* (Amnesty International Report, 19 November 1996; see also *Le Monde*, 20 November 1996). "The government and the Islamists kill innocents." They conduct terrible crimes against innocents in the name of "the fight against terrorism" or "the holy war", Amnesty reported. More than 50,000 people have been killed since 1992, and arbitrary arrests, disappearances and torture "belong to the order of the day". The report also warned that the emergence of so-called self-defence groups that were supported with arms by the government only had exacerbated the human rights violations and constituted a dangerous setback (Amnesty International Report, 19 November 1996).

Moreover, a new and crucial uncertainty entered the discourse on Algeria. It was no longer possible to identify those responsible for the killings of civilians. The security forces were dressing up in civilian clothes, just as Islamic groups often were carrying uniforms (Spencer 1996: 133; *The Economist*, 7 December 1996; *Le Monde*, 26 December 1996; Amnesty International Report, 19 November 1996). In spite of these atrocities, the international community had chosen to ignore the facts; turning their backs on the Algerian massacres and human rights violations (Amnesty International Report, 19 November 1996). How can Europe ignore the Algerian regime's responsibility for the killings, *Le Monde* (26 December 1996) also asked, and concluded: "The Europeans cannot be unaware of the nature of a regime that carries a heavy responsibility for the present situation; specifically the European Union should put pressure on Algiers because it cannot be suspected to have a hidden post-colonial agenda."[19]

These concerns were very different from those previously voiced. First, the killings and massacres were not inscribed into a "civil war scenario" where Islamic groups were killing civilians and government forces were pursuing terrorists. Rather, the government was now accused of being directly involved in some of the attacks on civilians. Second, it was no longer treated as a virtue and a given that "outside actors" should stay neutral with respect to the Algerian conflict. On the contrary, neutrality was turned into a vice; being read as an indication of indifference and passivity. The very notion of "outside actors" was questioned: the EU or the international community could not remain neutral or stay on the outside. Algeria was also "our" responsibility. By the end of 1996, we hence see the first articulations of the Algerian situation as an international problem, demanding international solutions. These calls for international involvement were, as we are to see, voiced with increasing intensity in 1997.

The problem: "Who Kills?" silence and truth

> Thousands of people – women and children, the poor and elderly – have been massacred with unspeakable brutality. Some of those lucky enough to have escaped having their throats cut or being burned alive in their homes have reached nearby security forces posts and called for help. In vain. Their cries have not been heard in their country, or beyond their national borders. Up to 80.000 people have been killed behind a virtual wall of silence on the part of the international community.
> (Amnesty International; FIDH; Human Rights Watch; Reporters sans Frontières, 15 October 1997).

The killings of civilians continued throughout 1997. Appalling massacres of whole villages including children and women were extensively reported in newspapers and commentaries. These descriptions were, however, troubled by uncertainties. Groups of what appeared to be Islamist guerrilla groups were, in the midst of night and sheltered by the dark, encircling villages, capping off access, and then carrying out carefully planned massacres on the inhabitants. But why did the security forces not come to their rescue, it was asked. How could these atrocities take place so close to army barracks and military installations? And why were journalists hindered from entering the barbaric sites? (See, for example, *Le Monde*, 8 January 1997; *Washington Post*, 18 October 1997.)

Western government officials were compelled to comment on these massacres and the uncertainties that surrounded them. Journalists and intellectuals openly suggested that the problem of Algeria had been silenced. Western governments had, it was suggested, deliberately refrained from speaking about "what to do" about Algeria's problems and the horrendous massacres which tormented the Algerian population (see, for example, Hervé de Charette, 27 January 1997; UK House of Commons Debate, 1 December 1997). Government officials had now to answer problems and questions that already had been discursively fixated by others. They were probed to respond to a situation, which already was framed within a moral and universal language; where particularistic national identities and boundaries were taken to hold less importance than common human sentiments. As one professor explained in *Le Monde*:

> The children who are slaughtered in Mitidja are Algerians, but symbolically they are Germans, Americans, Sudanese, Chinese, French ... To come to the rescue of the children of Algeria, to save them from the knife which cut their throats, is a moral imperative that is essential to everybody.
>
> (Addi Lahouari, 26 September 1997)

It was, accordingly, increasingly difficult to assert that the killings remained an internal affair of Algeria; that the proper locus of responsibility and action solely rested with Algeria. We were all – as fellow humans and moral beings – under attack.

This change of reference was, in particular, made possible by the question of "who kills", and by the writing of a history of international silence. Human rights organizations and academics had already in late 1996 started to raise doubts in terms of who was actually behind the killings, as pointed out in the previous section. These concerns were now also being voiced in newspapers, by politicians and in parliamentary debates. In late August a new massacre in Raïs, a small village just south of Algiers, caused the death of 300. The perpetrators had entered the village in the morning armed with hatchets and Kalashnikovs. They had mutilated, burned and shot the residents until half past two in the morning. The victims had cried out for help in vain, *Le Monde* reported. "People shouted. No help arrived. Yet the security forces were close by" (*Le Monde*, 1 September 1997). Just a week after, the inhabitants of a shantytown of Algiers were also brutally slaughtered by "unidentified assailants" (*Washington Post*, 9 September 1997). "Algerian officials have been unable to explain why police and army forces at barracks only a few miles from the carnage failed to respond during hours of shooting and arson" (*Washington Post*, 9 September 1997).

> The identity of those who committed these barbaric acts, these crimes against humanity, is not known for sure. In Algiers, the craziest rumours circulate about the possible backers. According to two hypotheses put forth by different sources, the villagers were massacred either by Islamists disguised as military, or by paramilitaries disguised as Islamists.
>
> (*Le Monde*, 26 September 1997)

The unknown perpetrators of the massacres were, of course, starkly condemned (see, for example, EU Declaration, 12 September 1997; Foley, US State Department Spokesman, 3 September 1997; Védrine, 1 October 1997). In the first parliamentary debate in the EU on the situation in Algeria, it was asked once again: "Why is it that some of these murders have taken place close to security positions; why is it that the military have not been able to protect their population?" (Debates of the European Parliament, 17 September 1997). This was also echoed in the US Foreign Relations Committee, and even French leaders referred to the situation in Algeria in terms of uncertainty and lack of truth: "the very challenging thing is that we do not know how to understand what is happening in Algeria. We do see a ghastly terror, a scandalous violence carried out against the population, but it is extremely difficult to identify what happens" (Jospin, 29 September 1997; see also Neumann, US Foreign Relations Committee, 1 October 1997).

Why was it difficult to know what was *really* going on? This was largely attributed to absence of freedom inside Algeria that enabled the Algerian government to build a virtual wall of silence and international isolation. Six years of repression and violence had created an environment of fear and manipulation of truth. Journalists and intellectuals had been killed, the opposition had been outlawed and the press had been censored (US Foreign Relations Committee, 1 October 1997; Human Rights Watch Report on Algeria, June 1997). Algeria had been contained from the rest of the world for years. Foreign embassies had been shut down, diplomats had fled the country along with foreign correspondents, Western airlines had suspended all flights, and visas were practically unobtainable (*Washington Post*, 9 September 1997). The bestiality had occurred behind "closed doors" (*Le Monde*, 26 September 1997; Reporters sans Frontières, March 1997: 22). Now, in the midst of these brutal massacres, the Algerian government was still denying journalists and the international press entry and accurate information. The numerous calls for an international investigation into the massacres and appeals for a UN special Rapporteur were also refused by the Algerian government.

Yet if the government did not have anything to hide, why were all types of international enquiries so vigorously denied, it was asked? The Algerian government was trying to silence the atrocities (*Le Monde*, 25 September 1997). "We have a right to know", the EU Parliament stressed in a statement to the press (News

Report EU Committee on Foreign Affairs, 25 September 1997). This quest for accurate knowledge was also voiced by a French government spokesman: "It is clear that the international community needs to know what goes on in Algeria" (Ministry of Foreign Affairs, Spokesperson's Statement, 10 November 1997).

Yet, the international community's apparent search for knowledge and truth was questioned. It was not merely the Algerian regime, which for years had attempted to silence the issue of Algeria; Western governments and the international community had also, critics argued, successfully participated in the construction of a wall of silence (*Le Monde*, 8 September 1997; *New York Times*, 3 September 1997; *Politiken*, 8 September 1997). These articulations of a shared responsibility for the silencing of Algeria were spurred by the UN Secretary-General's remarks on Algeria in late August. For the first time Kofi Annan spoke about the atrocities in Algeria and explicitly correlated silence and responsibility. Algeria was not a matter of "not knowing", but a matter of pretending not to know. By silencing the issue of Algeria, the international community had failed its responsibility towards the Algerians. It had failed the essence of what it meant to be human.

> It is extremely difficult for all of us to pretend that it is not happening, that we do not know about it and that we should leave the Algerian population to their lot. I think as compassionate human beings, as people with conscience and moral concerns, I think that we are all moved and concerned by what is happening in Algeria. Words may not be enough, but it is a beginning to let the victims know that third parties care.
>
> (Kofi Annan, 30 August 1997)

Kofi Annan's outcry on Algeria became a powerful point of reference. The Secretary-General had, it was argued, broken the silence and broken a taboo. Annan had shattered that apathy which the apparent lack of knowledge had legitimized (*Le Monde*, 25 September 1997). In the aftermath of Annan's speech, similar calls were made by the Vatican, by the UN Commissioner of Human Rights, by UNICEF and in several editorials (*Le Monde*, 1 October 1997). The *Daily Telegraph*, for instance, described the situation the following way:

> Kofi Annan, the Secretary General of the UN, has said that it may be time for the UN to intervene to stop the spiral of killing and atrocity ... Following the grotesque orgy of beheading and throat-cutting last week, which took at least 300 lives in two villages south of Algiers on one day, the Vatican has accused the international community of 'ice-cold indifference'. The military regime of President Liamine Zeroual has rejected Mr Annan's statement as unacceptable interference in Algeria's internal affairs. With no end in sight to the violence, in which up to 100,000 Algerians have died hideously, it is Mr Zeroual's statement which is unacceptable.
>
> (*Daily Telegraph*, 2 September 1997)

With reference to Kofi Annan's speech, journalists could now repeatedly point to "the fact" that the issue of Algeria had been ducked and cloaked, and ask Western politicians what they intended to do about Algeria without being charged with subjectivism and bias.

This stood in sharp contrast to the way that questions and answers were framed prior to Kofi Annan's speech. In January a journalist had, for instance, asked Charette whether the French government's silence on the issue of Algeria should be attributed to a fear of terrorism. In his answer Charette (30 January 1997) described the question as aggressive, as an expression of the journalist's individual preferences and as a very dubious infliction on Algeria's sovereignty: "I find your question particularly aggressive and one-sided. What do you want? That the government tells the Algerians what they have to do? Algeria is not France. It is necessary to understand this fact ... Algeria is a sovereign nation." Now, however it was possible to invoke Kofi Annan's analysis of silence and responsibility, to ask "what should be done?" (Ministère des Affaires Étrangères, 7 October 1997; see also Ministère des Affaires Étrangères, 1 October 1997, 23 September 1997; Jospin, 16 September 1997).

The establishment of silence, hence, became a defining element in the discourse on Algeria. Silence was equated with manipulation and cloaking of truth, attributed both to the Algerian government and to the international community. By pointing to the years of silence that has surrounded the Algerian crisis, the international community was invested with a partial responsibility for the way in which the conflict had developed in Algeria. Now that silence gradually was broken, it was argued, the international community had to act. It could no longer pretend that it did not know. The invocation of silence became a powerful move, which served to highlight that the "outside" had to become involved.[20] As we are to see below, the demand to do something was, however, foremost made possible by the articulations of the Algerian atrocities as a moral issue that transcended the confines of territorial boundaries and national identities.

This is our responsibility: this is us?

No, Algeria, it's not an internal affair.

(Robert Fisk, 5 November 1997)

The almost daily reports on horrible massacres committed by unknowns, by masked assassins without faces, seemed only to leave journalists and commentators with one solid point of reference: the victims. Photographs could neither be taken of the massacres nor of the sites where they had been perpetrated. The Algerian authorities refused access (*Le Monde*, 26 September 1997). Instead, newspapers were filled with testimonies of relatives and of those who had managed to escape the killings. Of mothers who had foetuses ripped from their wombs, of two-year-olds who were burned to death, of dwellers who in vain had cried out for help.[21] When will the international community react, yet another editorial demanded (*Washington Post*, 18 October 1997). Eighty thousand killed until today, how many new victims does it take before non-intervention becomes a crime, Addi Lahoura asked in *Le Monde* (26 September 1997).

The massacres should not only be seen as brutal attacks on the Algerian people, but on humanity at large; on all of us, it was argued. Being human therefore demanded involvement and undertaking one's responsibility (EU Parliament, 17 September 1997). "We cannot stand by and do nothing whilst assassinations are committed on a daily basis. It is our duty to act" (André-Léonard, French EU Parliament member, 17 September 1997).

> It cannot be denied that today it is also our responsibility and our countries' responsibility to put an end to this martyrdom ... It is not facile rhetoric to affirm that the struggle of the Algerian population hostage to violence, is our struggle.
>
> (Muscardini, Italian EU Parliament member, 17 September 1997)

Not to act was in this way represented as a crime; as a violation of the very essence of being human.

The obligation to act was, however, not depicted as a universal duty. Rather, it was inscribed as a specific responsibility arising from the fact that the Algerian state had defied its own moral obligations towards its citizens. Protecting the Algerians was foremost the task of the Algerian state. It was because the Algerian government had failed to fulfil its own responsibilities to the Algerian people; because it had been incapable of rescuing the victims of the massacres, or even been partly complicit in these killings, that the international community had to take its place. Under normal circumstances such duties belonged to the Algerian authorities, under normal circumstances moral agency belonged to the state. As Isabelle Adjani explained, at a European-wide demonstration and petition for Algeria,[22] "At a moment where a whole people, the Algerian people, does not know who to trust; does not know where to find refuge, it is up to us to be there. Global solidarity means to consider the Algerians as our brothers and sisters" (*Le Monde*, 11 November 1997).

In newspaper articles, one could similarly notice that references to the Algerian security forces now were put in inverted commas (see, for example, *Le Monde*, 11 November 1997). Amnesty International described Algeria as a "failed state" who was denying its citizens proper protection. Not out of lack of resources and infrastructure, but due to a lack of *will* (Amnesty International Report, 19 December 1997). Since the Algerian state did not live up to its most basic obligations, how could it portray itself as a sovereign state? (*Le Monde Diplomatique*, October, 1997; *Le Monde*, 11 November 1997, 21 November 1997). "When a state lets a child's throat be cut, when it is without capacity or will to protect it: then how can it invoke the principle of non-interference in the name of sovereignty" (*Le Monde*, 26 September 1997). Having failed to fulfil its moral duties in terms of providing security and protection, the Algerian state had failed the essence of statehood and, hence, the right to speak in the name of sovereignty and non-intervention.

International organizations and NGOs similarly questioned Algeria's claim to sovereignty. Not only because Algeria had failed its proper responsibilities of statehood, but also because human rights violations could not be considered an internal affair. The gross and brutal violations of human rights could not be protected by the principle of sovereignty:

> Human rights protection is not just an internal affair or an issue of national sovereignty. Algeria is not above international scrutiny. At a time when its citizens are being slaughtered en masse week after week, the government should welcome – not oppose – international attention aimed at helping to protect lives.
>
> (Amnesty International, 15 October 1997)

"The general secretary has the moral obligation to intervene where human rights are violated. When so many lives are lost it is never a purely domestic matter" (*Le Monde*, 8 September 1997). And at a meeting in New York between the Algerian foreign minister and Mary Robinson, the UN Human Rights Commissioner, she similarly emphasized, to the dismay of the Algerian minister, that human rights do not reside within national boundaries (*Le Monde*, 1 October 1997).

In another communiqué by Amnesty, it was stressed that the perpetrated violations in Algeria were unprecedented. In spite of the overwhelming attacks against civilians, the international community seemingly remained passive: "We cannot think of any other country where human rights violations are so extreme, where civilians have been targeted to such an extent, and yet where there has not even been international scrutiny let alone action by the international community" (Amnesty International News Release, 18 November 1997). The international community was hence once more granted moral agency and a duty to substitute the Algerian state. The international community was invested with a shared responsibility for the persistent killings. It was therefore difficult, if not impossible, to argue that the international community should stand passively by. The articulations of a moral imperative and the depiction of a situation in which helpless and innocent civilians were left alone to face unknown killers without any aid from their government made it very difficult to contend that nothing should be done.

However, by making a common distinction between "*devoir*" and "*pouvoir*", it was possible to recognize this moral imperative and yet to argue that it could not be pursued. Outside actors were in fact incapable of acting; of doing something. As Védrine (7 October 1997) explained: there is a difference between "what can be done" and "what ought to be done". Everybody who was demanding something *should* be done needed to ask what *can* be done (Védrine, 7 October 1997). "There is a certain reality", Védrine emphasized; a reality that makes intervention unfeasible. Everybody agreed with Kofi Annan that the current massacres in Algeria were dreadful and could not go on. Hitherto nobody had been able to formulate a proper solution. No one had been able to answer, "*que peut-on faire?*" (Védrine, 7 October 1997, 18 September 1997, 1 October 1997, 23 September 1997). By speaking reality to morality, realism to idealism, and particularity to universality,

Védrine did not dispute the moral imperative. This was, as noted, almost impossible, given inaction's equation with inhumanness. Instead, Védrine made morality dependent on *pouvoir*; on the possibilities of acting given the realities (particularities) of the situation.

But what did these apparent realities consist of? Which realities did all those speaking in the name of *devoir* have to realize? Algeria was an unidentifiable conflict, Védrine explained to a journalist with *Le Monde*, who as many others was asking why international force was not used to stop the war and help the victims of the massacres. The deployment of an international brigade was unthinkable as long as no one knew who this brigade was going to fight. All the uncertainties concerning the Algerian conflict made it impossible, Védrine (7 December 1997) emphasized: "If an engagement like that should come under way, it is necessary to answer why, for whom, against whom?" This type of justification was also echoed by American diplomats: "I'm not sure that outsiders can play a constructive role. As long as the situation on the ground is so fractious and murky, whose heads are we supposed to be banging together?" (*Washington Post*, 18 October 1997; see also UK Secretary of Commonwealth Affairs, 19 November 1997). As in 1995 it was seemingly the "nature of the conflict" which explained the impossibility of translating moral duty into action.

Foremost it was argued – as it had been throughout the 1990s – that Algeria was a sovereign and independent state. Algeria was not the "*demandeur*" (Védrine, 7 October 1997). Without Algeria's consent and without its explicit request for help it was very limited what could be done (UK House of Commons, 1 December 1997; see also Védrine, 23 September 1997). We cannot just intervene as if national sovereignty does no longer exist, Védrine (7 October 1997) further explained. The Algerian crisis had seemingly not crossed the domestic realm. "In the end, it is the Algerian people who must decide their nation's future", the US Assistant Secretary of State concluded after a long report on widespread extrajudicial killings, of torture and excessive use of force (Neumann, 1 October 1997). Similarly, the Secretary for Commonwealth Affairs condemned "unreservedly the violence which has prevailed", but then continued, "a solution to the serious problems in Algeria must come from the Algerians themselves" (House of Commons, 10 November 1997; see also Pasty, French member of European Parliament (UPE), 17 September 1997; Védrine, 4 December 1997).

This was to be repeated in the months to come. The international community, everybody, was deeply affected by the Algerians' predicament. But, it was not for "us" to tell the Algerians how they ought to solve their own problems, neither did we have a responsibility for the Algerians' current predicament (Jospin, 30 November 1997).

A short conclusion: the constitution of an object of non-intervention

We can now answer how Algeria emerged as an object of non-intervention demanding legitimations; how politicians were placed in a position where they had to legitimize what normally does not need to be legitimized.

As we have seen from 1992 to 1998 the representations of the Algerian crisis and what to do about the crisis, went through several shifts and turns. From 1992 to late 1996 Algeria was referred to as an object causing concern. It was, however, not so much the present situation, but rather expectations and fears about the future that caused concerns. The content of these concerns shifted over two periods. From 1992 to 1994 it was primarily Islamic terrorism and the ramifications of an Islamic takeover, which was to be countered and remedied. By 1995 the dichotomy between fundamentalist terrorists and regime was gradually dissolved and the subjects involved in the Algerian conflict exploded. The emergence of "moderate Islamists", the Rome platform and the references to innocent civilians made it increasingly difficult to suggest that there did not exist a democratic and peaceful alternative to the current regime and its policy of eradication and repression. The concern over Algeria's future started to move from the dangers of Islamists and terrorists to the prospects of democracy. The escalating violence was deemed as a partial result of the government's continued repression and its unwillingness to proceed towards democracy and dialogue. However, Algeria was not (yet) a question of dictatorship versus democracy. Rather, the Algerian situation was articulated as a murky and complex civil war, which made it impossible and unwanted to choose sides. What was needed was a balanced and neutral response. At this point in time, all voices still shared a presumption about the virtue and necessity of neutrality. The international community and Western governments were criticized for being partisan; in reality supporting the Algerian regime by continually providing economic aid and loans to the Algerian government. Yet, the provision of economic aid was also articulated as a neutral and necessary act; where a halt in this aid was positioned as equal to an economic embargo. By the end of 1996 the virtue of neutrality, however, started to be questioned.

Increasing reports of massacres conducted by unknown perpetrators against innocent civilians who were unprotected by the government, moved the Algerian conflict into something that could not be ignored; something which demanded action. Algeria was also an international problem and an international responsibility. The past was now written in terms of a continued silence, where governments and the international community were criticized neither for being neutral, nor for being partisan, but for being passive.

In late 1997 politicians and government officials, as we have seen, gradually had to legitimize what normally does not need to be legitimized: they had to justify why the international community *could* not possibly intervene.

6 Sovereignty and non-intervention

By 1998 Western leaders had to answer why intervention could not be undertaken in Algeria in the face of brutal massacres, which had cost the lives of at least 80,000 and left a whole population terrorized and terrified.

By legitimizing what normally does not need to be legitimized and pointing out what usually appears as obvious and normal, Algeria's sovereignty was on the one hand treated as a given, as something already in existence, its invocation being a mere innocent and nominal practice, which just designated what was already there. And yet by engaging in the very practice of legitimations, politicians were, on the other hand, recognizing that the meaning and boundary of state sovereignty was in dispute, that they – through their very references to Algeria's sovereignty – were enmeshed in a political practice, where they constituted and decided its meaning and content.

This recognition could of course never be displayed, if so the invocation would lose its power. If the contingency of sovereignty was revealed, then sovereignty/non-intervention would be open to political manipulation and decision, hence creating intervention as a viable political option. And, conversely, if sovereignty/non-intervention was displayed as a given, there would be no need to justify why intervention could not be carried out. Politicians were hence caught in paradoxical practice, where they simultaneously constituted state sovereignty as something given and natural, and as something contested and political.

How was this paradox handled? How could the contingency and politics of sovereignty at one and the same time be concealed and revealed, and yet not appear as a contradiction? In principle, an indefinite number of strategies may of course be employed. In Kosovo, as we saw in Chapter 4, combining simultaneous articulations of intervention and non-intervention was made possible by respectively speaking from the outside and the inside. In Algeria, however, as this chapter will show, state sovereignty was spoken of as a closed and fixed concept, and yet as something open to subjective construction through articulations of Algeria as the defining and omnipotent subject, and the international community as a reacting and powerless subject, being entirely dependent on what Algeria gave its consent to. Algeria was described as the ultimate subject entitled to identify the boundary between non-intervention and intervention and the meaning of its own sovereignty, while the international community could only mimic Algeria's own determinations of its boundary. As it will be shown, a "therapeutic relationship" between Algeria and the international community was established, where the international community was not allowed to judge, sanction or determine. Accordingly, Algeria was not something to be created or corrected by the outside, but something already there, to be conveyed and understood by the outside. The issue at stake was not how a future ideal or community could be realized, but how the community already in existence could be secured; how what was already in place could be protected from *its* outside and from *the* outside. The legitimations of non-intervention did, in this way, not simply revolve around a dichotomy of pro and contra intervention. Just as in Kosovo, notions of people and state, freedom and truth, might and right, Self and Other, unity and diversity were set in motion. The legitimations of non-intervention produced – yet only for a while – meaning to the concept of sovereignty.

This chapter will proceed by asking the same analytical questions as the synchronic chapter on Kosovo. Since Algeria is approached as an object of non-intervention, the first question, however, needs to be slightly modified. The main question is still how violation is represented, but the sub-question is not who is violating sovereignty, but instead how is the boundary drawn between violation and non-violation? Thus, the three analytical questions, previously outlined in Chapter 2, are: (1) How is violation represented? How is the boundary drawn between violation and non-violation? (2) Which community is constituted through that representation? (3) What are the conditions of possibilities for this community?

We cannot intervene: producing violation and non-violation

This section will address the first part of the three analytical questions, answering how a boundary was drawn between intervention and non-intervention. First, it will be spelled out which meaning intervention was given, which acts were identified as constituting a violation of Algeria's sovereignty, and hence also what was taken to be encompassed by Algeria's sovereignty. Second, it will be demonstrated how the invocation of help, opened up room for international action and made it possible to argue that the international community was "doing something". Third, it will be spelled out how international help produced those very objects and issues where Algeria needed help.

An indefinite boundary

The notion that we did not know what was really going on inside Algeria and that this lack of knowledge and transparency in itself blocked action had, as described in the former chapter, spurred calls for sending an enquiring or investigating mission to Algeria. Such a mission would, as a first step, allow improved knowledge of the situation – that is, of the proper responsibility for the killings – and hence in a second step, such knowledge would provide the means for further action (see, for example, *The Economist*, 10 January 1998). At the same time, there were also calls for international mediation between "the parties", or even of an international conference under the auspices of the EU, expanding on the ideas of dialogue and democracy developed in the Rome platform in 1995 (BBC News, 19 January 1998). Finally, it was also, once again, proposed that the economic aid to Algeria should be conditioned on the government's embrace of democracy and upkeep of human rights (Associated Press, 12 January 1998).

All of these proposals were, however, inscribed as interventionary acts; as acts that were intended to unjustly punish Algeria or as attempts to scrutinize and mingle in her internal affairs. The international community had no right to punish or sanction Algeria, it was contended, or to determine guilt and innocence. In fact, the very head of the EU Parliamentary delegation to Algeria stressed: "Algeria needs no judges, it needs help and comprehension" (Soulier, *Washington Post*, 12 February 1998). Intervention was taken to be impossible; to be synonymous with punishment and judgement, at the same time as intervention was given a seemingly indefinite content. How was this possible? Two interrelated strategies were employed, as it will be spelled out below: one which inscribed Algeria, qua its sovereignty, as that sole subject who was entitled to define the boundary over intervention and sovereignty, and another that through the invocation of a range of familiar dichotomies situated sovereignty on the side of reality.

Without Algeria's consent, or its explicit request, investigating missions could not be undertaken, it was argued. The international community could not, and would not, infringe on Algeria's sovereignty. "We cannot, we will not, assail Algerian sovereignty. Moreover, the Algerians, and not only the leaders, have rejected those who have maintained that they wanted to or proposed to interfere" (Védrine, 5 February 1998; see also Radio Free Europe, 27 January 1998). Algeria's refusal to allow any outside investigation was not a feeble attempt of state power to oppose truth; it was a unitary wish shared by all of Algeria to maintain integrity. Not only the Algerian government, but also the Algerian people and all of the parties of the Algerian Parliament, were refusing foreign intervention. Following the EU Parliament's visit to Algeria, it was thus concluded: "One thing was perfectly plain, the Algerian MPs whatever their political stripe, did not wish to hear any talk of an international committee of inquiry" (EU News Report, 11 February 1998). All Algerians were in agreement that this was a problem, which they themselves were capable of handling. "The Algerians are sufficiently unanimous in saying that it is a tragedy but that it is their problem, and they are sufficiently strong to overcome it" (Védrine, 7 March 1998). "We don't want anything from Europe. They should go home, said another man, expressing the over-riding opinion of Algerians", *The Times* (20 January 1998) equally reported.

As long as Algeria considered itself entitled to and capable of solving its own crisis, the outside could not impose itself upon Algeria, entering the Algerian conflict and forcing a solution through. It was impossible for the international community to engage in any act that was not in concurrence with the wishes and will of the Algerians, it was stressed. The Algerians cherished their sovereignty and therefore refused all forms of intervention: "The Algerians reject all interventions that are deemed to threaten their national sovereignty. For the Algerians, national sovereignty is a carrier of identity" (Védrine, 7 May 1998; see also Associated Press, 12 January 1998). As the US Assistant Secretary of State also explained to the Senate in a hearing on Algeria: "There is no way you can force this ... the international community, [does] not have any power to force someone in" (Neumann, 5 February 1998). In this way, the possibilities of international action were made dependent on Algeria's consent, which in turn was derived from Algeria's sovereignty. Because Algeria was a sovereign state, it – seemingly always a unity – was entitled to decide over the boundary of intervention and sovereignty.

This crucial tautology was, at the same time, related to the earlier distinction between *devoir* and *pouvoir*, drawing on a whole set of familiar dichotomies between the universal and the particular, feelings and practice, wishing and doing, policy and morality, opinions and foundations: the impetus to do something, to act according to human sentiments was strong and important. But it had to be turned into an effective and realistic policy, which was difficult indeed in the Algerian case, it was argued. "What is stronger than anything is this human sentiment. However, how are we to transform this profound and, I think, noble sentiment into useful and practical action: that is the whole problem" (Védrine, 10 January 1998; see also Associated Press, 12 January 1998). Those who were thinking "why is nothing done" needed to reflect upon just what the outside *could* do. Should it fight the Islamists? Facilitate a compromise with the Islamists? Or create an alliance with the democrats? Even if someone had an opinion in this regard, which foundation would serve to legitimize that the outside was infringing on Algeria's own rights and responsibilities; making its problems even worse, Védrine (5 February 1998) asked. In the last instance, we were not entitled to take the place of the Algerians: "We have no intentions of interfering and we will not call for an international inquiry. The Algerians will build their own future and *we will not try to take their place*" (italics added; Soulier, EU News Report, 12 February 1998). The US Assistant Secretary of State Neumann (5 February 1998) equally emphasized that even mediation demanded Algerian consent; it could not be enforced from the outside: "We have not sought to mediate. I think that is not a role you can take on without being asked to take it on. You've got to have the parties accept." Thus, intervention was relegated to the realm of the ideal, composed of feelings, wishes and opinions while Algeria's sovereignty was inscribed on the side of reality, policy and practice.

This, of course, implied that politicians were able to speak reality to morality, and practice to feelings. Thereby, they were on the one hand, recognizing the moral imperative of action, while on the other hand conveying action as a function of reality and possibility. Moreover, portraying the boundary of sovereignty/intervention as dependent on Algeria's own wishes and considerations, as a result of which actions Algeria approved of and gave its consent to, the content of intervention became completely plastic and could be stretched indefinitely. Intervention appeared as though it included all forms of (international) acts, and Algeria emerged as the only subject that was able and entitled to decide. The outside's ability to act as a subject became dependent on Algeria's portrayal of its own sovereignty and the corresponding competencies of the international community.

142   State sovereignty and intervention

The international community was, thus, almost stripped of any subject qualities, the "international" only appearing as an active subject by virtue of Algeria's beliefs, thoughts and definitions.

From intervention to help

If the international community was incapable of acting, if any response constituted an impossible violation of Algeria's sovereignty, the international community seemed to be left in a moral impasse, where it had to look passively on, while the massacres continued. But we do not want to be spectators to the Algerian drama, the French Minister of European Affairs Moscovici (16 February 1998) emphasized (see also Védrine, 10 January 1998). The international community does not intend to stand passively by. It is not indifferent to the suffering of the Algerians. "We are ready to help where we can ... we cannot stand silently by while these atrocities continue ... There are ways to do so that do not impinge on Algerian sovereignty", Martin Indyk emphasized (US Assistant Secretary for Near Eastern Affairs, 10 March 1998). "We want to know how we can help" (Cook, 14 January 1998; see also Cook, 15 January 1998, 26 January 1998).

Help was, thus, powerfully distinguished from intervention. Help was to do something, and yet not to intervene. Help could be provided in accordance with Algeria's sovereignty, in that Algeria itself was to define its own goals and we were to help them in achieving these goals. As it was explained in the US Sub-Committee on Africa: "We are focussing our efforts and looking for ways to help ... The challenge is for the Algerian Government and people to obtain their own goals. Any action we take is meant to be supportive" (US Committee Hearing on Algeria, 5 February 1998). In this way, it was still not for the outside to determine how the Algerians were to solve their problems. In fact, it was even not for the outside to define what the Algerians' problems consisted of. The international community was not to punish or sanction anyone, neither to define guilt and innocence, but to deliver support. As Soulier, head of the EU Parliamentary delegation to Algeria, had stressed, "Algeria needs no judges, it needs help and comprehension" (*Washington Post*, 12 February 1998; see also Védrine, 14 September 1998).

The task of the international community was to deliver help and assistance, without engaging in any prior judgements and definitions of the nature of the help required: "France is profoundly affected by the suffering of the Algerian people and we are ready to provide every kind of help which the Algerians would ask us for, and this in total respect of their sovereignty" (Védrine, 5 March 1998). "We have expressed several times our willingness to participate in any useful initiative if the Algerian leaders ask us to participate and to provide useful help" (Védrine, 5 February 1998).

The relationship between helper and helped, giver and receiver was in this way inversed. As Jenny Edkins has shown, in relation to food and relief aid, provision of help normally functions by creating a subject–object relationship, where the provider of help is the one who determines the help required and the nature of the problem to be alleviated. Food and relief aid are, in this way, instruments of control

Sovereignty and non-intervention   143

and subjectification (Edkins 2000: 76). Aid programmes define the problems to be relieved, for example, food shortage, and accordingly determine the content of help, for example, food aid. The recipient is, thus, prevented from defining the proper needs or the character of the help required. Here, however, it was Algeria only, who defined the content of help. The relationship between helper and helped, giver and receiver, subject and objects was turned on its head. It was not the international community who was creating the needs and demands of the Algerians by determining the nature of the help that Algeria was to receive. Rather than being a passive receiver, an object of help already defined by others, Algeria was instituted as a privileged subject deciding over the content of help. The provision of help was dependent on Algeria's conception of the problem at hand and the scope of the international help required. The helper became a passive giver and Algeria an active recipient.

Moreover, in contrast to relief and food aid programmes which via administrative technologies of power define the criteria to be fulfilled in order for aid to be provided and the means by which it is to be provided (Edkins 2000), the definition of help to Algeria was ideally to be found via "political" mechanisms of dialogue and understanding. To know which help Algeria was requesting, dialogue, it was argued, needed to be established between the international community and Algeria. Through conversation and listening, the international community was to learn and comprehend. The objective is "to listen and learn", Soulier underscored (*Washington Post*, 12 February 1998). Dialogue would allow us to achieve a better understanding of the situation and of the expectations of the Algerians. It would help us "to better understand the situation in Algeria as well as the expectations of the Algerians with regard to the international community" (Védrine, 16 April 1998). Being committed to learn and listen, the dialogue was seemingly to be open-ended, based on the issues which the Algerians themselves wanted to discuss: "We are happy to discuss all matters relevant to ending the suffering of the Algerian people and are ready to listen to all concerns that the Algerian authorities wish to put to us" (BBC, 15 January 1998).

Three "missions of dialogue" were sent to Algeria: first, a delegation from the EU Troika; second, a delegation from the European Parliament; and third a so-called UN Panel of Eminent Persons. All three delegations were – via dialogue with the Algerian government and society – to find out where Algeria needed help. "Our intention is that this mission will demonstrate the concern across the peoples of Europe for the suffering of the Algerian people and explore whether and how Europe can help" (Cook, 15 January 1998) The key objective is to "identify if, and how, Europe might help ... to improve our understanding of the problems faced by the Algerian Government and its people so that the General Affairs Council of Foreign Ministers may have a better informed discussion on how the European Union could react to the recent violence and what it might do to help" (EU Presidency Press Release, 20 January 1998).

Neither of these visits to Algeria hence had, it was continually emphasized, an investigating or enquiring nature: "The mandate is straightforward. It will be seeking to facilitate contacts apart from the politicians, with representatives of civil society. It's not being sent out as an international commission of inquiry" (CNN, 9 January 1998; see also UK Parliamentary Debate, 26 December 1998). Even the UN Panel Mission was stripped of any pretence of investigation or inquiring. Instead, it was to achieve an improved understanding of the situation: "The panel mission will contribute to a better *understanding* of the complex situation" (italics added; EU Statement, 8 July 1998). In the official aim of UN Panel Mission it was equally stated that the purpose was to "gather information on the situation in Algeria" (UN Report of Eminent Panel, 16 September 1998). Algeria could only be referred as an undefined "situation" since it was the very dialogue with Algeria, which was to determine what the situation consisted of, and thus where help was needed.

The UN Panel's "information gathering" was just as the EU's, to be achieved through talks with representatives of the Algerian government and organizations of the Algerian civil society. In contrast to the parliamentary hearings on Algeria, where human rights organizations, foreign diplomats and experts on the region were summoned to testify on Algeria's predicament, the findings of the UN report were solely to be based on conversations with Algerian representatives inside Algeria. It was the Algerians themselves who were to teach the international community about their predicament, and "we were to listen and learn". Information, learning and understanding were in this way equated, while being differentiated from investigation/intervention. Investigation was drawing on a *judicial-police* language, where facts were to be collected, responsibility appropriated and evidence found by an external authority. The invocation of learning, understanding and help drew, however, on what might be called a *therapeutic discourse*. This discourse produced the international community, not as an *"external judge"* engaged in a police operation, but rather as a *"helping therapist"* who was to understand and depict the Algerian conflict from within. The UN Panel was to create and recreate the Algerians' conceptions, demands and feelings, rather than establishing the truth of the events or apportioning guilt and innocence. The Algerians were inscribed as narrators of their own stories and views, and the Panel appeared as an empathetic listener. Hence, phrases such as "They considered", "They stressed" "They believed", "We listened", "We heard" appeared again and again (for these phrases see UN Panel Report, 16 September 1998, p. 18).

Algeria became, in short, the foundation of knowledge about itself. In order for outside actors, whether in the form of Western government officials, the UN Panel representatives or the EU delegations, to render authority to, and verify, their conclusions and descriptions of the Algerian events, they had to appeal to what the Algerians perceived, believed and told. Outside actors could not take the position as narrators of truth or even of information. Only the Algerians themselves could claim to constitute the source of knowledge about themselves. Accordingly who was defined as part of the Algerians' Self was to have important ramifications.

In which areas did Algeria require help? And hence which understanding had the dialogue provided of the problem(s) to be alleviated in Algeria? Foremost, terrorism was singled out. The report of the EU Troika as well as the more extensive UN report both identified terrorism as the key problem, which Algeria needed international support to combat. The EU Council concluded on the basis of the Troika mission's report that it hoped that international support would place "the Algerian government in a better position to engage in finding the solution to the terrorist problem" (EU Council 1998). This was equally expressed in the UN Panel report's conclusions:

> We would like to state, first, our categorical rejection of terrorism in all its forms and manifestations. Terrorism has been condemned outright by the international community and is illegal under international law. Algeria *deserves the support of the international community* in combating this phenomenon. We also condemn any form of extremism or fanaticism that might be offered as a pretext for the acts of terrorists. There is no excuse for terrorism.
>
> (italics added; UN Panel Report, 16 September 1998)

References to human rights violations, extrajudicial killings, disappearances and torture *did* appear in the UN report. But it was frequently underscored that human rights violations could not be put on par with the crimes committed by the fundamentalist terrorists. Those Algerians, which the Panel had interviewed, including members of Algerian human rights organizations all argued, according to the report, that "there were violations of human rights by some government agents, but they protested strongly against equating the crimes of the terrorists with the excesses committed by government agents." Concluding on the status of human rights, the report cited an Algerian woman: "Because of the importance of the issue", the report emphasized, "we would like to cite the words of one of our interlocutors who does not belong to any part":

> What the Islamist terrorists have committed are crimes against human species. Violations of human rights are sometimes committed by Governments. But the acts committed by the terrorist Islamic groups are crimes against humanity. In Algeria the power is not quite democratic and we fight and struggle against it for more democracy. But that does not mean that we want the Afghan veil. I tell you this as a woman. We cannot have dialogue with such terrorists.
>
> (UN Panel Report, 16 September 1998)

This quotation was neither commented on nor qualified. It was therefore an open question as to whether the Panel shared the view that human rights violations constituted a lesser crime than terrorism or whether the Panel attempted to refrain from judgement all together; only allowing the "Algerian voices" to be heard.[1] This ambiguity and uncertainty in terms of the subject(s) actually making the conclusions – the Panel or the interviewed Algerians – appeared throughout the report. What was described as government excesses and violations of rights were, by several of the interviewed, explained as unfortunate – yet unavoidable – outcomes of the fight against terrorism. When Algeria was in the midst of a life and death struggle against terrorism, human rights violations could neither be averted nor have first priority. Security was a prior condition of other goals such as freedom, law and rights. When Algeria's very survival was at stake, rights could legitimately be sacrificed on the altar of security (UN Panel Report, 16 September 1998, p. 18).[2]

Having relegated human rights violations to a second priority, or even to an inevitable consequence of the struggle against terrorism – creating a "hierarchy of crimes" – terrorism emerged as the main problem to be combated whereas principles of human rights emerged as mere residual questions of how terrorism was fought.[3] "Fighting" for human rights did not appear as an *end* in itself, but rather as a question of how the goal of eradicating terrorism was reached. To put it simply, the conclusion of the UN report did not address how the international community was to help the Algerians in its pursuit of democracy and human rights, but how the international community could help Algeria carry out its fight against terrorism, and yet attempt – as far as possible – to pay tribute to law and rights. Terrorism was that very issue where, as the report stressed, "the Algerians deserved our help and support" (UN Panel Report, 16 September 1998, p. 18).

Through dialogue with the Algerians, it was established in which areas Algeria needed the help of the international community and in the very same move it was established what the problem in Algeria consisted of. As the EU Presidency declared, following the publication of the report:

> The European Union takes note of and welcomes the detailed report of the United Nations Panel of Eminent Persons ... In this context the European Union repeats its categorical condemnation of terrorism in all its forms and manifestations and remains supportive of the Algerian Government's efforts to consolidate democracy and protect its citizens from terrorism.
> (Declaration by the EU Presidency, 22 September 1998)

In sum, legitimizing why intervention could not be undertaken, a boundary was drawn between intervention and non-intervention. Intervention came to include an endless list of international actions, its very meaning dependent on which acts Algeria gave its consent to and did not give its consent to. Yet, the positioning of help on the side of non-intervention granted the international community a possibility to leave the moral impasse and emerge as a subject capable of *re*-acting. By drawing on a therapeutic discourse, help became – just as intervention – to be dependent on Algeria's own conception and definition of the support required.

Yet, in order to articulate Algeria as a subject entitled to grant consent to certain international acts while refusing others; as a subject the international community had to listen to and comprehend; who was able to convey it own problems, rather than these being determined by others, Algeria had to be represented as a free, open and democratic society. Only by assuming that the Algerians were speaking freely and with one voice, could intervention be articulated as an unfounded attempt to take Algeria's place. In other words, such articulations would rely on a specific construction of the Algerian community. This construction will be the topic of the next section.

The constitution of an Algerian community

Which presumptions about the nature of the Algerian community did the inscription of help rely on? This will be answered in two steps: first, it will be spelled out how the Algerian society was constituted as an open and plural society; second, how this diversity presumably was represented in governmental institutions, hence allowing for articulations of an Algerian unity.

Algeria, it was stressed, was a diverse society composed of different cultural and linguistic groups, and different political views; a society where French, Arabic and Kabylian mixed, where Islam and modernity met (FCO Background Brief; US Sub-Committee Hearing; UN Panel Report, 16 September 1998; EU News Report, 18 February 1998). Algeria, Soulier emphasized, was at the "confluence of Western modernity and the traditions of the Arab-Muslim world" (EU News Report, 18 February 1998). These various components of Algerian identity were also reflected in Algeria's new constitution, where Islam, Berberism and Arabism all were stipulated as fundamental characters of the Algerian people (UN Panel Report, 16 September 1998, p. 6).

Diversity was, however, not a source of dispute and friction, but of pride and richness. Multiplicity was part of the Algerian people's very identity. As the UN Panel report (16 September 1998, p. 17) emphasized "Many Algerians of all walks of life and shades of opinion ... took great pride in their linguistic and cultural diversity, which is part of their national heritage." These differences were also freely expressed in political debates. Algeria was marked by lively and pluralistic discussions: "We could see for ourselves that there was a pluralistic and vibrant press in Algeria" (UN Panel Report, 16 September 1998, p. 17). Equally, it was emphasized that Algeria had a flourishing civil society, composed of various organizations and movements. "Labour organisations, professional associations, women's groups, human rights groups, a free press and humanitarian organisations already active in Algeria are also agents for constructive change. These things exist. They are a tribute to the Algerian people" (US Committee Hearing on Algeria, 5 February 1998). The diversity of Algerian society was, hence, properly represented and freely played out on all levels. Opinions and views could be discussed in the press and in the parliament, through public institutions rather than in secrecy: "Discussion among the Algerians now takes place in the Parliament rather than in the streets. After one year of Parliament's existence there has been tangible evidence that dialogue and reconciliation are possible by working together" (UN Panel Report, 16 September 1998). The many references to the need of the Algerians to engage in dialogue, which had appeared ever since 1995, hence disappeared. Dialogue was presumably already under way in the Algerian Parliament and everyday life. Dialogue was seemingly only necessary between the international community and Algeria; not between the Algerians. Or to put it differently, it was the international community and Algeria that now were to reach an understanding, rather than the Algerians. The Algerians were already engaged in debate and exchange.

On the cover of the UN Panel report, Algeria was, thus, portrayed as the archetype of Mediterranean idyll. The cover showed a map of Algeria overlaid by a large photo in blue and white colours resembling a typical postcard for tourists visiting North Africa. The photo depicted an apartment in oriental-style, with ornamented French balconies, open windows and curtains blowing in a light breeze. Here there appeared to be no signs of violence, friction or bloodletting, but of a tranquil Mediterranean atmosphere, welcoming the outside to enter the Algerian "home".

This description of Algeria as a tranquil society in which the people openly could, and did, express their opinions and identity was also reproduced in the reports by the EU and UN delegations: "Everyone in Algeria had the opportunity to express themselves freely", it was concluded by the EU delegation (EU News Report, 11 February 1998). "A striking feature of our talks was the freedom with which they were conducted" (EU News Report, 11 February 1998). "All the Algerians, including those on the government side, spoke with complete freedom" (EU News Report, 18 February 1998). The UN report did not explicitly comment on the relative freedom and truth with which the interviewees spoke, but in the conclusion of the report it was stressed: "We are satisfied that Algerian society is capable of expressing political views and discussing them within the framework of legality" (UN Panel Report, 16 September 1998, p. 20). Moreover, as we saw above, the statements of the interviewees – whether these were representatives of parliament, the army or an "unpartisan Algerian woman" speaking against the "Afghan veil" – were all left uncommented and unquestioned. In accordance with the logic of a therapeutic discourse, none of the citations were complemented or contrasted with additional "data" or testimonies from Algerians in exile, journalists or human rights organizations having operated or operating in Algeria. The interviews were neither treated as expressions of something hidden nor as manipulated and repressed voices, but as authentic and genuine expressions of the Algerians, reflecting their own perceptions and opinions.

As noted, the interviews and conversation with the Algerians were articulated as mere efforts to achieve a better understanding of the events and sentiments in Algeria, yet the statements obtained were at the same time used to convey the reality of what was going on inside Algeria. They relinquished responsibility and apportioned innocence. Thus, both the UN report and the EU report concluded, on the basis of their interviews inside Algeria, that the accusations of government involvement in the massacres were unfounded: "Independent citizens with whom we spoke accepted that the responsibility for the violence being committed lay with the radical extremist" (UN Panel Report, 16 September 1998, p. 13). Soulier similarly quoted one of the religious representatives, whom the EU delegation had met, who said: "Don't keep on asking us who is killing who. We know and the victims know too." Thereafter the report concluded: "Nobody, when speaking to us pointed a finger at the army" (EU News Report, 12 February 1998).[4] The reports in this way employed what can be called a "double-perspective". Both reports mixed and oscillated between a judicial and what I call a therapeutic discourse simultaneously, where the aim of the reports was merely to achieve an understanding of the events, and yet also to establish the truth of the events. Hereby, the conversations with the Algerians could, on the one hand, appear as mere expressions of how the Algerians themselves perceived and narrated their predicament and problems, and on the other hand, as testimonies which legitimately referred to judicial concepts such as crime and innocence. The judicial categories did not need to be related to judicial-police methods such as establishing proof, carrying out independent fact-finding, and/or collecting technical and forensic evidence. Instead "therapeutic methods" of diagnosing were applied; such as conversation, listening and self-description.

This "double-perspective" and ambiguity in terms of the aims of the report was equally apparent in the way that the Panel described its visit to two massacre sites in Benimessous and Ain Khalil. These descriptions seemed, on the one hand, only to be descriptions of how the occupants of the villages – and especially the security forces and Gendarmerie – perceived and narrated what had taken place. On the other hand, the detailed descriptions of the atrocities and how they had been carried out "borrowed" the terminology of a "judicial investigation" into a massacre; again without backing up these descriptions with additional and/or conventional methods of investigations (UN Panel Report, September 1998, pp. 13–14). It appeared sufficient, as we saw above, to establish that the Algerians were speaking freely. By inscribing Algeria as a realm of freedom and by using therapeutic means of method, the interviewees were granted a position as authoritative narrators of themselves.

If we preliminarily compare this to the way the testimonies of Kosovar Albanians were used in the media and in the US Congress to establish proof of ethnic cleansing, it was only Kosovar Albanians in exile or refugees who had fled Yugoslavia who were taken to be witnesses of truth. The moment they were outside of Yugoslavia, and hence outside of Milosevic's repression and manipulation, they were taken to be able to accurately depict the situation inside Yugoslavia. Here, however, it was the very fact that the Algerians were residing inside Algeria, which gave them a privileged position to convey the nature of the Algerians' problems to the international community.

The presumption of freedom – and hence of the possibilities of truth – were closely intertwined with enunciations of the Algerian government as – at least on the verge of becoming – democratic and representative of Algerian society. As in Kosovo, freedom, truth and representation were taken to be necessary conditions for one another. Since the governmental institutions were democratic and representative, there was no need to distinguish between government and people. Or rather Algeria, Algerian government and Algerian people could be used interchangeably since the former reflected the latter. One could seemingly unproblematically refer to what the "Algerians" perceived as an infringement on their sovereignty; which international initiatives "they" granted and did not grant their consent to; and which help and support "they" perceived necessary. By assuming a convergence between government and people, it was possible to determine that the government's rejection of outside investigations represented a collective wish of all Algerians to oppose outside intervention, rather than a hidden attempt by the regime, or by some particular fraction of Algerian society, to hinder outside scrutiny. By assuming this convergence it could be established that international help against terrorism was directed at – and benefited – Algeria as a whole.

The presumption of the diversity of the Algerian people being reflected in governmental institutions did not only allow for a convergence between people and government, but was also articulated as a sign of the democratic nature of Algeria as such. Algeria had now, it was emphasized in an EU News Report (12 February 1998), a multi-party system where political exchange could be undertaken: "In recent years Algeria has seen significant changes. It now has an elected president, an elected parliament in which 10 political parties are represented ... There is a lively debate in parliament. There is also ostensible separation of the executive branch from the military and judicial branches. Democracy is making progress." "The Algerian parliament is a reality, we have met it", the EU News Report (12 February 1998) similarly introduced its account of the situation in Algeria. These institutions served as vital forums of debate allowing the plurality of views to be expressed and reconciled. As Védrine (16 April 1998) noted, "The Algerians have elected and pluralistic institutions at their disposal where a debate has been initiated" (see also Védrine, 5 February 1998). Through these institutions "conflicting viewpoints could be articulated and compromises facilitated" (Neumann, US Sub-Committee Hearing, 5 February 1998).

On the other hand, it was simultaneously recognized that full democracy had yet not been achieved: "Algeria is not yet a democracy but neither is it a one-party state of the *past*" (italics added; US Committee Hearing on Algeria, 5 February 1998). "Indeed, the organization of political power does not yet fully correspond to the norms of European countries, where freedom has been forged over centuries of battle. But honesty obliges the observation that Algeria has set out on the road towards democracy" (Jack Lang in *Le Monde*, 5 March 1998). Algeria was progressing towards the telos of democracy, but had not yet reached its final stage. It had transcended its past, but not yet arrived at its future.

Democracy and pluralism were new and fragile in Algeria, but an indication of Algeria having crossed the threshold of its past. Just as Neumann, in the US Committee Hearing, distinguished Algeria's past from its present, so did the EU Parliamentary delegation report appear under the name "A wind of change". "The discussions with the political parties showed that a wind of change appeared to be blowing through Algeria. All parties, of both the government side and the opposition, stressed their commitment to the current democratic process", Soulier emphasized (EU News Report, 11 February 1998). The articulations of a plural, free and democratic society, gave content and direction to the future.

Whereas the future seemed to hold the promise of democracy and peace, Algeria's past was, however, written as a long history of turmoil, violence and repression. The past had been marked by a perpetual struggle for freedom, in which the Algerian people first had fought a long and bloody war for independence against France and later for freedom against the FLN state (see, for example, UN Panel Report, 16 September 1998; US Committee Hearing; FCO Background Brief; *The Times*, 5 December 1998). This inscription of Algeria's past did not only portray the present as different from the past. It created a yardstick by which Algeria's progress could be measured and the current state of freedom and democracy appreciated. Algeria became positioned in a different place, as having moved on, but the people were at the same time invested with a particular predilection for independence and autonomy. And hence a corresponding anxiety for losing it. Because the Algerians had fought hard for their freedom, they were particularly sensitive about their independence and dignity. "The Algerians answer that they are a great country; an independent country which has won its independence under difficult conditions" (Védrine, 7 March 1998; see also Védrine, 7 May 1998, 11 May 1998). "The Algerians are very proud of their independence, they are not going to accept tutelage from anybody", the US Ambassador similarly explained to the Associated Press (12 January 1998).[5] Having struggled for their identity and independence, the Algerians were not willing to sacrifice it easily: "The soul of Algeria is to be free: resistant to colonial occupation; resistant to the assassins who wanted to imprison her through violence; resistant to external interferences" (Jack Lang in *Le Monde*, 5 March 1998).

Algeria was, in sum, articulated as a democratic, open and pluralistic community. This made it possible to refer to Algeria as a whole; as a unified subject speaking with one voice. Yet, how could these articulations of a harmonious, free and united society be combined with the simultaneous articulations of gruesome massacres, of people living in constant fear of being butchered; of the presence of Algerian extremists and terrorists moved by a fanatic and repressive vision of society? This will be the topic of the next section.

Conditions of possibility

> Algiers should neither become Kabul nor return to the frozenness of one-party regimes.
>
> (André Glucksmann and Romain Goupil in *Le Monde*, 4 April 1998)

Drawing on poststructuralist insights on constructions of Self and Other, this section will argue that the Algerian community only could be portrayed as a plural, tolerant and free society by articulating fundamentalist terrorism as the society's other side. Through a series of binary oppositions, fundamentalism was articulated as a radical Other, as a threat and enemy to the Algerian Self. At one and the same time fundamentalism was the very condition of possibility for articulations of a coherent Algerian identity, and yet this very condition was in itself constituted as a threat to Algeria's continued existence. I will go through these two elements in turn, first describing how fundamentalist terrorists were differentiated and excluded from the Algerian community, and then describing how this Other was articulated as a threat only to be countered by extermination.

The Algerian terrorists were articulated as essentially non-political and un-representable. The terrorists seemed to be motivated by violence itself; lacking any alternative political vision or ideology of change. Violence rather than being a means to a political end had become an end in itself: "The Algerian terrorism is unique in that it is not pursuing a specific objective", the UN Panel report (16 September 1998, p. 7) established.[6] Whereas terrorist acts in the beginning had been directed at the institutions of state, it was now aimed at "the entire population" (UN Panel Report, 16 September 1998). Innocent civilians were massacred, raped and mutilated without seeming reason. As an editorial in the *Washington Post* (15 January 1998) asked: "Which ideology could serve to justify that eight year olds were killed?" The fundamentalists had proven themselves unwilling to forsake violence and to embrace the Algerian Constitution, and thus they could not be described as anything less than terrorists. The FIS leaders had, the UN report concluded, no intentions of joining a meaningful dialogue with President Zeroual; having categorically rejected to respect the laws of the Republic and condemn terrorism (UN Panel Report, 16 September 1998, p. 5). FIS could and should therefore not be represented or listened to. They had excluded themselves from representation. During the EU Parliamentary delegation's visit to Algeria, Soulier received an envelope with a message from FIS. According to the *Washington Post* (12 February 1998) the letter was dismissed with the following justification: "We have no sympathy for a movement that promotes violence. By unanimous decision of the nine-member delegation, Soulier tore up the envelope without opening it" (see also *Le Monde*, 20 February 1998).[7] By equating FIS, fundamentalists and terrorists, FIS was not only excluded from political representation and dialogue, but was granted no legitimate voice, and no position of speech in relation to the international community. When the UN Panel delegates and others referred to what the "Algerians" wanted, perceived and told, this did not include FIS. Dialogue could not, Bernard Lévy similarly emphasized in one of his comments in *Le Monde* (12 February 1998), be initiated with people who were killing civilians. This was equally backed up by the Algerian woman quoted in the UN report. As she explained to the panel: "I tell you this as a woman. We cannot have dialogue with such terrorists. We cannot condemn women to their vision of society. We would not like to be compelled to live like that" (UN Panel Report, 16 September 1998, p. 17).

The Islamist terrorists were, in short, positioned outside of politics. They were rendered as unrepresentable voices due to their use of violence and their lack of a legal and legitimate political agenda. Due to their anti-democratic nature they could not be allowed to enter the normal and democratic processes of dialogue and compromise now taking place among the Algerians. The fundamentalists were the very antithesis of democracy and thus of politics: "By definition a democrat rejects violence. However, the Islamists are prepared to kill in the name of a millennial utopia that regards the individual as a terrestrial means to a celestial end" (*Le Monde Diplomatique*, February 1998).

At the same time as Islamists were described as the other side of politics, they were also compared to the most villainous dictators and movements of the twentieth century; embodying similar authoritarian tendencies and ideologies as Nazi Germany, the Taliban regime in Afghanistan, post-revolutionary Iran and Cambodia during Pol Pot's reign. The Islamists in Algeria, *The Times* reported, shed and prohibited the most banal objects of everyday life, wearing glasses, for instance, as signs of Western decadence. Under their rule "women are murdered for failing to cover their hair with traditional Islamic chador and children butchered for attending schools where the syllabus is considered too secular" (*The Times*, 10 January 1998; see also *Le Monde*, 7 March 1998). The terrorists wanted to "force people into mental regress by imprisoning them inside a regressive and mythical ideology from another age" (Jack Lang in *Le Monde*, 5 March 1998). The Islamists, Glucksmann moreover explained, were prepared to exchange the current government with a totalitarian regime equivalent to those in Iran and Afghanistan (*Le Monde*, 4 April 1998). Algeria was fighting against that "theological political extremism" which had marked the twentieth century from Hitler to the Taliban to GIA (Glucksmann in *Le Monde*, 4 April 1998). Algeria had no other choice than to fight the "Khmer Verte" (Lévy in *Le Monde*, 12 February 1998).

Islamists were, thus, invested with the exact opposite characteristics as the Algerian community. Through a chain of binary oppositions, they were distinguished from the Algerian Self and thereby granted no actual voice within, or in relationship to, the Algerian Self, being compared to some of the most totalitarian movements of the twentieth century. Yet, they were still located inside of Algeria in a territorial sense. Being constituted as a subject residing within the territory of Algeria, but outside of the Algerian community, they were shaped as an *internal Other*; who constituted a physical threat, as well as a threat to the shared values and identity of the Algerian community (Campbell 1992).

Speaking of Islamists as a threat and danger to the Algerian Self, of course, added one more element to the radicalization of Algeria's internal Other, while also shaping the way in which this Other could be approached. As we have already seen above, attempts to engage in dialogue or even to listen to Islamic radicals were excluded. They had, it was stressed, proven themselves unworthy of consideration and dialogue. As the *Washington Post*, for instance, reported from Algeria: "The real enemy is Islamic fundamentalist. There are men who are sick here. That is why a peaceful resolution of the warfare is impossible. You can't have dialogue with throat killers" (*Washington Post*, 13 February 1998). "In this difficult battle it is necessary that the terrorists know that they will see no complacency, no concession, no weakness from our side" (Jack Lang in *Le Monde*, 5 March 1998). Such metaphors of the battlefield were also invoked in commentaries and official reports, where the relationship between Algeria and the "fundamentalists" were spoken of in terms of battle, struggle, fight, eradication and elimination. "The extremists and terrorists", Neumann (5 February 1998) emphasized in the US Hearing, have to be "isolated and eventually eliminated". "For some years, unfortunately, France has contributed to isolate *Algeria*, when it was the fundamentalists who should have been isolated" (italics added; Védrine in Canal Plus, 7 March 1998; see also *Washington Post*, 9 January 1998, 30 January 1998).

The so-called Islamic fundamentalists were thus articulated as a subject who was unable to reform and normalize; who had to be struggled with and fought against rather than accommodated or reasoned with. This brought the relationship between Self and Other into a zero-sum realm. The relationship between fundamentalists and the Algerian community became a matter of which identity was to survive and prevail in the future, where the existence of one excluded the existence of the other. If the Islamic fundamentalists – very often equated or correlated with terrorists – were not eliminated or contained, Algeria would become a new Kabul, where women were segregated, minds imprisoned, and freedom dissolved, and hence the very identity of Algeria extinguished.

By vesting the so-called fundamentalist or radical Islamists within Algeria's territorial boundary, yet externalizing them from the Algerian Self, Algeria could be portrayed as a plural, open and democratic society, while extremism, intolerance and violence could be attributed to the Other. In this sense, the Algerian Other became the condition of possibility for the Algerian Self. But at the same time, the existence of the Algerian Other was articulated as that very force threatening the continued identity of the Self. If Algeria was to remain and develop its plural, democratic and modern community, radical Islamism had to be eliminated.

A preliminary conclusion

Let us briefly return to the paradox outlined in the introduction to this chapter. If sovereignty is readily apparent and its content already given, there is no need to justify why intervention cannot be undertaken. Only by recognizing that sovereignty is under pressure does non-intervention need to be legitimized. Yet to embrace the contingency of sovereignty would, of course, dissolve the power of its invocation; rendering sovereignty a source of political dispute rather than a natural boundary. The legitimizations therefore had to articulate sovereignty in a way which at the same time rendered Algeria's sovereignty an already clearly defined entity in the world, and yet a concept always open to political decisions.

How was this difficult task carried out? As this chapter has shown, by making the boundary between non-intervention and intervention a result of which acts Algeria granted its consent to and did not grant its consent to, the power to decide, convey and judge was seemingly transferred to Algeria alone. Algeria was articulated as the sole subject able to decide the content and extension of its sovereignty. At the same time, it was the very sovereignty of Algeria which granted Algeria the right to refuse and approve various international acts in relation to itself. Placing the capability to judge and decide with Algeria, Algeria was depicted as *the* subject able to depict the nature of its problems. Combined with invocations of a "therapeutic discourse" this meant that there was seemingly only one perspective and one vantage point through which Algeria's problems could be understood, namely that of Algeria. Algeria could only become known and diagnosed through its own narration about itself; through an effort to understand, or as it were overtake, the perceptions and feelings of the Algerians. It, however, had to be presumed that Algeria constituted an unproblematic unity. Whereas differences on the inside, as we saw in the case of Kosovo, could be evaded and shed by speaking from the outside – from an "international perspective" – in Algeria this was made possible by the articulations of a spatio-ethical outside. Algeria could, in a double-move, be referred to as a unity, by constructing a congruence between people and government and relegating that which was not represented, outside of Algeria; residing as a radical different identity from the Algerian Self. Algeria emerged as a tranquil, plural and democratic Self, by posing violence, intolerance and totalitarianism with the Other. What Algeria feared told us what Algeria was (Campbell 1992).

7 Contrasting constitutions

How did politicians and others come to legitimize intervention in Kosovo and non-intervention in Algeria? How could the content of state sovereignty emerge as something to be defined by Algeria itself, whereas the competencies and boundaries of Yugoslavian sovereignty appeared to be a matter of international consensus and commonly held norms? How could gross violations of human rights, extrajudicial killings and massacres be portrayed as a clear foundation for international involvement in terms of Kosovo and not in Algeria? Before engaging with these comparative questions, it might be useful to recapture some of the arguments regarding the limits and possibilities of comparative analysis within a context of discourse analysis.

Usually comparative analyses are carried out by selecting a number of prior variables to be contrasted and compared. On the basis of a set of theoretical notions or hypotheses a certain number of factors, variables or themes are singled out, and the case analysis is subsequently written and compared according to these common themes. Instead of delineating, on a prior theoretical level, a set of (universal) variables through which to read and compare the two cases, the two cases have been analysed separately; thereby letting them emerge in their own historical specificity and contingency. As argued in Chapter 2, only on the basis of this separate analysis of Kosovo and Algeria can the comparison be made, if we wish to refrain from imposing a common prior perspective and coherence upon the writing of the two cases.

While the aim is neither to explain causally nor to generalize on the basis of two cases what might constitute the universal conditions of possibilities for intervention and non-intervention, the objective is however to point to some of those *specific* discursive differences and similarities which constituted intervention as a necessity in Kosovo and an impossibility in Algeria, and to those differences and similarities in the way that sovereignty and intervention were established. This will be carried out in two steps: first, by making a comparison of the diachronic chapters in terms of the historical processes of selections and constitutions that rendered Kosovo as an object of intervention and Algeria as an object of non-intervention; second, by comparing the synchronic chapters in terms of the differences and similarities in the constitutions of sovereignty. This will at the same time serve as a summary of the main insights of the previous chapters.

Diachronic comparison: murky conflict and lucid genocide

At first sight Kosovo and Algeria may seem to display some striking similarities. They both went through processes of conflict escalation and internationalization, both were at first referred to as international concerns, and later in terms of civil wars to be remedied by dialogue and negotiations, and finally in terms of massacres and persecutions of innocent civilians. Algeria as well as Kosovo were both in the late 1990s taken to be marked by human rights abuses, repression and extrajudicial killings, placing a moral responsibility on the part of the international community to act. Yet, Kosovo led to an international intervention and Algeria did not. Thus, as this section will argue, references to massacres of innocent civilians, brutal oppression and lack of democracy constitute powerful discursive moves, but they are not to be conflated with "magic words", which in themselves will spur certain international actions or make some events appear clear-cut. It is not sufficient simply to speak in the name of morality and humanity. Using the "same words" will not necessarily make up the same discursive construction. By way of an analogy, we might say that when building two constructions, for instance, two houses, the bricks and material used might be identical, but the way they are related and positioned in relation to one another construct two different buildings. Although the bricks (signifiers) are identical, it is their specific internal relations to other bricks that grant them meaning, and hence constitute different buildings (discourses). This analogy obviously echoes the poststructuralist argument concerning the constitutions of meaning, but it is worth emphasizing once more, in order to refrain from attributing the same significance to apparent similar words, or to infer too easily a causal link between representations of conflicts and policies (see also Hansen 2006). With these cautions in mind, we can now move to the diachronic comparison.

Kosovo and Algeria were both at the beginning of 1990s referred to as international concerns; as situations that needed to be followed closely. These concerns were to a large extent predicated on scenarios about the future, rather than on evaluations of the present. It was not so much the *present* being of Yugoslavia and Algeria that caused concern as their potential being.

The nature of the two concerns was, however, articulated very differently. Kosovo was taken to be a powder keg of ethnic tensions, which threatened to explode into ethnic war due to discriminations and violations of the Kosovar Albanians' rights within Serbia, thereby repeating the horrors of Bosnia and Croatia. Although fears were also expressed of Algeria turning into a civil war, the primary concern was soon portrayed as Islamic fundamentalism and radicalism. It was feared that a violent Islamist uprising, or possibly revolution, would turn the hitherto secularly minded government into an Islamic state. This government, it was feared, would possibly be guided by the *Sharia* and anti-Western sentiments. An Islamist takeover, emulating the revolution in Iran in 1978/1979, would not only have severe consequences for the workings and stability of the Algerian society, it was argued, but also for the West and France in particular. In contrast to Kosovo, it was therefore extremely difficult to voice concerns over the future state of democracy and the present human rights situation. Such concerns were taken to be indicative of a dangerous embrace of the ideology of FIS and Islamists in general.

In both Kosovo and Algeria future scenarios were based on analogies with prior historical experiences, drawing so-called lessons from the wars and massacres in the Balkans in terms of Kosovo, and the Islamic revolution in Iran, and even the "evil empire" and the Cold War, in terms of Islamic fundamentalism in Algeria. Taking the past into the present powerfully served to portray the potential future as something to be avoided and remedied. If the causes of ethnic conflict in the case of Kosovo and the causes of the Islamic revival in the case of Algeria were identified, then one would also possess the cure. But the means to be employed in order to remedy respectively ethnic tensions and Islamic extremism were evidently taken to be very different.

In Kosovo, the roots of ethnic war were presumably founded in violations of human rights, especially minority rights. It was due to the Serbian suppression of Kosovar Albanian rights that tensions were mounting between Serbs and Kosovars. The aim was therefore to see that rights were observed, not to carve out an independent state of Kosovo. It is not national or ethnic distinctions and affiliations, which constitute the basis of viable modern states, but democracy and respect of human rights, it was argued. The extensive monitoring mechanisms set up under the auspices of the OSCE and the UN were to assure that Kosovar Albanian rights were observed, by closely watching and reporting on the conduct of (S)FRY. Surveillance was to establish what was really going on inside Kosovo, as well as restraining the behaviour of the Serbian authorities. The constant international gaze was to be a means of Yugoslavian reform.

In Algeria, a somewhat similar logic of cause and remedy operated. Yet, very different international institutions and practices were invoked. Islamic fundamentalism and terrorism were primarily articulated as symptoms of socio-economic discontent rather than signs of political discontent or an embrace of political Islam. Algeria's ruined economy, the rate of unemployment and the poor housing conditions were, from this perspective, interpreted as causes of FIS success and as conducive conditions for further "islamization". If fundamentalism and terrorism were to be contained, the Algerian economy would need to be recovered. International aid, loans and rescheduling of debt were to provide "the Algerian economy" with sufficient resources to control and fight Islamic fundamentalism.

Thus, whereas Kosovo was portrayed as a matter of political reform, Algeria was largely taken to be a matter of economic reform. Kosovo and Algeria were, in this sense, projected into different realms marked by different logics and institutional practices: Kosovo was addressed within the forums of CSCE and the UN committees of human rights, and Algeria within the IMF and in connection with EU development assistance and loans. The point here is not that Kosovo was defined more openly than Algeria simply by being portrayed as a question of political reform. Both fixations brought closure and had important ramifications for the way that the two cases were debated in the years to come. As argued in Chapter 3, identifying Kosovo as a question of human rights and democracy effectively sustained Kosovo's constitutional status as part of Yugoslavia. It secured that independence and statehood were not issues to be debated. Similarly, for Algeria, explaining the cause of Islamic resurgence in terms of economic and social deprivation served to distinguish politics from economics, and to depict economic aid and rescheduling of debt as vital and non-political measures, which were not "recovering", aiding or supporting a distinct subject but the Algerian economy.

While the situation in Kosovo in the beginning of the 1990s seemed to require that neutral and objective information on the reality of the human rights situation for the Kosovar Albanians was collected, assessed and reported, in Algeria everybody seemingly knew what was going on. Algeria was a conflict composed of only two parties: fundamentalist terrorists and government. Between these two fronts, "There was nothing", as Pasqua explained. By depicting the actors involved in the Algerian conflict in terms of a dichotomized battle between the government forces and the terrorists, raising critique against the Algerian authorities was quickly translated into an embrace of, or support to, fundamentalists and terrorists. Obviously coupling terrorism and Islamic fundamentalism made it almost impossible to enounce issues of human rights or democracy, or to voice alternative representations of the nature of the conflict at hand or the subjects involved.

However, in the wake of the Rome platform in 1995 the dichotomized battle was slowly dissolved. The meeting between the opposition parties, including FIS, did not only nuance the depiction of a coherent and violent Islamist front, who collectively was unwilling to engage in compromise and employ peaceful means, but in its wake, increasing references were made to civil war scenarios. The multiplication of political actors displayed not only the frictions and differences between the Islamic movements, but also that the various Islamic fractions and parties were at war amongst themselves, competing for resources and territorial control; being moved by different political goals, if any at all. Civilians were hence caught between the security forces and the various Islamist fronts. Yet, whereas the invocation of terrorism and civil war contributed to the moving of Kosovo from a national to an international problem, this was not the case in Algeria. Although Algeria also was marked by references to the plight of innocent civilians, calls for government restraint in its pursuit of and crackdown on the terrorists, and by endless appeals for negotiation and dialogue, Kosovo was taken to necessitate international involvement, whereas this was taken to signify untimely interference in the case of Algeria. These differences have especially to be seen in light of earlier articulations and how historical lessons from previous international engagements in the Balkans and Algeria were invoked.

Bosnia, in particular, served as a powerful reference point in the discourse on Kosovo. The Western response, or rather lack of response, to the Bosnian genocide and Serbian aggression was interpreted as an instructive lesson for the international community; a lesson which had taught "us" about the consequences of acting too late and being too complacent. Bosnia had shown what happens when the international community approach the Serbs and Milosevic by strategies of appeasement, and had proven the success of using the threat of force and intervention. With the upsurge of violence in Kosovo, the Bosnian experience was taken to recur. The potential future fear, which the human rights monitoring had been intended to remedy, appeared to have become a reality, and the international community was continually called upon "to do something". Non-involvement and neutrality had, qua the supposed lesson of Bosnia, been infused with derogatory connotations, whereas intervention and the use of force were seen as signs of a "political will" to act, and as recognition of the international community's responsibility. The combination of the invocation of the lesson of Bosnia, and the previous articulations of the content of the international concern, made it extremely difficult to portray the situation in Kosovo as an internal affair of the FRY.

In Algeria references to international involvement or outright intervention were invested with very different connotations. France's colonial history and the traumatic war of independence rendered any calls for internationalization as imprudent inflictions of Algerian sovereignty; as mere attempts to realize postcolonial goals and aspirations. Non-interference was inscribed as a virtue and closely coupled with an ideal of neutrality. As we saw in Chapter 5, already in the immediate aftermath of the annulment of the parliamentary elections, neutrality and non-interference were taken to go hand in hand. Although the international community, and France in particular, was criticized for providing large amounts of economic aid to the Algerian regime, the critique of the provision of economic aid was equally founded in the ideals of neutrality and non-intervention. The continuous channelling of economic resources was flawed exactly *because* it did not constitute a neutral and balanced posture. All voices in that way seemed to share the virtue of neutrality and non-interference. When policies were criticized, it was for not being neutral enough, in contrast to Kosovo where policies were criticized for not being sufficiently activist. Algeria was for a long time not a question of "how can we act", but of "how can we secure not to act". As Juppé (11 August 1994) explained, "Sometimes I hear people say: but what does France do? When will she act? We have no intention at all of acting in Algeria. The problem belongs to the Algerians."

Moreover, not only was France's traumatic engagement with Algeria taken to demand international neutrality and non-involvement, but France's historical and cultural ties with Algeria were at the same time taken to grant France a special and defining role in how outside actors were to approach Algeria. France was articulated as the proper, natural and authoritative site from where policies and responses were to be stipulated and debated in Europe as well as in the United States. At the same time, France was to respond neutrally and in a balanced manner to the Algerian events; to obey strictly to the notions of non-interference and Algeria's treasured sovereignty. As a result, it was unclear who was to respond to the Algerian crisis, besides Algeria itself. As Hastings explained: "The United States treats Algeria as if it is a European problem, Europe treats it as if it is a French problem, and the French cannot make up their minds" (US Hearing, House of Representatives, 5 February 1998). The articulations of France's history and ties with Algeria came to serve as double binds or restraints on the possibilities of voicing (alternative) responses to Algeria.

In 1997, Algeria and Kosovo were both marked by uncertainties. Or rather in both cases it was still very open what the conflicts consisted of, and which subjects could be identified as guilty and innocent. The doubts that had been raised in terms of who was actually behind, and responsible for, the massacres in Algeria had forcefully moved the discourse on Algeria, and enabled the hitherto shared virtue of neutrality to be questioned. But this did not seem to make it any easier to decide who was to be blamed. In Kosovo the competing representations of ethnic war and ethnic cleansing equally made it highly contentious to attribute guilt and innocence. The absence of unequivocal distinctions between perpetrators and perpetrated, guilt and innocence, thus, haunted the discourses on Kosovo and Algeria. If Kosovo was an ethnic war, and if both sides were unwilling to negotiate and compromise, who was the international community to punish, it was asked. How could the use of force persuade the Kosovar Albanians to enter negotiations? Similarly, in Algeria, it was asked whom the international community was to target and, as it was put, whose heads it was going to bang together? Devoid of a clearly identifiable conflict and enemy, intervention could not be undertaken. In both cases interventionary measures were assumed to be a matter of sanctioning an already identified guilty subject; of engaging in punitive action. By equating intervention with sanctions and punishment, articulations drew on a legal discourse requiring both that an innocent subject could be defined – all subjects could not be guilty – and that unambiguous judgements could be made of who was guilty.

One of the important differences, in this respect, was that in the case of Kosovo a whole range of markers and demands had been voiced in the form of Security Council resolutions and in connection with the Rambouillet talks. Such markers could subsequently be used as a foundation for determining compliance and non-compliance, and thus guilt and innocence. As argued in Chapter 3, Kofi Annan's report on whether FRY had complied with the Security Council resolutions in October 1998 was open for very different interpretations, just as the criteria for NATO's use of force changed during the Rambouillet talks.[1] But the absence of international demands and conditions with respect to Algeria implied that no references could be made to formal international decisions or resolutions. No international actors had furnished a particular threshold or boundary, which could be crossed, or specified a set of conditions that had to be obeyed or complied with by the parties of the conflict.[2] Hence, although Kosovo and Algeria both had emerged as international problems in 1997, the situation in Kosovo was continually surveyed, assessed and judged under the auspices of the UN and NATO and with reference to the Security Council resolution, while the situation in Algeria mainly was a topic of national parliamentary debates, sub-committee hearings and reports of NGOs.

While the nature of the events in Kosovo was still disputed in the fall of 1998, uneasily oscillating between ethnic war, humanitarian catastrophe and ethnic cleansing, the massacre of Racak – in which forty-five civilians were killed – is often inscribed as a turning point that established that Milosevic's forces were carrying out ethnic cleansing, and hence displayed Milosevic's true intentions (Knudsen 1999b; Judah 2000; Chomsky 1999). Yet, during the subsequent talks at Rambouillet, references to ethnic cleansing virtually disappeared from official statements. Instead, Rambouillet became inscribed as a sign that the Kosovar

Albanians were willing to compromise and pursue peace, in contrast to Milosevic and the Serbian government, as well as a sign that the international community had employed all available means of diplomacy. Although NATO had not achieved a mandate from the UN Security Council, with reference to the Rambouillet talks and to previous diplomatic initiatives, the language of humanitarian intervention and "just war theories", could endlessly be invoked.

As in Kosovo, although on a much larger scale, the massacres of whole villages – which had marked Algeria ever since 1996 and killed up to 80,000 – did not in themselves spur calls for international intervention. Rather, it was the question of "who kills who?" that at least implicitly related the Algerian government to the massacres, and this in turn placed a moral responsibility on part of the international community. Since the Algerian people were left without protection from their own government, being daily confronted with barbaric massacres, international passivity would amount to an affront on the very essence of humanity. The feelings of human revulsion, indignation and of the need to do something were taken to be commonly shared, while the responsibility for acting according to these sentiments was taken to belong to the international community.

In this way, the issues at stake (morality and the content of being human) and the subject capable of undertaking moral responsibility (the international community) were depicted in somewhat similar terms in Kosovo and Algeria. But in stark contrast to Kosovo, a clear distinction was invoked between *devoir* and *pouvoir*. While no one questioned *devoir* – that the international community ought to do something – Western officials, in particular, questioned the possibilities of actually doing something. In Kosovo, no distinctions were made between "should" and "could", idealism and realism. With references to Milosevic's violations and disregard of the UN Security Council resolutions and diplomatic attempts to furnish a peaceful resolution, it could be established that Milosevic had not given the international community any options other than intervention; that the use of force was a last resort. The "could" had, in other words, been narrowed down to one possibility, which appeared to amount to a necessity.[3]

While references to massacres against innocent civilians and the invocation of a universal language of the good, the moral and the human – resembling the legitimations of the Kosovo intervention – did not in itself provoke a military intervention in Algeria, it did, however, demand that non-intervention was legitimized. Thus, although no linear or causal relation can be drawn between *representations* of a conflict and *responses* to that conflict, as Hansen (2006) also has pointed out, it can be argued that references to massacres and gross violations of human rights constitute powerful discursive moves, which cannot easily be ignored (Malmvig 2001b). As spelled out in the synchronic chapter on Algeria, which we are to turn to shortly, it was virtually impossible to refuse to engage with the question of "doing something". Politicians had to legitimize why non-intervention did not constitute indifference and why non-intervention was not an inhuman and immoral act.

In sum, the legitimations of intervention in Kosovo and of non-intervention in Algeria had their own historical specificities and points of emergence, which conditioned future responses; making some articulations possible while excluding others. Although similar articulations and discursive strategies can be detected between the two, we have also seen how apparently similar words and references were given different meanings and significance; how their meaning depended on previous articulations and relations to other signifiers. The discourses on Kosovo and Algeria both went through gradual selections of possibilities and narrowing of representations and responses, but they each had their own specific histories.[4]

Synchronic comparison: sovereignties

Legitimizing intervention and non-intervention was neither merely a matter of arguing in favour of, or against intervention, nor simply an issue of when, or whether, state sovereignty can be transcended. The legitimations of intervention and non-intervention related sovereignty to grand questions of responsibilities and capabilities, might and right, future and past, inclusion and exclusion; producing – albeit only temporally – meaning to the concept of sovereignty.

To disentangle how sovereignty was related to these questions and concepts, three questions were asked to each of the two cases: How is violation of sovereignty represented? Which community is constituted through that representation? And what are the conditions of possibilities for this community? It is with reference to these three questions that the constitution of sovereignty now will be compared.

Turning to the first question, namely how the violation of sovereignty was represented, Milosevic, it was established, had transgressed his sovereign powers. He had violated his right to sovereignty by employing power and force outside of the confines of law. Having used his powers as a mere tool, committing extrajudicial killings and gross violations of human rights, he had abused his right to rule. Milosevic could not take away the rights of his citizens by force, and thereafter speak in the name of sovereignty. Sovereignty does not give political leaders the right to terrorize their people and extrajudicial killings can never be an internal affair, it was established. Through a discourse of rights a boundary to sovereign power was drawn. Law was installed as the code that state power ideally was to obey. It was taken to be a – or the only – means that regulates the relationship between people and government, as well as that code through which rule should be judged and evaluated. Law and rights were peoples' protection against repressive governments and misuse of state power. Law constituted the privileged point from where state power – synonymous with Milosevic's power – could be scrutinized and assessed.

Yet, which type of law served as the basis for drawing a boundary between legitimate and illegitimate sovereign power was left ambiguous. By the invocation of genocide it could, however, be established that Milosevic had clearly violated his powers. Genocide functioned as that undisputed marker and legal basis upon which a limit to sovereign power could be safely determined; leaving no one in doubt that power had been brutally abused and the most basic rights violated. While the references to genocide concealed hard questions of the involvement of boundaries and laws with subjectivity, power and interpretation, it did also open a new set of questions. Being a legal category and closely associated with

Holocaust, genocide called for proofs and evidence. It had to be proven that genocide was indeed taking place in Kosovo; that events were represented accurately. Since politicians were not taken to be objective "representers" of truth, but rather inscribed as potential manipulators engaged in "war-rhetoric", truth was to be established through neutral and objective means, such as eyewitness accounts and photographs from inside Kosovo. We were to *see* what was going on, in order to verify the truth. Genocide, thus, did not only depoliticize the determination of the confines of state (Milosevic's) sovereignty, but it also demanded that the events in Kosovo could be established as corresponding strictly to the legal definition of genocide, while also resembling the images and unique status of Holocaust.

In Algeria, however, there did not appear to exist any *external* foundation from where state power could be evaluated, or from where the boundary between internal and external affairs could be safely determined. The confines of state sovereignty – and conversely the content of violation – were dependent on the authorities Algeria granted itself. Algeria's sovereignty appeared to determine Algeria's sovereignty. Algeria's sovereignty, however, also seemed to determine the competencies and actions of the international community. Algeria's consent was assumed to be a pre-condition for international action, and the boundary of Algeria's autonomy and independence could therefore be stretched infinitely; Algeria became her own foundation.

The inscription of Algeria as the place and subject from where consent, authority and definitions originated was closely coupled with what was called a therapeutic discourse. Algeria was not to be judged according to a legalistic code of law and right, as in the case of Kosovo, but helped in accordance with a therapeutic code of listening and understanding. Through dialogue and conversations the Algerians were to convey their own perceptions of their predicament to the international community, and the international community was in turn to listen and learn. Only on this basis could the international community comprehend and diagnose what the problems in Algeria consisted of and where Algeria needed help; not in order to take the place of Algeria, as it was continuously emphasized, but in order to put oneself in Algeria's place. Hence, in contrast to Kosovo, where judicial evidence and neutral documentation were inscribed as means of verification and representation, here it seemed to be (the Algerians') perceptions that constituted the authentic source of representation.

Through the conversations with Algerians, it was determined that fundamentalist terrorism was the primary problem of Algeria. Fundamentalist terrorism threatened the very existence and identity of Algeria. It was the survival of the Algerians and ultimately the identity of the Algerian state that was at stake. Under such conditions of life and death, questions of human rights violations and extrajudicial activity had to take on second priority it was argued. The crimes of the Islamists could not be compared with the violations of judicial rights committed by the security forces. The latter could not be put on par with the atrocities of terrorism. In contrast to Kosovo, it was the security of the people – and thus of Algeria as a whole – which was inscribed as the guiding imperative of the use of state power and force.

However, the point is not that this hierarchy of security over rights and law constituted a conscious effort on the part of the UN and EU delegations to conceal and subdue, but rather that the articulations of the Algerian situation – as a matter of security and survival – brought Algeria's crisis into a realm of emergency and exception, where all other considerations could be constructed as of an inferior nature. By explicitly comparing security against rights, inscribing the Algerian people as the referent object of security, while attributing rights to a matter of whether "government agents committed excesses" in its struggle against terrorists, it appeared as obvious that the security of "the Algerians" had to be guaranteed before other goals could be pursued and rights strictly observed.

There seemed to be no external point from where Algeria's crisis could be evaluated or judged. If "non-Algerians" were to speak about Algeria, they had to appeal to what the "Algerians" wanted and perceived, while hastily emphasizing that no one intended to take "the place of the Algerians". This forcefully restrained attempts of "external" criticism and scrutiny, while also indicating that it was unproblematic to refer to the Algerians as an indivisible unity speaking with one single voice. In other words, the continual references to the "Algerians" did not only reproduce the Algerians as the only ground from where one could legitimately talk about Algeria, but the articulations also came to presuppose that no friction or incongruence existed between people and government, society and state.

In Yugoslavia, by contrast, a sharp distinction was made between the people and state. The state was equated and personified by Milosevic, and sovereignty was turned into a possession of Milosevic, which he had misused and employed to his own purposes and against his own citizens. In Algeria, sovereignty belonged to Algeria as a whole. Sovereignty was articulated as a treasured part of Algeria, which the Algerians had fought hard to achieve; as a defining characteristic, which protected the identity of the Algerians and secured Algeria's independence, autonomy and will.

The source of conflict, tension and violence was in both cases relegated to a place outside of the Algerian and Yugoslavian communities. It was not inherent ethnic differences among the Serbs and Kosovar Albanians that had caused the barbaric attacks and repression of the Kosovar Albanians, but Milosevic's skilful manipulation and repression. In fact, the Serbian people were victims of Milosevic's suppression too. Kosovars and Albanians had lived together in peace for centuries. It was Milosevic who had hindered the Serbs and Kosovar Albanians to realize their potential and true identity. Being contrasted with what was described as Milosevicism, the Serbian community was inscribed as a potential tolerant, multi-ethnic, inclusive and pluralistic society. As in Algeria differences in terms of religion or ethnic affiliations were not taken to be sources of conflict, but signs of a strong and rich society united by common values of democracy, tolerance and pluralism.

NATO accordingly insisted that it had no quarrels with the Serbian people. It was not the people of Serbia that were punished and targeted, but Milosevic and his regime. How was this possible? This partly rested on articulations of a sharp distinction between Milosevic and the Serbian people and on the invocations of a present, and yet potential; a repressed, but yet already existing, pluralistic community. But this inscription was also dependent on the articulations of freedom as a condition of responsibility and truth. Since the Serbian people, as the Kosovar Albanians, were not free, since they were subjected to power, they did not have access to truth, and could hence not be judged or punished. The absence of democracy, of a free media, of debate and freedom of expression, made the Serbs oblivious of, and without responsibility for, what was being done in their name. It served to turn Serbs and Kosovars alike into passive objects with "no voice"; with an identity and will which had to be interpreted and represented, and thus constituted by NATO. In Algeria the inverse logic of freedom and truth operated. Since the Algerians' wishes, perceptions and opinions were inscribed as the natural foundation of representations, it had to be shown that the Algerians were free and truthful narrators of what was really going on; that the Algerian community was composed of a plurality of voices and organizations, which were able to express themselves and engage in lively debate. In contrast to Kosovo where interpretation and judgement had to be made due to the overwhelming exercise of power and repression of truth, with respect to Algeria, statements were to be taken at face value. Here, the so-called outsiders were not in a position to question statements delivered in freedom. They were primarily to listen and learn.

When compared, the articulations of the Algerian and Yugoslavian communities have some similar traits. Both were portrayed as on the verge of becoming plural, tolerant and democratic societies, and in both cases societal differences were inscribed as sources of strength. Diversity was articulated as the foundation of a modern, open and accepting community, in contrast to Milosevic's anachronistic ideal of homogeneity and the Islamists' and terrorists' medieval vision of a totalitarian *Sharia* state. Yet, whereas the Serbian community was inscribed as slumbering and repressed, uneasily oscillating between reality and potentiality, the Algerian community had seemingly crossed the threshold of its past. While the Yugoslavian identity had to be given a voice, where only NATO was able to interpret and determine its future, the Algerians were granted a privileged voice.

Turning to the third question of conditions of possibility, as pointed out, it was difficult to advance that Serbia already was a plural and tolerant community where Serbs and Kosovar Albanians were living in peaceful coexistence. Instead, it was claimed that the two groups were not inherently nationalistic, barbaric or discriminating; that no intrinsic characteristics hindered them from becoming a modern European community. How could potentiality in this way be turned into reality? Democracy was the condition of possibility for plurality, tolerance and peaceful coexistence. Yet, democracy would demand the removal of Milosevic. Serbia could only evolve into its proper self with the help of NATO. By the dual inscription of the Yugoslavian community as both present and absent, the conditions of possibilities were already in place and yet had to be created. On the one hand, this community already existed since the Serbs and Kosovar Albanians were not inherently nationalistic, violent and intolerant, but on the other hand, their identity could not be realized without democracy, and democracy could not be installed if

Milosevic remained in power. Agency could not be placed with the community itself, because it was not yet a proper self, and only NATO could therefore help it to full realization.

The Algerian community similarly fluctuated uneasily between presence and absence. As in the case of FRY, it was of course difficult to depict the Algerian community only in terms of tranquillity, plurality and openness. Instead of referring to potentiality, one spoke in terms of an Algerian opposite. This opposite was constructed as a constitutive outside, where Islamic fundamentalism served both as the condition of possibility for the Algerian Self, and as the very condition threatening the identity of that Self. The fundamentalist terrorists were articulated as if standing outside of the Algerian community and politics. They were supposedly unrepresentable and not to be granted a voice within Algeria. By relegating and attributing violence, fanaticism, intolerance and suppression to Islamic fundamentalists, the Algerian community was invested with the opposite characteristics of openness, tolerance and diversity. Algeria appeared as a unity, and yet in constant danger of being overtaken and subdued by its radical Other. In contrast to Yugoslavia, it was, accordingly, not a matter of realizing a Self, but of combating a threat to the Self.

Few denials were made of the fact that NATO was engaged in an intervention in Kosovo, and that this intervention indeed was illegal. Yet, a distinction was drawn between legality and legitimacy. Albeit NATO's intervention did not conform strictly to present international law, it did honour and fortify present norms and values of the international community. Legitimacy was not solely dependent on law, it was contended. Law and judicial technicalities could not override morality and ethics. Law had to correspond to the good and right rather than the other way around. Even lawyers of international law, who determined the intervention as illegal, immediately assured everyone that from a moral perspective, intervention was the only and justified choice. This in turn required that NATO was able to establish that it was moved by good and righteous intentions, rather than by particularistic interest and power, which was an impossible task since the surface could always be interpreted in light of the hidden; since the universal could always be read as particular, and since values and morality could always be turned into an expression of interest.

In Algeria, morality, values and ethics were similarly at stake; demanding that something should be done in the face of brutal massacres and unprecedented barbarity. Rather than legality, morality was here contrasted with possibilities and realities. The sovereignty of Algeria was articulated on the side of reality; as that foundational principle which necessitated that the international community did not act blindly on the basis of moral indignation and sentiments. Sovereignty and non-intervention were not portrayed as tedious and anachronistic details of international law, but as crucial questions of respecting the very identity, particularity and independence of Algeria.

As we have seen throughout, Algeria's sovereignty was in this way turned into the final centre of articulations. Intervention was taken to be impossible; not because non-intervention constituted a valuable principle – for example, by assuring international order and regulating state interaction – but because any act which Algeria perceived as an intervention would infringe on Algeria's own will and independence. The ultimate community of reference was not the international community, as in the case of Kosovo, but Algeria itself.

In Kosovo, law was separated from morality and the violating subject was turned around. It was FRY who had violated the basic norms and rules of the international community, rather than NATO. Ideally there should have been a Security Council mandate, it was argued, but FRY's conduct and blatant violation of the appeals of the international community and the numerous UN Security Council resolutions turned FRY into a rogue and disobedient state, which could not claim the protection of legal sovereignty. FRY had given up the right to sovereignty. To voice a claim to sovereignty was therefore merely a dubious attempt to furnish a protective shield behind which the committed atrocities were to be hidden.

In Algeria, appeals had also been voiced for the need for greater knowledge and information. Similarly, it was argued that Algeria should *allow* the international community access to, and knowledge of, Algeria's predicament. The crucial point, and difference was, however, that authority was vested with Algeria. It was Algeria alone who could decide to which extent and on what conditions the international community could be allowed entry. It was Algeria who, qua its sovereignty, was to grant prior consent. Algeria's refusal of fact-finding missions or envoys of UN special rapporteurs were not taken to be feeble attempts of the Algerian government to use sovereignty as a protecting "shield", or as a dubious attempt to hide atrocities. They were rather taken to be a legitimate concern shared by *all* Algerians of protecting their independence and strong identity. Again, the references to what all Algerians wished and perceived were important. Only by presuming that all Algerians spoke with one voice, was it possible to speak in terms of "protecting identity and independence", and thereby hiding any references to a torn society, or a repressive regime invoking sovereignty for cloaking and concealing purposes.

In contrast to the case of Kosovo, Algeria did not disobey or violate any international norms or demands. The international community's identity, future or values were not taken to be afflicted. The international community was presumably concerned and indignant over what happened to the Algerians, but it was not itself directly affected. The fight against terrorism and fundamentalism was a particular fight, ultimately being the Algerians' fight, which the international community would help and support, but a fight that it was not itself involved in. It was the survival and future of the Algerian community which essentially was at stake, not that of the international community.

NATO's intervention was, in contrast, articulated as a universal battle between good and evil, past and future, democracy and dictatorship, tolerance and hatred. It was identified as one of those defining moments which would decide the content and identity of the community of states; which would determine which rules and norms were to prevail; and which values and beliefs states' actions were to be guided by in the future. The intervention would decide the future of all of "us". By deciding to act NATO had proven that states are not only moved by power, interest and gains. The international community was by this very act moved one more step in the right direction, where interest and values would merge into one, and peaceful existence would prevail.

Although these values were inscribed as universally shared, it was only democratic states whose conduct was guided by values of tolerance, freedom and peace. Captured between particularity and universality, presence and future, agency and structure, it was argued that the full realization of the future international community would demand that ultimately all states became democratic. It was assumed that the natures of states determine their actions and, hence, in turn the very character and identity of the international community. Albeit the future was defined as belonging to democracy, this future would not emerge if "we" sat on the sidelines of history. History was to be made by democracies and safe from democracies.

Comparing the legitimations of intervention and non-intervention in Kosovo and Algeria, we have now seen how sovereignty on the one hand rendered meaning to these very legitimations, and on the other hand how these very legitimations rendered meaning to sovereignty, albeit in very different ways. Where sovereignty was located; what was encompassed by sovereignty; which rights and status sovereignty bestowed on the sovereign subject, and in relation to whom; when and how sovereignty could be violated were answered in two different ways. What may be the implications of these differences and ambiguities? This will be addressed in the next and concluding chapter.

8 Sovereignty intervened

This book began by framing the intervention in Kosovo and the non-intervention in Algeria as questions of sovereignty's spatial contingency. State sovereignty, this book has shown, does not only vary over time but also in space. State sovereignty is daily (re)made and, paradoxically, one of those practices where this takes place is when (non)intervention is legitimized.

Hitherto, practices of non-intervention have been read as non-events in International Relations. In fact, they have not been analysed as practices at all. Non-intervention is presumably the normal state of affairs, which only affirms that international politics works as it is supposed to, hereby withdrawing non-intervention from academic questioning and debate. This book has argued that this rests on a hierarchical relationship between sovereignty and intervention. Sovereignty and intervention function as a binary pair, where the former resides on the side of the good and normal which just is and must be, while intervention resides on the side of the pathological and problematic, which always is in need of justification. To legitimize intervention is to reproduce this logic, albeit in a paradoxical manner. By engaging in the act of justification, intervention is reinstalled as a dangerous and abnormal act reaffirming the normality and legitimate being of sovereignty, and yet in the same move sovereignty is violated. Legitimations of non-intervention do not escape this paradoxical logic: by providing justifications for what usually does not need to be legitimized, pointing to the sacred nature of sovereignty and the principle of non-intervention, such articulations silently recognize the shaky, contingent and political nature of what they simply claim to signify and represent. Legitimations of non-intervention simultaneously treat sovereignty as given and undisputed, and yet in need of justification and representation.

How did such paradoxical practices contribute to constitutions of sovereignty in the cases of Kosovo and Algeria? The legitimations of (non)intervention reproduced many of International Relations' familiar concepts and binary pairs of people and state, representation and repression, freedom and truth, legality and legitimacy, past and present. Yet, the combinations and relations between the concepts invested state sovereignty with very different meanings. The legitimations produced different answers to what constitutes a violation of state sovereignty; which competencies and authorities states have, and in relation to whom; what falls within and outside of a state's internal affairs; who has the (unquestioned) authority to decide over this differentiation and on which grounds. Within the same time span, but in different spaces, we were faced with different answers to where, and with whom, political and moral responsibility resides; who can decide the future of, and provide for, domestic communities; what is to be provided, and who can represent and speak on behalf of national and international communities.

What may be the implications of these different answers? If sovereignty is so fluid and plastic that it does not only vary across time but also across space, what may this connote about the status and importance of the concept today? From an "imperial" perspective in many ways close to the one adopted in this book, it could be read as an indication of the increasing irrelevance of state sovereignty. The contingency and openness of sovereignty may serve to emphasize that we have already moved beyond a world of state sovereignty, into a world of imperial world domination, where a logic of *Empire* has supplanted the modern logic of the state system (see especially Hardt and Negri 2000). Along some of the same lines, Foucault (1977c: 121) argued nearly thirty years ago that political theorists should acknowledge that sovereignty belongs to the past and by "busying ourselves" with the problem of state sovereignty, we are in fact ignoring the multiple power networks that reach beyond the state. On a very different basis, (neo)realists reach a similar conclusion in terms of the relationship between sovereignty and political power. Here the spatial contingency of sovereignty may testify to the conclusion that sovereignty is little more than "organized hypocrisy". Sovereignty is, as it has always been, an unstable construct that can be violated and bended whenever power and interest dictates so. Sovereignty is not what we make of it, power is what makes it (Krasner 1999).

Yet, this book has sought to point in a third direction; emphasizing neither the general demise of sovereignty nor its irrelevance in light of power and interest. Instead, it has suggested that we should look to the political consequences of specific invocations of sovereignty, and hence to its power. As Bartelson indicates in the Foreword to this book, when sovereignty has lost its uncontested meaning, we should ask how sovereignty works in specific historical and political contexts. We should look to how the concept of sovereignty is used in various sites, whether that may be states in the Middle East who currently stress that democracy only can come from within and cannot be imposed from outside, or the Bush administration's calls for a global war on terror. It is hence yet too early to cut off the king's head simply by refusing to busy ourselves with state sovereignty. What we need is not to kill the sovereign king and his predecessors, but to appreciate and investigate the politics involved, when sovereignty is invoked.

Notes

Introduction

1 All French quotations have been translated by Henrik Breitenbauch and the author. Statements by Western government leaders, spokespersons, international organizations and NGOs cited in the text and indicated as e.g. (Bush, 15 April 1999) have all been downloaded from official governmental and institutional websites in the period 1998–2002 from the following URL addresses: www.USIA.gov, www.doc.diplomatie.fr, www.fco.gov.uk, www.un.org, www.nato.org, www.europarl.eu.int, www.europa.eu.int, www.hrw.org (Human Rights Watch). CSCE reports and statements have been quoted from the collection of statements by Marc Weller, *The Crisis in Kosovo 1989–1999: From Dissolution of Yugoslavia to Rambouillet and the Outbreak of Hostilities*, Cambridge University Press (1999).

1 Sovereignty as discourse

1 For more detailed discussions of the epistemological and ontological assumptions of poststructuralists see, for example, Edkins (1999), Smith *et al.* (1996), Bartelson (1995), Shapiro (1981, 1984), and Ashley (1989, 1996).
2 I will for the sake of convenience use the terms poststructuralist and poststructuralism throughout this book to denote a group of authors who share a set of basic epistemological assumptions. There are, of course, extensive debates over what is to be understood by poststructuralism, how, if at all, it differs from postmodernism, and what is to be understood by a poststructuralist epistemology (see, for example, Smith 1996: 29ff). Similarly, as it often has been pointed out, the invocation of grand names such as Foucault and Derrida causes problems since neither Foucault nor Derrida have applied the label "poststructuralist" to describe the work they have undertaken (see, for example, Campbell 1992; Edkins 1999).
3 As Foucault (1990: 54) noted "a critique is not a matter of saying that things are not right as they are. It is a matter of pointing out on what kinds of assumptions, what kinds of familiar, unchallenged, unconsidered modes of thought the practices we accept rest."
4 These are important qualifications of the poststructuralist position, which, however, often seem to be forgotten. Negri and Hardt, for instance, in their much acclaimed book *Empire*, construct a category called postmodernists – largely synonymous with those authors whom I call poststructuralists – and claim that these postmodernists have not achieved their self-proclaimed goal of working for liberation and emancipation (*sic*). Instead, postmodernists have, according to Negri and Hardt, come to speak the language of capitalism and reproduced the ideology of the world market. Based on the above account it should appear as evident that Negri and Hardt have misread the aims of, at least most, poststructuralists, buying into what Foucault has termed the blackmail of Enlightenment. This gives Negri and Hardt a seemingly novel position of speech,

wherefrom they can deliver the promise of liberation of the oppressed. In the end, I will claim, Negri and Hardt (2000: 138–59) undertake a classical Marxist analysis with a poststructuralist touch, celebrating the productive capabilities of the poor.
5 As Foucault (1984b: 46), for instance, notes in *What is Enlightenment*: "We have to turn away from all projects that claim to be global or radical ... the claim to escape from the system of contemporary reality so as to produce the overall programs of another society of another way of thinking, another culture, another vision of the world, has led only to the most dangerous traditions."
6 As Simons also effectively argues, by relegating the power to determine which practices are to be considered legitimate and non-legitimate to political philosophy, Habermas' position might well result in political paralysis and run counter to those ideals of emancipation and liberation, which he embraces. It disempowers, Simons (1995: 116) argues, those "non-intellectuals who may feel the need to resist but who are unable to justify themselves before the judicial authority of the state and academy ... What happens to all those others who cannot articulate reasons for resistance in terms he [Habermas] would accept? What do we do with the people whom we do not respect because they seem to be irrational, and thus opposed to what we are, as rational subjects? What price do we pay for applying communicative rationalities of government to ourselves?" In terms of the "academy" Smith (1996: 13) has equally argued how appeals to reason may serve as instruments of power, rather than an emancipating force. "Those who swim outside these safe waters [outside of positivism] risk more than simply the judgement that their theories are wrong; their entire ethical or moral stance may be ridiculed or seen as dangerous just because their theoretical assumptions are deemed unrealistic. Defining common sense is the ultimate act of political power."
7 Of course, many more studies have been carried out than are cited. This is, however, not the place to engage in a general overview of all poststructuralist studies within International Relations, neither is the present account to be seen as constituting a complete account of all the insights and analyses made by the works cited.
8 Within International Relations constructivism has come to be defined rather narrowly, as a school associated with the works of especially Katzenstein, Adler, and Wendt, to be differentiated from poststructuralist, as well as neo-realist and neo-liberalists. Outside the discipline, constructivism is, however, usually taken to be a much broader category. It is seen as an umbrella term, which also includes what we in International Relations would describe as poststructuralists.
9 Poststructuralism, Jackson and Sørensen (1999: 237), for instance, argue, does not "provide any foundation of knowledge", and hence cannot distinguish between fact and value, objective and subjective. The world has become pure chance and contingency, and all knowledge subjective and biased. Krasner – as Sørensen and Jackson – accepts that the world, or at least part of it, can only become meaningful through our intersubjective understanding of it. Following Searle, Krasner (1999: 49) however, argues that poststructuralists have failed to realize that there can be "a subjective ontology but an objective epistemology" (see also Jackson and Sørensen 1999). The cardinal point of critique, in other words, rests on the modern distinctions between epistemology and ontology, subjectivity and objectivity, where the production of objective knowledge, the very ability to distinguish between true and false, apparently can be carried out in a realm free of this world's intersubjective constructions. Investigators can, Krasner (1999: 49) concludes, make objective judgements. In contrast, I assert that this book cannot claim to make objective representation of representations, which can be verified or falsified from an extra-discursive position. We cannot, on the one hand, purport that the world is (discursively) socially constructed and, on the other, argue that how we gain and validate knowledge about these social constructions are not. This does not imply that anything goes as I will argue for in the next chapter. But it implies that what counts and does not count as knowledge, who can claim to speak in its name, what differentiates it from, for instance, superstition, rhetoric or religion, cannot be set outside of discourse –

174 Notes

or intersubjective understandings – but must equally be seen as a discursive construct whose boundaries and content have varied across time and space. Knowledge, to put it crudely, is no less a social construction than nation-states, money or marriage.

10 This is not to argue that such an exercise would be fruitless and irrelevant, but since this book is very "empirical" in its scope, it does not leave room for such discussions, which easily would risk becoming superficial and evident.

11 As it often has been emphasized, where some see Foucault's archaeological and genealogical strategies as mutually exclusive, reading the archaeology as a failed strategy which Foucault himself refused after his "archaeology of knowledge" (Dreyfus and Rabinow 1982), others, including me in this book, argue that one can find traces of genealogical thinking in Foucault's early work as well as an application of archaeological "methods" in his genealogical work.

12 As Lene Hansen (1997: 323) has also argued: Walker indicates that the emerging change in the conceptualization of time, eroding the distinction between time inside (as progress) and time outside (as repetition), opens up a rearticulation of the inside/outside construction, but "Walker does not expand on what this means in more detail."

13 While I agree with Bartelson – and Rabinow and Dreyfus – that the regularities of discourses only are to be seen as regularities that reside within discourse and which can only be described, rather than being turned into explanations, Bartelson's argument for complementing the archaeological strategy with a genealogical one, seems at times unclear. By arguing that a genealogical strategy has to be introduced because the archaeology strategy does not furnish us with "an external point from which to explain discontinuity" (Bartelson 1995: 72) Bartelson unfortunately comes to indicate that he, as well, is searching for a causal explanation of the emergence of discourses: an aim that is consistent neither with Bartelson's epistemology nor with Nietzsche's and Foucault's delimitation of the genealogical project. In practice, however, as we are to see below, Bartelson's analysis of the transition and succession of discourses does not operate with a causal logic of explanation, but rather points to those discursive tensions, paradoxes and limits within, as well as between, the discourse on knowledge and sovereignty, which makes the transition from one discourse to another possible. If one is to point to a "hidden causality" in Bartelson's analysis it is perhaps to be located on the sovereignty/knowledge axis, where, although the two are mutually constitutive and respectively sustain one another, it is ultimately prior epistemic transformations which move the discourse on sovereignty. The initial change seems to arise from changes in the criteria and foundation of knowledge, not from a rearticulation of sovereignty moving knowledge. In short, it is knowledge that tends to explain changes in sovereignty, rather than sovereignty explaining changes in knowledge. This is, of course, not surprising. Even though Bartelson contends that sovereignty and knowledge are mutually constitutive, that they stand in a circular relationship to one another, and that both, in this sense, must be construed as objects of investigation and held open to variation, it is after all sovereignty which is the study object rather than knowledge.

14 The importance of, and the exact distinction between, a Foucauldian archaeology and genealogy has caused much debate. The difference between the two seems in Bartelson's interpretation mainly to be one of accounting for (or even explaining) discursive change, introducing a historical dimension to the archaeological strategy (Bartelson 1995; see also Åkerstrøm 2002). Others have stressed that it is really a matter of emphasis, since Foucault's archaeological project also had a historical ambition evident from his early empirical work on medicine and madness for example (Connolly 1984: 155; Edkins 1999: 42). Even others suggest that the sizing difference should be found in Foucault's introduction of the power/knowledge nexus (Simons 1995: 27; Sheridan 1980: 116). This reading can also be found with Dreyfus and Rabinow (1982: 103ff), but they in particular see a difference in terms of the position of the investigator – detached spectator versus an involved investigator – arguing that archaeology is subordinated to genealogy. Foucault himself also offered a multiplicity of interpretations of his works and the relative priority

which should be attributed to genealogy or archaeology respectively; at times they were to be seen as complementary, at others distinct, while in a third reading all of his work was said to be genealogical, yet addressing different domains, first a domain of truth, second of power, and third of ethics (see, for example, Foucault 1984a: 386). If we are to conclude on these various readings, it seems that there is no need to read archaeology and genealogy in terms of reversal or progression, or as inherently incompatible strategies where one has to choose between the former or latter. The two can be combined, albeit the aim of the combination may differ. I will return to this point in the next chapter.

15 This is the second point where Bartelson departs from Foucault. Bartelson argues that Foucault's conceptualization of power/knowledge invests power with a capability to explain everything, and yet itself remain immune from explanation, residing in an uncontaminated point outside of discourse. Bartelson (1995: 80–4) proposes that we still ought to see power/knowledge as mutually constitutive – as Foucault did – but yet as a relationship within discourse, rather than a relationship between discourse and power. Power, however, tends in Bartelson's analytic to be read as synonymous with articulations of sovereignty or as a product of the articulations of sovereignty. Bartelson thus writes: "Above all the discourse on sovereignty is a discourse on power ... The discourse on sovereignty is a discourse on the varying attributes and changing locations of power within political discourse, but power is not the essence or the source of its truth, rather it is the discourse on sovereignty ... that tells us what power is within each ... historical episode." Although I agree with Bartelson that power should be turned into a product of discourse, the problem is that one cannot at the same time contend that the meaning and fixation of power takes place through discursive articulations and historical battles between interpretations, while also contending that sovereignty is a discourse on power telling us what power is. This amounts to a definition of power as sovereignty, and sovereignty as power, refraining us from appreciating that there has existed and does exist other articulations of power than the ones correlated with sovereignty, exactly what Foucault so violently opposed. Bartelson's genealogy is a genealogy of sovereignty and not of power, of the interdependence and productive circuit between knowledge and sovereignty, and although "truth is power, and power is truth", that does not mean that sovereignty and power need to be turned into one, in order to render the circuit intelligible.

16 Heralding the end of Man, Foucault (1972: 211) thus declared "You may have killed God ... but don't imagine that ... you will make a man that will live longer than he." In the *Archaeology of Knowledge and the Discourse on Language,* Foucault famously announces the death of Man, demonstrating how the modern episteme with Man and his doubles has been swept away – this in fact seemingly constituting the condition of possibility for his account of the sciences of Man in the first place (Foucault 1972: 130; Rabinow and Dreyfus 1982: 86). Bartelson (1995: 248), on the other hand, seems to suggest that we still are captured by the modern episteme, although it is shaky and criticized from many points.

17 In this respect it should also be noted that it is not entirely clear how change comes about in Bartelson's analysis. As I described in the Introduction, Bartelson wishes to explain the transition from one discourse to another, without relying on a metaphysical and all-present force of power. Instead, change is to be *explained* through battles over truth. Bartelson does not elaborate on what he understands by "battles" – is it, for instance, to be seen as antagonistic battles between competing discourses in the sense of Laclau and Mouffe (1985) or as those combats of progression which Foucault rejected? This is not only analytically undefined, but the very battles are in fact difficult to detect in the empirical analysis. As I suggested above, discourses seem rather to transform as a result of paradoxes, tensions, unsolved problems and limitations, than through open discursive battles.

18 This is not the place to engage in a long dispute over the differences and controversies between Foucault and Baudrillard. Yet, I will briefly argue that it is uncertain why Baudrillard only should be applied to the last two cases or why he should be applied at

all. If, as it sometimes seems, Baudrillard's order of simulation is necessary in order to analyse our contemporary age, this would imply that previously – prior to our post-representational age – truth and ultimate signified somehow existed, whereas truth now has ceased to exist and signified only can be seduced and manipulated. Although Baudrillard – and Weber – contends that the opposition between real and unreal collapse into one another due to "too much reality", distinctions between real and seduced, produced and simulated, reality and hyper-reality are sneaked in through the backdoor, with all the unfortunate ontology they entail when Foucault is criticized and the Baudrillardian perspective sought qualified. Or to put it differently, by arguing that truth only is seduced, Weber comes to imply that there exists – or has existed – such a thing as un-seduced and un-manipulated truth, and that Weber herself somehow is able to make the privileged distinction. In short, Weber comes to prise herself open to the often-voiced critique of Baudrillard (see, for example, Christensen 1999; Doty 1996). Moreover, as Doty (1996) also has argued, there might not exist such a radical difference between Foucault and Baudrillard. When Weber (1995: 126) following Baudrillard, for instance, writes: "Signs continue to circulate, and their exchange continues; however, rather than exchanging for 'the real' signs now exchange for signs of the real – for truth effects", it seems reasonable to argue that Foucault would agree, or at least that he would not subscribe to a view where signs refer to the "real".

19 This form of argumentation is a good example of the (mis)readings which the Baudrillardian approach may give rise to. By stressing the fabrication, staging and artificiality of the request by OECS and the consequent mere *construction* of the community of OECS, Weber comes to imply that the communities of judgement and foundational sources of sovereignty during Wilson and the Concert of Europe were somehow less constructed and more real.

2 Analytical strategies

1 As Neumann (2000: 3) also has stressed: "we need a new literature on method precisely because we need a plurality of ways to organise science."
2 As Foucault (1977a: 146) cautions, "genealogy does not pretend to go back in time to restore an unbroken continuity that operates beyond the dispersion of forgotten things; its duty is not to demonstrate that the past actively exists in the present, that it continues secretly to animate the present, having imposed a predetermined form to all vicissitudes."
3 Although poststructuralists in International Relations generally have abandoned the quest for explanations, Wæver (2000) and Holm (1999) have notably sought to draw in the other direction, contending that it is indeed possible to explain and even (negatively) predict change within a poststructuralist framework.
4 Thus, I only analyse the legitimations of the Kosovo intervention during those relatively few months of 1999 of NATO's campaign. The following debate over the legitimacy of the intervention, which has been carried out in many academic journals, books and in several reports by government agencies and "think tanks" are hence not included. In the case of Algeria, I similarly only analyse those legitimations of non-intervention which were made in 1998, when Algeria drew world attention. Hence, the period after Bouteflika was elected as President and Algeria seemed to have emerged into peace and reconciliation is not included.
5 This first question is divided into two sub-questions where I, in the case of Kosovo, ask "Who is violating sovereignty?", and in the case of Algeria ask "How is the boundary drawn between violation and non-violation?".
6 However, although I have primarily restricted myself to texts understood in the traditional sense – as written sources – this should not be conflated with any ontological distinction between "the textual" and "the non-textual". Everything is text, designating that everything can be analysed as text. Thus, at times I also include and analyse press photographs, book covers and satirical drawings as text.

Notes 177

7 However, it should be stressed that the discursive field cannot be neatly ordered solely on the basis of those voices that spoke against or in favour of an intervention. For instance, commentators such as Robert Fisk or Bourdieu who both argued for international involvement in the Algerian crisis relied on and reproduced many of the same crucial discursive assumptions as the legitimations of non-intervention. For example, that outside actors were not to take the place of the "Algerians", that Algeria was to create its own future and that the outside was not to judge this proud and independent people (see Chapters 5 and 6; Fisk, 5 November 1997; Bourdieu, 3 September 1997).

8 It should be noted in this respect that calling for an intervention in Algeria meant something entirely different than in Kosovo. While intervention in Kosovo became a question of using military means, to bomb Yugoslavia, in Algeria it was economic sanctions or investigating missions, which were inscribed as interventionary measures. This might explain some of the difference between the position of "left-wing intellectuals" with regard to Algeria and Kosovo.

3 From object of observation to object of intervention

1 From the beginning of the intervention, references to genocide, ethnic cleansing and crimes against humanity circulated simultaneously. They were not, however, as the next chapter will outline, articulated as competing representations, but rather as overlapping or synonymous categories.

2 This form of warning was reiterated by the Clinton administration in 1993 and 1994 (Clinton, 17 May 1993, 14 January 1994, 19 February 1994).

3 Whereas all states can be said to be objects of this ever-watchful gaze and of yearly evaluations of their human rights performance by non-governmental organizations, such as Amnesty International and Human Rights Watch, or by the so-called Special Thematic Rapporteurs of the United Nations High Commissioner for Human Rights, only states which are considered to be in a particular situation of crisis will be singled out for monitoring by the Country Rapporteurs of the UNHCR or required to report on their human rights records by the various treaty committees.

4 However, the reports of the CSCE Mission of Long Duration were, in contrast to the reports of the UN and NGOs, not made available to the general public or to the press (Weller 1999a).

5 As Der Derian has argued in terms of intelligence systems, so one might argue in terms of human rights reporting: Much of its power lies in the presumption of representational truth (Der Derian 1992: 31). Yet, in contrast to intelligence systems, which rely on and produce a shield of secrecy, where power works because the gathering of knowledge is hidden, human rights monitoring rests on transparency and openness. The powerfulness of monitoring is an effect of it being made known and visible to all.

6 Just a month before, SFRY's membership of the UN had been suspended. The suspension of SFRY was a follow up on the decision by the Arbitration Commission, which had established that SFRY had ceased to exist. The Security Council and the General Assembly now also confirmed that Serbia and Montenegro could not be considered as exclusive successor of the SFRY. They (Serbia and Montenegro) had emerged as new states, which had to apply anew for membership of the UN (SC Resolution 777, accepted by the General Assembly GA NO 47/1 1992).

7 This was the first time in the history of CSCE that a member state was excluded.

8 Throughout the years of 1992–1996 the establishment of a UN field office in Belgrade was similarly denied.

9 The UN Special Rapporteur also continued to report to the Human Rights Committees and local human rights organizations within FRY equally carried out investigations and reporting (Weller 1999a).

10 For instance, "Request the Secretary General to seek ways and means ... to establish an adequate international monitoring presence in Kosovo" (UN Sub-Commission

178 *Notes*

Resolution 1996/2, 19 August 1996) or "Calls upon the Special Rapporteur to continue to monitor closely the human rights situation in Kosovo and to pay special attention to this matter in reporting"(UN Sub-Commission Resolution 1995/10, August 1995).

11 The UN embargo was imposed on Yugoslavia in 1992. It was related specifically to Belgrade's support to the Serbs in Bosnia-Herzegovina and not to Kosovo.

12 Although the UN embargo had been lifted following the Dayton Accord, the US had still kept what was referred to as the "outer wall of sanctions"; that is to say sanctions which hindered the FRY from applying for loans with IMF and the World Bank.

13 The EU had kept its arms embargo in place even after the adoption of UN Resolution 1021 (Council of the European Union, Common Position on Arms Export to the Former Yugoslavia, 26 February 1996).

14 Russia and China had strongly objected to any phrase that would specify Kosovo as a threat to peace and security.

15 In that way she came characteristically, and in contrast to earlier articulations, to portray Kosovo as an independent political community from that of Serbia, and thereby to install the Kosovar Albanians as a majority and the Serbians as a ruling minority. In the beginning of the 1990s, as we have seen, the situation of the Kosovars was however represented as a question of safeguarding minority rights within Serbia, hence reproducing the Kosovars as a minority in relation to the Serbian majority.

16 At the same time the EU established a new ban on investments in FRY, and later on all flights between FRY and EU (Cardiff European Council Presidency Conclusions, 15 June 1996). France and Britain also attempted to draft a new Security Council resolution. In contrast to NATO's threat of force, this future resolution was, however, described as a warning to the *parties* of the possibility of authorizing further measures, if violence was not reduced (BBC News, 11 July 1996).

17 As one international lawyer noted: "Indeed one is immediately struck by the degree to which the efforts of NATO and its member states follow the 'logic of', and have been expressly linked to the treatment of the Kosovo crisis by the Security Council ... A reading of the relevant Council Resolutions together with the respective pronouncements of NATO (members) might lead an observer to conclude that the two sides acted in concert. The most remarkable illustration of this is the way in which SC Resolution 1203 (1998) welcomed and endorsed the agreements between NATO/OSCE and FRY brought about by the unauthorized NATO threats" (Simma 1999: 354).

18 Yet, many American and British officials did not apply the exception or emergency argument. The British Foreign Minister, for instance, stressed, "A limited use of force is justifiable in support of the purposes laid down by the Security Council but without the Council's express authorisation when that is the only means to avert an immediate and overwhelming [humanitarian] catastrophe" (UK Parliamentary Testimony, November 1998). Similarly the US argued that that the existing UN resolutions, which FRY was in blatant violation of, constituted a sufficient ground for intervention (see also Guicherd 1999: 26).

19 The Holbrooke agreement was to be monitored on the ground by a special OSCE verification mission (KVM) and by daily NATO overflights. They were to verify and monitor the withdrawal of Serbian forces, the maintenance of cease-fire, the return of the refugees, and oversee and supervise local elections. Moreover, as part of the Holbrooke package, Milosevic was also to reach a political agreement with the Kosovars based on the previous proposal by Ambassador Hill and the Contact Group. On 24 October Holbrooke's deal was adopted by the Security Council in Resolution 1203 and on the 25 October the OSCE mission was formally established. This mission – composed of 2,000 unarmed verifiers – was to monitor the cease-fire and the withdrawal of Serbian forces, along NATO's aerial observation of compliance, and it was to supervise and run the local elections in Kosovo.

20 In fact, especially American politicians were met with questions of why the United States should involve itself and turn the war in Kosovo into its own problem (Clinton, 23 February 1999; Kissinger in *Washington Post*, 22 February 1999).

4 Sovereignty and intervention

1 We were, hence, faced with the well-known narrative of a potentially reformed, recognizable "Other", who, with the help and guidance of the West, could develop into "Us" (Oxford, 1999: 688). Serbs and Kosovars it seemed could neither act on their own nor have any political agenda on their own (see also Zizek 1999).
2 As Charney (1999) argues "In the Nicaragua case, the International Court of Justice found that to challenge a rule of international law, the state practice relied upon must be clearly predicated on an alternative rule of law; but NATO has not justified its actions on the basis of a specific rule of law – even humanitarian intervention – new or old. Throughout the campaign, NATO offered no legal justification for it. Yet, some attempts were made to the effect that the intervention was legal. Notably through references to customary and humanitarian law it was sought proven that there indeed was a legal basis for NATO's intervention (see, for example, Albright, 20 April; Henderson, British Minister for the Armed Forces, 22 April; Christopher Greenwood, 28 March 1999).
3 Vedrine (4 April 1999), for instance, explained: "Our principle is that the recourse to force, should be authorized by the Security Council [...] It normally has the monopoly on the legal and legitimate use of force. Yet, basically, there can be cases of extreme urgency, of very great gravity, in which one of the permanent members of the Security Council, in this case Russia or China, for reasons of profound political disaccord; for reasons of domestic politics, cannot give explicitly its accord to the entirety of the process. Thus, it is a dilemma ... Is it for this very important juridical reason – which, faced with a tragedy, can seem formalistic – should one say that one cannot act? Or is it in that very moment that one must remember that there is after all a certain legitimacy to act, to advance in spite of everything?"
4 Habermas (1999: 268), for instance, argued: "The case at hand shows that universalist justifications do not by necessity always function as a veil for the particularity of undeclared interest ... neither the motive of securing and extending its sphere of influence as ascribed to the United States, not the motive of finding a new role attributed to NATO, and not even the motive of establishing a 'European Fortress' as a way of preventing waves of immigration, can explain the decision to undertake such a serious, risky and costly intervention."
5 As Bartelson (2001: 18) also has argued, anyone speaking in terms of universality, attempting to move from particularity to universality is captured by a tragic predicament, in that it can always be interpreted as an expression of particularity. The structure of the pluralistic system of states limits most effectively the credibility of any attempt of universalistic legitimations.
6 The mere titles of Chomsky's and Mccgwire's comments are telling: "The current bombings: behind the rhetoric" and "Why did we bomb Belgrade?". Mccgwire (1999: 22), for instance, writes in his conclusion, "We were told that Kosovo was a new kind of war – one designed to protect values not interest. But is this factually correct? [Mccgwire then moves on to describe what is factually correct, to describe the real purpose of the intervention]. The purpose of NATO's intervention was to pre-empt a civil war, a war that would trigger George Bush's Christmas warning about US action to defend vital interest in the Balkans. The second objective, demonstrating NATO's continuing utility and future potential, was clearly concerned with public relations, not values. And as a final refutation, the resources allocated to SACEUR were intended to force Milosevic to agree to the deployment of a NATO force in Kosovo, and were not designed to avert a humanitarian disaster."

5 From object of concern to object of non-intervention

1 FIS had been legalized as a political party in September 1989, after the instalment of a multi-party system and a new constitution. In June 1990 Algeria held its first free, multi-party local elections. FIS won 55 per cent of the communes and 853 town halls out of

180   *Notes*

    1,539. The local elections were followed by parliamentary election in December 1991. The first round was won by FIS, with 47.42 per cent of the votes cast, but with only 24.50 per cent of registered voters (Martinez 2000: 20).
2 In an interview in *Le Monde* (22 February 1992), Michel Rocard, the former Prime Minister, explained "you [may] have remarked that I have been very prudent in my comments on the coup. I have a number of Arab friends for whom it was justified. We, with our culture of human rights, think that the interruption of a democratic process is necessarily dangerous for what follows; that only the democratic process can resolve the evils brought about by the very people who would have wanted to profit from this process in order to try to destroy it: but all this supposes that a certain level of democracy had been attained and I do not think that Algeria is at that level."
3 In very simplified terms: in the former, democracy is primarily defined through those formalized procedures by which collective decisions are made. The identification of an act as democratic or not, hence, depends on the procedures by which it is reached. The result of the ballot box is accordingly democratic if the votes have been cast freely and fairly regardless of the result. In the latter, however, democracy is also "dependent on the outcomes not simply the processes through which they are reached" (Cohen 1996: 95). The outcome of an entirely democratic procedure may in other words be defined as undemocratic if it violates the substance of democracy, for example, if it infringes on the principle of equality by allowing religious, sexual or class discrimination. And in the case of Algeria, according to the argument, if the party elect abolishes the electoral process (Cohen 1996; see also Habermas 1999b; Held,).
4 *Intégrisme* and *intégristes* function as the antithesis of secularism, of *laïcité* in a French context. Hence, *intégrisme* carries negative connotations, being inscribed as a threat against one of the core values of the Republic. To some extent *intégrisme* resembles the English term "fundamentalism".
5 GIA is a rival Islamic military group to AIS (Armée Islamique du Salut, the military wing of FIS) which was founded in 1992 shortly after the annulment of the second round of the parliamentary elections and the outlawing of FIS.
6 GIA had, for instance, in *Le Monde* (17 November 1993) warned that those who were cooperating with the regime would be viewed as accomplices in the crimes committed by the Algerian authorities, hence constituting potential targets of GIA reprisals.
7 In April 1994 Algeria obtained a new IMF agreement; an additional one billion dollars were provided from France in 1994. In May the EU granted 150 million ECU to Algeria, and in December EU provided another 5.5. billion ECU to Algeria (Spencer 1996).
8 Amnesty reported in October that, "Since the proclamation of the state of urgency in February 1992 the situation of human rights has continuously deteriorated." The security forces, Amnesty contended, had executed "several hundred civilians in an extra-judiciary manner". Amnesty equally reported that systematic torture was common, and that the judicial process at the Special Courts (for those accused of terrorism) violated the most basic legal principles (*Le Monde*, 26 October 1994). In the US Sub-Committee on Africa the Secretary of Near Eastern Affairs also reported that, "Excesses by government security forces in their efforts to contain the insurgency continue. We are disturbed by reports of extra-judicial killings, torture and detention without trial. The United States condemns violations of basic human rights by all sides" (Pelletreau, US Assistant Secretary of State to the House Sub-Committee on North Africa, 3 October 1994).
9 Derrida, although a supporter of the appeal cautioned, in a speech to the two committees, that the several references to non-intervention and the portrayal of the crisis as being the Algerians' own, could come to serve as an unfortunate alibi for inaction: "the Appeal says that solutions belong to the Algerians alone, a correct claim in principle, but it adds several times that these solutions cannot be born in isolation of the country. This reminds us of what must be made explicit in order to draw its consequences: political solutions do not depend in the last instance on the citizens of this or that nation-state. Today, with respect to what was and remains up to a certain point a just imperative,

that is non-intervention and the respect of self-determination (the future of Algerian men and women of course in the end belongs to the Algerian people) a certain manner of saying it or of understanding it runs the risk of being, from now on, at best the rhetorical concession of a bad conscience, at worst, an alibi. Which does not mean that a right of intervention or of intrusion, granted to other states or to the citizens of other states as such, should be reinstated. That would be inadmissible. But one should reaffirm the international aspect of the stakes and of certain solidarities that tie us all the more in that they do not only tie us as citizens of determinate nation-states" (Derrida 2002: 304). Thus, although Derrida in that way refused to make the Algerian nation foundational of the political, he, however, quickly re-emphasizes that the future belongs to the Algerian people and that a right to intrusion or intervention should not be granted to other states, thus equally oscillating uneasily between "human solidarity" and "self-determination", the self of course being the Algerian people (Derrida 2002: 304).

10 Of course, phrased this way, it was more a choice between evil and less evil than an insoluble dilemma. It was even possible to depict the situation as an obvious choice. One journalist in *The Times* (12 July 1994), for instance, portrayed the situation in Algeria the following way: "On one side are those fighting to install an Islamic republic along Iranian lines. Pitted against them is the ruling elite which is determined to pursue reforms aimed at liberalizing the country."

11 This rigid opposition between regime and terrorists was also endlessly reproduced in the media. For example, "[This is a] dirty war that pits the fundamentalist gunmen against the military government of president Zeroual" (*The Times*, 2 April 1994); "Islamic fundamentalist groups have steadily intensified their campaign to overthrow the secular regime through violence" (USIA, 4 April 1994); "Nowhere more than there [Algeria] does political Islam now appear, in Western eyes, as the new villain, successor to communism and the evil empire; nowhere more than there do Islamists themselves, or their extreme factions, deem themselves so viscerally, so genetically, at war with another civilization – that of the 'unbeliever, the Crusader, the Jew' ... Yet it only dramatizes what is already known, that the deepening Algerian crisis is likely to spill over into Europe, and France first of all, more disruptively than Palestine ever has, and that it poses a moral and political dilemma of an excruciating, all-but-insoluble, kind" (*Guardian*, 28 December 1994 quoted from Esposito 1995: 190).

12 Sant Egidio is a non-governmental organization founded in Rome in 1968 by a group of high school students. Officially it is an "international lay organization" of the Catholic Church. Its official aim is to serve the poor and dispossessed. Since the late 1980s the organization has, however, also contributed to peace-making efforts, notably in Mozambique (see www.santegidio.org). The parties of the talks were FIS, FFS (Front des Forces Socialistes), FLN (Front de Libération Nationale), Ennahda (moderate Islamic party), and MDA (Mouvement Démocratique Algérien). The regime had also been invited to the talks but had rejected participation.

13 MIA (Mouvement Islamique Armé), GIA (Groupement Islamique Armé), MEI (Movement pour l'Etat Islamique) and AIS (Armée Islamique du Salut) were all founded after the annulment of the elections in 1992. GIA is perhaps the best known of these groups in the West due to its proclaimed war (Jihad) against the West and in particular against France. According to Martinez (2000: 179ff), MIA and AIS are distinct from the other groups in that they share a goal of bringing FIS back into politics through a re-legalization of the party and an overthrow of the military regime, yet the two groups conduct their "warfare" differently: MIA mainly through guerrilla war as GIA, AIS attempting to emulate the model of the ALN during the War of Independence against France.

14 In fact, the British foreign ministry only issued one statement following the Rome platform, which merely "noted" the results of the meetings in Rome. The US administration "urged the Algerian government to consider the National Platform, or St. Egidio document put forth by Algeria's opposition parties. This could serve as a basis for discussion of a process by which Algeria's crisis could be brought to a peaceful conclusion and a

process of national reconciliation launched" (Welch, US Deputy Assistant Secretary of State for Near Eastern Affairs, 11 October 1995).
15 The National Pact was of course deemed by the Algerian government as an interference in the internal affairs of Algeria and as an attempt of foreign manipulation, just as Mitterand's proposal was portrayed as an effort to realize old colonial dreams in Algeria (*Le Monde*, 20 January 1995, 8 February 1995).
16 Mitterand's proposal was inscribed by the French government as a potential interventionary act rather than a position between indifference and intervention. It was, for instance, noted: "And thus we have shown interest in everything which would permit the start of this dialogue, but we have also said: no interference in the domestic Algerian matters" (Juppé, 7 February 1995).
17 Yet, while French politicians as well as commentators and journalists now emphasized that France was the worst suited to react to Algeria, the US administration continued to project France – and Europe at large – as the primary actors in relation to Algeria, who had, it was argued "the greatest interest in the region". "While U.S. interests in North Africa, and specifically in Algeria, are extensive and continuing, those of France may be greater ... I do not see us as on any confrontation course, with France or the Europeans on issues of the region. The U.S. Administration wants to stay closely cooperative with the Europeans" (Pelletreau, 15 November 1995).
18 On 25 July the first bomb exploded at the St. Michel station killing eight and wounding eighty-four; six additional bomb attacks were carried out in Paris in 1995 and one in a Jewish school in Lyon (Villeurbane).
19 A referendum on a new constitution was concurrently held in November. The referendum was boycotted by several opposition parties. There were wide allegations of fraud, also by UN observers. In particular, it did not seem credible, it was argued, that 85 per cent had voted in favour of the new constitution.
20 My point is not to establish that Algeria *was* or had *been* silenced. Silence and silencing do not have an ontology on their own. Silence is not the forbidden and unsaid, rather silence is part of the "said" part of discourse, and the interesting question is therefore what function references to silence may have in any given discourse, rather than whether something *is* silenced or not. The former "Foucauldian question" demands that silence is granted a hidden place, behind or underneath of the said, which the theorist somehow has a special access to. Foucault (1967: 27) thus writes in *History of Sexuality*, "Silences are an integral part of the strategies that *underlie* and permeate discourses" (italics added). It should be noted however that Foucault explicitly denies any binary division between the said and the unsaid, and hence also grants silence a place inside discourse. Yet, it remains unclear how the unsaid can be identified.
21 One press photo in particular came to circulate in the world press. The photo (la Madone de Bentalha) was taken in the wake of the massacre in Bethala. It displayed a grief-stricken mother leaning against the wall outside of a morgue in Zirmili. She had lost all of her eight children in the massacre. The press photo won the following year a first prize as the best press photo of the year. It was later revealed as fraud (*Le Monde*, 23 July 1998).
22 A group of French intellectuals and actresses, among others Pierre Bourdieu, Benjamin Stora, Gérard Depardieu and Isabelle Adjani, set up an organization "A day for Algeria". Demonstrations were arranged all over France, and in major European cities on 10 November.

6 Sovereignty and non-intervention

1 The panel, hence, equally reported "Representatives of several women's organisations who are leading figures, stressed and underlined that a clear distinction should be made between what was described as crimes against humanity committed by fanatical terrorists and excesses committed by Government agents. While recognizing that in a democratic society the rule of law must prevail and the excesses should not be tolerated, they

considered, nevertheless, that the barbaric acts committed by fundamentalist terrorists against innocent people warranted priority attention" (UN Panel Report).
2 Claire Spencer has in her analysis of the UN Panel Mission equally pointed to the effects of merely reporting the explanations and statements of the interviewed without any commentary, concluding that the Panel came to echo the analysis of Algerian authorities, endorsing the same meaning to words such as terrorism (Spencer 1998).
3 This hierarchization of crimes was equally invoked in several commentaries. Bernard Lévy, for instance, continually underscored, in his comments and articles on Algeria, that several French intellectuals were banalizing and excusing the crimes of what he referred to as the "*Khmer vertes*" by putting the Algerian government's human rights violations into the same basket as the crimes by the Islamists (*Le Monde*, 12 February). A similar analysis was made in the US Sub-Committee hearings on Algeria, where Neumann (5 February 1998) argued, in response to a question of what the US could do if the Algerian government's human rights record did not improve: "We do not want to be put in the place where the Algerian Government rather than those who we think are doing the majority of the killings, becomes the object of our ire. I think that is not a policy course that makes a lot of sense. So we are looking for ways to help the Algerian Government, as a friend, understand that we could do more."
4 In a number of controversial articles in *Le Monde*, Bernard Lévy equally concluded on the basis of conversations with civilians as well as government representatives during a visit to Algeria – by the invitation of the Algerian government – that the government was not complicit in the massacres against civilians. With reference to the Algerians' own estimations, Hubert Védrine also established that everyone knew who was behind the killings: "Des nombreux Algériens estiment en effet que les responsables des massacres perpétrés sont clairement identifiés" (Védrine, 14 September 1998).
5 Robert Fisk, a well known commentator and correspondent on the Middle East, even inscribed the Algerians as a particularly proud and intelligent people, as apparently demonstrated during their battle of independence against France, and therefore not to be judged and taught by anyone: "The Algerians were fighting and killing Frenchmen in their battle for independence. But one reason the French loathed – and I suspect in many cases still hate – the Algerians is because the Algerians are not a backward, ignorant people. They are intelligent – far too intelligent for Frenchmen to tolerate. The Francophone veterans who fought the French read Camus and Molière. Tragic though their circumstances have become, Algerians are quick-witted, bright, discerning people. They deserve better than to be lectured by us" (*Independent*, 5 November 1997).
6 Luis Martinez in his book on the Algerian Civil War, makes a somewhat similar – although more sophisticated – analysis of the terrorist movements in Algeria. Arguing that rather than being moved by an Islamic ideology, groups, such as GIA, were moved by a quest for power and wealth, by a war rationale of accumulating ever more resources. Accordingly, Matinez refer to the Islamic groups as "political bandits" rather than religious zealots, extremists or fundamentalists.
7 The UN Panel report however did point out that they would have wished to meet with some of the representatives of FIS, but that the Algerian authorities had refrained the Panel from such a meeting because FIS by a court decision had been dissolved in 1992 and therefore fell outside the framework of legality (UN Panel Report: 2).

7 Contrasting constitutions

1 As argued in Chapter 3, in the initial phase of the Rambouillet talks the Serbian and Albanian delegations were both to sign the accord, but after three weeks of failed negotiations it was, however, only if the Serbian delegation refused to sign that NATO would resort to means of force.
2 As we saw in Chapter 5, calls had of course been made to all sides in the Algerian conflict of the necessity of engaging in dialogue, of refraining from using violence; and

with respect to the government, to couple security measures (use of force) with further democratization. These calls were, however, always framed as encouragement and appeals, they were not articulated as demands that would result in sanctions if they were not complied with.

3 On one hand, it was asserted that NATO was not responsible for the intervention, that Milosevic's refusal of all peaceful solutions placed the responsibility for the intervention on him; on the other hand, it was equally argued that it indeed was the responsibility of NATO to intervene, that turning our backs on the Kosovar Albanians would amount to a refusal of our moral responsibility.

4 It should be stressed that by "gradual conflict escalations and internationalisation", I do not mean to invoke a linear or inevitable history. For instance, as we saw in the case of Kosovo, at the end of 1998 following the deal between Holbrooke and Milosovic, and the deployment of the OSCE forces, the problem of Kosovo was largely interpreted as having been solved. Similarly in Algeria, the presidential elections in 1995 were articulated as a sign that democratic progress and peace had now reached Algeria.

Bibliography

Adler, Emmanuel (1997). Seizing the Middle Ground: Constructivism in World Politics. *European Journal of International Relations*, **3**, 3, pp. 319–63.
Akehurst, Michael (1984). Humanitarian Intervention. In Bull, Hedley (ed.), *Intervention in World Politics* (pp. 95–118). Oxford: Clarendon Press.
Åkerstrøm Andersen, Niels (1994). Institutionel Historie – en introduktion til diskurs og institutionsanalyse. COS-rapport 10. Copenhagen: COS.
—— (2002). *Discursive Analytical Strategies*. Bristol: Policy Press.
Alford, C. Fred (2000). What would it Matter if Everything Foucault Said about Prison were Wrong? Discipline and Punish after Twenty Years. *Theory and Society*, **29**, 1, pp. 125–46.
Ali, Tariq (1999). Springtime for NATO. *New Left Review*, **234**, pp. 62–75.
Ambos, Kai (1999). Comment: NATO, the UN and the Use of Force: Legal Aspects. *European Journal of International Law*, Discussion Forum at www.ejil.org/journal/Vol10/No1/coma.html
Andersen Erslev, Lars (1997). Middelhavet er blevet moderne. *Udenrigs*, **3**, pp. 63–9.
Anleu, Sharyn (1999). Sociologist Confront Human Rights: The Problem of Universalism. *Journal of Sociology*, **35**, 2, pp. 198–212.
Ashley, Richard (1987). The Geopolitics of Geopolitical Space: Towards a Critical Social Theory of International Politics. *Alternatives*, **12**, 4, pp. 403–34.
—— (1988). Untying the Sovereign State: A Double Reading of the Anarchy Problematic. *Millennium*, **17**, 2, pp. 227–63.
—— (1995). The Powers of Anarchy: Theory, Sovereignty, and the Domestication of Global Life. In Der Derian, James (ed.), *International Theory: Critical Investigations* (pp. 94–129). London: Macmillan.
—— (1996). The Achievements of Post-Structuralism. In Smith, Steve, Ken Booth and Marysi Zalewski (eds), *International Theory: Positivism and Beyond* (pp. 240–53). Cambridge: Cambridge University Press.
Ashley, Richard and R. B. J. Walker (1990a). Reading Dissidence/Writing the Discipline: Crisis and the Question of Sovereignty in International Studies. *International Studies Quarterly*, **34**, 3, pp. 367–416.
—— (1990b). Introduction. Speaking the Language of Exile: Dissident Thought in International Studies. *International Studies Quarterly*, **34**, special issue, p. 259.
Barkin, Samuel J. (1998). The Evolution of the Constitution of Sovereignty and the Emergence of Human Rights Norms. *Millennium*, **27**, 2, pp. 229–52.
Bartelson, Jens (1995). *A Genealogy of Sovereignty*. Cambridge: Cambridge University Press.
Bartelson, Jens (1996). Short Circuits: Society and Tradition in International Relations Theory. *Review of International Studies*, **22**, 4, pp. 339–60.

Bartelson, Jens (1998). Second Natures: Is the State Identical with Itself? *European Journal of International Relations*, **4**, 3, pp. 295–326.
—— (2001). *A Critique of the State*. Cambridge: Cambridge University Press.
Beck, Ulrich (1992). *Risk Society. Towards a New Modernity*. London: Sage.
Biersteker, Thomas and Cynthia Weber (eds) (1996). *State Sovereignty as Social Construct*. Cambridge: Cambridge University Press.
Bigo, Didier (2001) Internal and External Security(ies): The Möbius Ribbon. In Mathias, Albert, Bigo Didier, Heisler Martin, Kratochwil Fritz, Jacobson David and Lapid Yosef (eds) *Identities, Borders and Orders*. Minneapolis: Minnesota University Press.
Bishai, Linda (2000). From Recognition to Intervention: The Shift from Traditional to Liberal International Law. Paper presented at ISA International Convention, Los Angeles, CA.
Bourdieu, Pierre (1997). Dévoiler et divulger le refoulé. In Jurt, Joseph (ed.), *Algérie – France – Islam* (pp. 21–30). Paris: l'Harmattan.
Brügger, Niels, Knut Ove Eliassen and Jens Erik Kristensen (eds) (1995). *Foucaults Masker*. Århus: Modtryk.
Bull, Hedley (1977). *The Anarchical Society: A Study of Order in World Politics*. London: Macmillan.
Burchell, Graham, Colin Gordon and Peter Mille (eds) (1991). *The Foucault Effect*. London: Harvester.
Cahoone, Lawrence (ed.) (1996). *From Modernism to Postmodernism: An Anthology*. Oxford: Blackwell.
Campbell, David (1992). *Writing Security: United States Foreign Policy and Politics of Identity*. Manchester: Manchester University Press.
—— (1993). *Politics Without Principle: Sovereignty, Ethics, and the Narratives of the Gulf War*. Boulder: Lynne Rienner.
—— (1994). The Derritorialization of Responsibility: Levinas, Derrida, and Ethics After the End of Philosophy. *Alternatives*, **19**, pp. 455–84.
—— (1996). Political Prosaics, Transversal Politics and the Anarchical World. In Michael Shapiro and Hayward Alker (eds), *Challenging Boundaries: Global Flows, Territorial Identities* (pp. 7–32). Minneapolis: University of Minnesota Press.
—— (1998a). *National Deconstruction. Violence, Identity and Justice in Bosnia*. Minneapolis and London: University of Minnesota Press.
—— (1998b). Why Fight: Humanitarianism, Principles, and Post-Structuralism. *Millennium*, **27**, 3, pp. 497–521.
Caney, Simon (1997). Human Rights and the Rights of States: Tery Nardin on Nonintervention. *International Political Science Review*, **18**, 1, pp. 27–37.
Canguilhem, George (1994). The Death of Man, or Exhaustion of the Cogito? In Gutting, Gary (ed.), *Cambridge Companion to Foucault* (pp. 71–91). Cambridge: Cambridge University Press.
Charney, Jonathan (1999). Anticipatory Humanitarian Intervention in Kosovo. *Vanderbildt Journal of Transnational Law*, **32**, pp. 1231–48.
Charvet, John (1997). The Idea of State Sovereignty and the Right of Humanitarian Intervention. *International Political Science Review*, **18**, 1, pp. 39–48.
Chenal, Alain (1995). La France rattrapée par le drame algérien. *Politique Etrangère*, **2**, pp. 415–26.
Chomsky, Noam (1999). *The New Military Humanism. Lessons From Kosovo*. Monroe, ME: Common Courage Press.
Chopra, Jarat and Thomas Weiss (1992). Sovereignty is No Longer Sacrosanct: Codifying Humanitarian Intervention. *Ethics and International Affairs*, **6**, pp. 95–117.

Christensen, Ove (1999). Hinsides politikken – Jean Baudrillard og det transpolitiske. In Carsten Bagge Laustsen and Anders Berg-Sørensen (eds), *Den ene den anden det tredje* (pp. 51–68). København: Forlaget politisk revy.
Cohen, Joshua (1996). Procedures and Substance in Deliberative Democracy. In Benhabib, Seyla (ed.), *Democracy and Difference: Contesting the Boundaries of the Political* (pp. 95–119). Princeton: Princeton University Press.
Connolly, William E. (1984). The Politics of Discourse. In Shapiro, Michael J. (ed.), *Language and Politics* (pp. 139–67). Oxford: Basil Blackwell.
—— (1985). Michel Foucault: An Exchange. *Political Theory*, **13**, 3, pp. 365–76.
Constantinou, Costas (1998). Before the Summit: Representations of Sovereignty on the Himalayas. *Millennium*, **27**, 1, pp. 23–53.
Crenshaw, Martha (1994). Crisis in Algeria. *Mediterranean Politics*, **1**, pp. 191–211.
Culler, Jonathan (1983). *On Deconstruction*. London: Routledge.
Danish Institute of International Affairs (1999). *Humanitarian Intervention. Legal and Political Aspects*. Copenhagen: Danish Institute of International Affairs.
Deleuze, Gilles (1988). *Foucault*. Minnesota: University of Minnesota.
Denham, Mark E. and Mark Owen Lombardi (eds) (1996). *Perspectives on Third World Sovereignty: The Postmodern Paradox*. NY: St. Martins Press.
Der Derian, James (1987). *On Diplomacy*. Oxford: Basil Blackwell.
—— (1989). The Boundaries of Knowledge and Power in International Relations. In Der Derian, James and Michael J. Shapiro (eds), *International/Intertextual Relations* (pp. 3–10). Lexington: Lexington Books.
—— (1990). The (S)pace of International Relations: Simulation, Surveillance and Speed. *International Studies Quarterly*, **34**, pp. 295–310.
—— (1992). *Antidiplomacy. Spies, Terror, Speed and War*. Cambridge: Blackwell.
Derrida, Jacques (1970). Semiologi og grammatologi. In Madsen, Peter (ed.), *Strukturalisme: En antologi* (pp. 241–61). København: Rhodos.
—— (1978). *Writing and Difference*. London: Routledge.
—— (1981). *Positions*. Chicago: University of Chicago Press.
—— (1992). Force of Law: The "Mystical Foundation of Authority". In Carlson, Gray David, Drucilla Cornell and Michel Rosenfeld (eds), *Deconstruction and the Possibility of Justice* (pp. 3–67). New York: Routledge.
—— (1997). *Politics of Friendship*. London: Verso.
—— (2002). Taking a Stand for Algeria. In Anidjar, Gil (ed.), *Acts of Religion* (pp. 300–8). New York: Routledge.
Diez, Thomas (2001). Europe as a Discursive Battleground: Discourse Analysis and European Integration Studies. *Cooperation and Conflict*, **36**, 1, pp. 5–38.
Dillon, Michael (1995). Sovereignty and Governmentality: From the Problematics of the "New World Order" to the Ethical Problematic of the World Order. *Alternatives*, **20**, pp. 323–68.
—— (1998). Criminalising Violence Internationally. *Millennium*, **27**, 3, pp. 543–67.
Doty, Roxanne (1996). Simulating Sovereignty–Intervention, the State, and Symbolic Exchange. Book Review. *American Political Science Review*, **90**, 1, pp. 237–8.
—— (1997). Aporia: A Critical Exploration of the Agent-Structure Problematic in International Relations Theory. *European Journal of International Relations*, **3**, 3, pp. 365–92.
—— (2000). Racism, Desire and the Politics of Immigration. *Millennium*, **28**, 3.
Dreyfus, Hubert L. and Paul Rabinow (1982). *Michel Foucault: Beyond Structuralism and Hermeneutics*. London: Harvester Wheatsheaf.
Dunn, John (1994). The Dilemma of Humanitarian Intervention: The Executive Power of the Law of Nature, After God. *Government & Opposition*, **29**, 2, pp. 248–62.

Dyrberg, Torben Bech, Dreyer Hanse, Allan and Torfing, Jacob (eds) (2000) *Diskursteorien på arbejde*. Samfundslitteratur, Frederikberg C: Roskilde Universitets Forlag.
Edkins, Jenny (1999). *Poststructuralism and International Relations: Bringing the Political Back In*. London: Lynne Rienner.
—— (2000). *Whose Hunger: Concepts of Famine, Practices of Aid*. Minneapolis: University of Minnesota Press.
Edkins, Jenny, Nalini Persram and Veronique Pin-Fat (eds) (1999). *Sovereignty and Subjectivity*. London: Lynne Rienner.
Eide, Espen (2000). NATOs Kosovokrig-ett år etter. *Internasjonal Politikk*, **58**, 1, pp. 27–62.
Esposito, John L. (1998). *Islam and Politics*, 4th edn. Syracuse: Syracuse University Press.
Esposito, John and Piscatori, James (1991). Democratization and Islam. *The Middle East Journal*, **45**, 32, pp. 427–44.
Falk, Richard (1997). State of Siege: Will Globalization Win Out? *Foreign Affairs*, **73**, 1, pp. 123–36.
Farer, Tom (2000). Restraining the Barbarians: Can International Criminal Law Help? *Human Rights Quarterly*, **22**, 1, pp. 90–117.
Feyerabend, Paul (1975). *Against Method. Outline of an Anarchistic Theory of Knowledge*. London: Verso.
Finnemore, Martha (1996). Constructing Norms of Humanitarian Intervention. In Katzenstein, Peter (ed.), *The Culture of National Security: Norms and Identity in World Politics* (pp. 153–85). New York: Colombia University Press.
Fisk, Robert (1999) Lies and More Damned Lies. How to Manipulate Hearts and Minds. *Le Monde Diplomatique*, August.
Flynn, Thomas (1994). Foucault's Mapping of History. In Gutting, Gary (ed.), *The Cambridge Companion to Foucault* (pp. 28–46). Cambridge: Cambridge University Press.
Flyvbjerg, Bent (1991). *Rationalitet og magt: Det konkretes videnskab Bind I*. Aarhus: Akademisk Forlag.
Forsberg, Tuomas (1996). Beyond Sovereignty, Within Territoriality: Mapping the Space of Late-Modern (Geo) Politics. *Cooperation and Conflict*, **31**, 4, pp. 355–86.
Foucault, Michel (1970a). *The Order of Things. An Archaeology of the Human Sciences*. New York: Vintage Books.
—— (1970b). Diskurs og diskontinuitet. In Madsen, Peter (ed.), *Strukturalisme* (pp. 145–62). København: Rhodes.
—— (1972). *The Archaeology of Knowledge & the Discourse on Language*. New York: Panthenon.
—— (1977a). Nietzsche, Genealogy, History. In Bouchard, Donald (ed.), *Language, Counter-Memory, Practice* (pp. 139–64). New York: Cornell University Press.
—— (1977b). *Discipline and Punish. The Birth of the Prison*. New York: Vintage Books.
—— (1977c). *Power/Knowledge: Selected Interviews and Other Writings 1972–1977*. London: Harvester.
—— (1978a). Politics and the Study of Discourse. *Ideology and Consciousness*, **3**, pp. 7–26.
—— (1978b). About the Concept of the "Dangerous Individual" in 19th Century Legal Psychiatry. *International Journal of Law and Psychiatry*, **1**, 1, pp. 1–18.
—— (1979). Governmentality. *Ideology and Consciousness*, **6**, pp. 5–21.
—— (1981). Questions of Method: An Interview with Michel Foucault. *Ideology and Consciousness*, 1981, **8**, pp. 3–14.

—— (1984a). Polemics, Politics and Problematisations: An Interview. In Rabinow, Paul (ed.), *The Foucault Reader* (pp. 381–90). London: Penguin Books.
—— (1984b). What is Enlightenment? In Rabinow, Paul (ed.), *The Foucault Reader* (pp. 32–50). London: Penguin Books.
—— (1990a). *The Will to Knowledge. The History of Sexuality*, vol.1. London: Penguin Books.
—— (1990b). *Michel Foucault, Politics, Philosophy, Culture: Interviews and Other Writings 1977–1984*. New York: Routledge.
—— (1991). *The Order of Things: An Archaelogy of the Human Sciences*. London: Routledge.
—— (1994). Security, Territory and Population. In Rabinow, Paul (ed.), *Ethics, Subjectivity and Truth: Essential Works of Foucault 1954–1984 Vol. I* (pp. 67–72). New York: The New Press.
—— (1995a). Tænkningen af det udenfor. In Brügger, Niels, Knut Ove Eliassen and Jens Eri Kristensen (eds), *Foucaults Masker* (pp. 47–65). Århus: Modtryk.
—— (1995b). Las Meninas. In Brügger, Niels, Knut Ove Eliassen and Jens Erik Kristensen (eds), *Foucaults Masker* (pp. 85–96). Århus: Modtryk.
—— (1998). Aesthetics, Method and Epistemology. In Faubion, James D. (ed.), *Essential Works of Foucault 1954–1984*. New York: The New Press.
Fowler, Ross Michael and Julie Marie Bunck (1996). What Constitutes the Sovereign State? *Review of International Studies*, **22**, 4, pp. 381–404.
Frank, Manfred (1989). *What is Neostructuralism?* Minneapolis: University of Minnesota Press.
Fuglsang, Martin and Asmund Born (2000). En Bemærkning om Udsagnet. *Grus*, **59**, pp. 71–77.
George, Jim (1994). *Discourses of Global Politics: A Critical (Re) Introduction to International Relations*. Boulder, CO: Lynne Rienner.
Gowan, Peter (1999). The NATO Powers and the Balkan Tragedy. *New Left Review*, **234**, pp. 83–105.
Guichard, Catherine (1999). International Law and the War in Kosovo. *Survival*, **41**, 2, pp. 19–34.
Habermas, Jürgen (ed.) (1987). Questions Concerning the Theory of Power: Foucault Again. In *The Philosophical Discourse of Modernity* (pp. 79–108). Oxford: Polity Press.
—— (1999a). Bestiality and Humanity: A War on the Border between Legality and Morality. *Constellations*, **6**, 3, pp. 263–72.
—— (1999b). Three Normative Models of Democracy. In Cronon, Ciaran De Grieff Pablo (ed.), *The Inclusion of the Other: Studies in Political Theory* (pp. 239–52). Cambridge MA: MIT.
Hansen, Lene (1997a). R.B.J. Walker and International Relations: Deconstructing a Discipline. In Wæver, Ole and Iver B. Neumann (eds), *The Future of International Relations Masters in the Making?* (pp. 316–36). London: Routledge.
—— (1997b). A Case for Seduction? Evaluating the Poststructuralist Conceptualization of Security. *Cooperation and Conflict*, **32**, 4, pp. 369–98.
—— (1998). *Western Villians or Balkan Barbarism? Representation and Responsibility in the Debate over Bosnia*. Copenhagen: Institute of Political Science.
—— (2000). Past as Preface: Civilizational Politics and the "Third" Balkan War. *Journal of Peace Research*, **37**, 3, pp. 345–62.
—— (2006). *Security as Practice: Discourse Analysis and the Bosnian War*. London, Routledge.

Bibliography

Hardt, Michael and Negri Antonio (2000). *Empire*. Cambridge, MA: Harvard University Press.
Held, David (1987). *Models of Democracy*. Cambridge, MA: Polity Press.
Hoffmann, Stanley (1984). The Problem of Intervention. In Bull, Hedley (ed.), *Intervention in World Politics* (pp. 7–28). Oxford: Clarendon Press.
—— (1996). *The Ethics and Politics of Humanitarian Intervention*. Notre Dame, Indiana: University of Notre Dame Press.
Hollis, Martin and Steve Smith (1991). *Explaining and Understanding International Relations*. Oxford: Clarendon Press.
Holm, Ulla (1996). *The French Garden is No Longer What it Used to be*. Working Papers 10. Copenhagen: COPRI.
—— (1998). Algeria: France's Untenable Engagement. *Mediterranean Politics*, **3**, 2, pp. 104–14.
—— (1999). *Det Franske Europa*. Århus: Center for europæiske kultur studier, Århus Universitet.
Howarth, David (1995). Discourse Theory. In Marsh, David and Gerry Stoker (eds), *Theory and Methods in Political Science* (pp. 115–34). London: Macmillan.
Howorth, Jolyon (1996). France and the Mediterranean in 1995: From Tactical Ambiguity to Inchoate Strategy? *Mediterranean Politics*, **1**, 2, pp. 157–75.
Huysmans, Jef (1995) Migrants as a security problem: dangers of "securitizing" societal issues. In Miles, R. and D. Thränhardt (eds), *Migration and European Integration: The Dynamics of Inclusion and Exclusion*. London: Pinter Publishers.
—— (1997). James Der Derian: The Unbearable Lightness of Theory. In Neumann, Iver B. and Ole Wæver (eds), *The Future of International Relations: Masters in the Making?* (pp. 337–58). London: Routledge.
—— (2000). The European Union and the Securitization of Migration. *Journal of Common Market Studies* **38**, 5, pp. 751–77.
ICISS (2001). The Responsibility to Protect. Report of the International Commission on Intervention and State Sovereignty. Ottawa, ON: International Development Research Centre.
Ignatieff, Michael (2000). *Virtual War*. London: Chatto and Windus.
Jackson, Robert and Sørensen, Georg (1999). *Introduction to International Relations*. Oxford: Oxford University Press.
Joffe, George (1994). The European Union and the Maghreb. *Mediterranean Politics*, **1**, pp. 22–45.
Johnson, Barbara (1998). Translator's Introduction. In Derrida, Jacques (ed.), *Disseminations* (pp. vii–ix.). London: Athlone Press.
Jørgensen, Marianne Winther and Louise Phillips (1999). *Diskursanalyse som teori og metode*. Frederiksberg: Samfundslitteratur/Roskilde Universitets Forlag.
Judah, Tim (1999). Kosovo's Road to War. *Survival*, **41**, 2, pp. 5–18.
—— (2000). *Kosovo: War and Revenge*. New Haven and London: Yale University Press.
Katzenstein, Peter (ed.) (1996). *The Culture of National Security: Norms and Identity in World Politics*. New York: Columbia University Press.
Keohane, Robert (ed.) (1986). *Neorealism and Its Critics*. New York: Columbia University Press.
—— (1988) International Institutions: Two Approaches. *International Studies Quarterly* **32**, 4, pp. 379–96.
Kjær, Peter (1996). *The Constitution of Enterprise*. Stockholm: Stockholm University, Department of Political Science.

Kjær, Peter and Åkerstrøm, Andersen Niels (1996). Institutional Construction and Change: An Analytical Strategy of Institutional History. COS-rapport 5/1996.
Knudsen, Tonny Brems (1999a). Humanitær Intervention uden FN? *Udenrigs*, **54**, 2, pp. 36–56.
—— (1999b). *Humanitarian Intervention and International Society*. Århus: Institute of Political Science, University of Aarhus.
Kouchner, Bernard. (1999). Establish a Right to Intervene Against War, Oppression. *Los Angeles Times*, Monday, October 18.
Krasner, Stephen D. (1993). Westphalia and All That. In Goldstein, Judith and Robert Keohane (eds), *Ideas and Foreign Policy: Beliefs, Institutions, and Political Change* (pp. 235–64). Ithaca and London: Cornell University Press.
—— (1995). Sovereignty and Intervention. In Lyons, Gene M. and Michael Mastanduno (eds), *Beyond Westphalia? State Sovereignty and International Intervention* (pp. 228–49). Baltimore and London: The Johns Hopkins University Press.
—— (1999). *Sovereignty. Organised Hypocrisy*. Princeton: Princeton University Press.
Kuusisto, Riika (1999). *Western Definitions of War in the Gulf and in Bosnia: The Rhetorical Frameworks of the United States, British and French Leaders in Action*. Helsinki: The Finnish Society of Sciences and Letters and The Finnish Academy of Science and Letters.
Laclau, Ernesto (1993a). Discourse. In Goodin, Robert E. and Philip Pettit (eds), *A Companion to Contemporary Political Philosophy* (pp. 431–7). Oxford: Basil Blackwell.
—— (1993b). Power and Representation. In Poster, Mark (ed.), *Politics, Theory and Contemporary Culture* (pp. 277–97). New York: Columbia University Press.
—— (1996). Deconstruction, Pragmatism, Hegemony. In Mouffe, Chantal (ed.), *Deconstruction and Pragmatism* (pp. 47–68). London: Routledge.
Laclau, Ernesto and Chantal Mouffe (1985). *Hegemony & Socialist Strategy: Towards a Radical Democratic Politics*. London: Verso.
—— (1987). Post-Marxism without Apologies. *New Left Review*, **166**, pp. 79–106.
Laustsen, Bagge and Ole Wæver (2000). Defence of Religion: Sacred Referent Objects for Securitization. *Millennium*, **29**, 3, pp. 705–39.
Lyons, Gene M. and Michael Mastanduno (1993). International Intervention, State Sovereignty and the Future of International Society. *International Social Science Journal*, **138**, November, pp. 517–33.
—— (eds) (1995a). State Sovereignty and International Intervention: Reflections on the Present and Prospects for the Future. In *Beyond Westphalia? State Sovereignty and International Intervention* (pp. 250–66). Baltimore and London: The Johns Hopkins University Press.
—— (1995b). *Beyond Westphalia? State Sovereignty and International Intervention*. Baltimore and London: The Johns Hopkins University Press.
Macdonell, Diane (1986). *Theories of Discourse*. Oxford: Basil Blackwell.
Malmvig, Helle (1999). Når det nationale bliver internationalt: Om vold i og imellem stater. *Politica* **31**, 1, pp. 43–58.
—— (2000a). Humanitær intervention. Retlige og politiske aspekter. *Økonomi & Politik* **73**, 3, pp. 90–2.
—— (2000b). *The False Dilemma? Between Sovereign Foundations during Legitimations of Intervention*, Arbejdespapir 2000/1. København: Institut for Statskundsakb.
—— (2001a). Kuusisto on Western Definitions of War in the Gulf and in Bosnia. *Cooperation and Conflict*, **36**, 1, pp. 135–41.
Malmvig, Helle (2001b). The Reproduction of Sovereignties: Between Man and State During Practices of Intervention. *Cooperation and Conflict*, **36**, 3, pp. 251–72.

Bibliography

March, James G. and Johan Olsen (1989). *Rediscovering Institutions: The Organisational Basis of Politics*. New York: Free Press.

Martinez, Luis (2000). *The Algerian Civil War 1990–1998*. New York: Columbia University Press.

Mccgwire, Michael (2000). Why did We Bomb Belgrade? *International Affairs*, **76**, 1, pp. 1–23.

McHoul, Alec and Wendy Grace (1993). *A Foucault Primer*. London: UCL Press.

Mearsheimer, John (1995). The False Promise of International Institutions. *International Security*, **19**, 3, pp. 5–49.

Milliken, Jennifer (1999). The Study of Discourse in International Relations: A Critique of Research and Methods. *European Journal of International Relations*, **5**, 2, pp. 225–54.

Morgenthau, Hans J. (1973). *Politics among Nations: The Struggle for Power and Peace*. New York: Alfred A. Knopf.

Munro, Alan (1996). British–Algerian Relations, Past and Present. *The Journal of Algerian Studies*, **1**, pp. 20–28.

Neumann, Iver B. (1996). *Russia and the Idea of Europe: A Study in Identity and International Relations*. London: Routledge.

—— (2001a). *Mening, materialitet, makt. En innføring i diskursanalyse*. Bergen: Fakboksforlaget.

—— (2001b). From Meta to Method: The Materiality of Discourse. Paper presented at the 42nd Annual Convention of the International Studies Association,Chicago, IL, February 2001.

Nietzsche, Friedrich (1956). *The Birth of Tragedy & The Genealogy of Morals*. New York: Doubleday.

Ohmae, K. (1995). *The End of the Nation State: The Rise of Regional Economics*. New York: Free Press.

Orford, Anne (1999). Muscular Humanitarianism: Reading the Narratives of the New Interventionism. *European Journal of International Law*, **10**, 4, pp. 679–711.

Parekh, Bhikhu (1997a). The Dilemmas of Humanitarian Intervention: Introduction. *International Political Science Review*, **18**, 1, pp. 5–7.

—— 1997b). Rethinking Humanitarian Intervention. *International Political Science Review*, **18**, 1, pp. 49–69.

Paul, Darel (1999). Sovereignty, Survival and the Westphalian Blind Alley in International Relations. *Review of International Studies*, **25**, 2, pp. 217–31.

Pedersen, Ove K.(1983). V*idenskabsproblemet*. København: Aurora.

—— (1995). Problemets anatomi – Eller problemet, der er et problem. *Tendens*, **7**, 1, pp. 1–11.

Persram, Nalini (1999). Coda. In Edkins, Perram and Pin-Fat (eds), *Sovereignty and Subjectivity* (pp. 163–75). London: Lynne Rienner.

Pharo, Per Frederik (2000). Nato og Kosovo-krisen: Mellem pest og kolera. *Internasjonal Politikk*, **58**, 1, pp. 3–26.

Philpott, Daniel (2001). Usurping the Sovereignty of Sovereignty. *World Politics*, **53**, 2, pp. 297–324.

Piertse, Jan N. (1997). Sociology of Humanitarian Intervention: Bosnia, Rwanda and Somalia Compared. *International Political Science Review*, **18**, 1, pp. 71–93.

Polat, Necati (1998). Poststructuralism, Absence, Mimesis: Making Difference, Reproducing Sovereignty. *European Journal of International Relations*, **4**, 4, pp. 447–77.

Poster, Mark (1984). *Foucault, Marxism and History: Mode of Production versus Mode of Information*. Cambridge, MA: Polity Press.

Provost, Lucile (1996). *La Second Guerre d'Algérie. Le quiproquo franco-algérien*. Paris: Flammarion
Purvis, Trevor and Alan Hunt (1993). Discourse, Ideology, Discourse, Ideology, Discourse, Ideology. *The British Journal of Sociology*, **44**, 3, pp. 473–99.
Rabinow, Paul (1987). *The Foucault Reader*. Harmondsworth: Penguin.
Raffnsøe, Sverre (1999). Historie- eller diskursanalyse? En introduktion til Foucaults Les mots et les choses og L'archéologie du savoir. COS-rapport. Copenhagen: COS.
Ramsbotham, Oliver (1997). Humanitarian Intervention 1990–5: A Need to Reconceptualize? *Review of International Studies*, **23**, 4, pp. 445–68.
Ramsbotham, Oliver and Tom Woodhouse (1996). *Humanitarian Intervention in Contemporary Conflict*. Cambridge, MA: Polity Press.
Roberts, Adam (1996). *Humanitarian Action in War*. Adelphi Papers 305. Oxford and New York: Oxford University Press.
Roberts, Hugh (1995). Algeria's Ruinous Impasse and the Honourable Way Out. *International Affairs*, **71**, 2, pp. 247–67.
—— (1999). Algeria's Veiled Drama. *International Affairs*, **75**, 2, pp. 383–92.
Rosenau, James N. (1995). Sovereignty in a Turbulent World. In Lyons, Gene M. and Michael Mastanduno (eds), *Beyond Westphalia? State Sovereignty and International Intervention* (pp. 191–227). Baltimore and London: The Johns Hopkins University Press.
Rosenau, Pauline (1990). Once Again into the Fray: International Relations Confronts the Humanities. *Millennium*, **19**, 1, pp. 83–110.
Ruf, Werner (1997). Perspectives de la crise en Algérie. La responsabilité internationale. In Jurt, Joseph (ed.) *Algérie – France – Islam* (pp. 225–40). Paris: l'Harmattan.
Said, Edward (1978). *Orientalism*. New York: Vintage Books.
—— (1999). Protecting the Kosovars? *New Left Review*, **234**, pp. 76–82.
Sarup, Madan (1988). *An Introductionary Guide to Poststructuralism and Postmodernism*. Hertfordshire: Harvester Wheatsheaf.
Saussure, Ferdinand (1966). *Course in General Linguistics*. New York: McGraw-Hill.
Shapiro, Michael J. (1981). *Language and Political Understanding*. New Haven: Yale University Press.
—— (1984). *Language and Politics*. Oxford: Basil Blackwell.
—— (1988). *The Politics of Representation: Writing Practices in Biography, Photography, and Policy Analysis*. Madison, Wisconsin: The University of Wisconsin Press.
—— (1990). Strategic Discourse/Discursive Strategy: The Representation of "Security Policy" in the Video Age. *International Studies Quarterly*, **34**, pp. 327–40.
Sheridan, Alan (1980). *Michel Foucault: The Will to Truth*. London: Tavistock.
Shinoda, Hideaki (2000). The politics of legitimacy in international relations: The case of NATO's intervention in Kosovo. First Press, www.theglobalsite.ac.uk
Simma, Bruno (1999). NATO, the UN and the Use of Force: Legal Aspects. *European Journal of International Law*, **10**, 1, pp. 1–22.
Simons, Jon (1995). *Foucault & the Political*. London and New York: Routledge.
Smith, Steve (1996a). Paradigm Dominance in International Relations: The Development of International Relations as a Social Science. *Millennium*, **16**, 2, pp. 189–204.
—— (1996b). Positivism and Beyond. In Smith, Steve, Ken Booth and Marysi Zalewski (eds), *International Theory: Positivism and beyond* (pp. 11–44). Cambridge: Cambridge University Press.
Smith, Steve, Ken Booth and Marysia Zalewski (eds) (1996). *International Theory: Positivism and beyond*. Cambridge: Cambridge University Press.

Spencer, Claire (1993). *The Maghreb in the 1990s*. Adelphi Paper. London: Oxford University Press (on behalf of the International Institute for Strategic Studies).
—— (1996). Islamism and European Reactions: The Case of Algeria. *Mediterranean Politics*, **2**, pp. 121–40.
—— (1998). The End of International Enquiries? The UN Eminent Persons' Mission to Algeria July–August. *Mediterranean Politics*, 3, 3, pp. 126–33.
Stora, Benjamin (1995). *Histoire de l'Algérie depuis l'indépendance*. Paris: La Découverte.
—— (2001). *La Guerre Invisible Algérie, années 90*. Paris: Presses de Sciences Po.
Todorova, Maria (2000). The Balkans: From Invention to Intervention. In Buckley, William Joseph (ed.), *Kosovo Contending Voices on Balkan Interventions* (pp. 159–72). Michigan/Cambridge: Wm. B. Eerdmans Publishing Company.
Torfing, Jacob (1999). *New Theories of Discourse: Laclau, Mouffe and Zizek*. Oxford: Blackwell.
Tovias, Alfred (1996). The EU's Mediterranean Policies under Pressure. *Mediterranean Politics*, **2**, pp. 9–25.
Vedby Rasmussen, Mikkel (2000). *A Time for Peace*. Copenhagen: University of Copenhagen Institute of Political Science.
—— (2003). *The West, Civil Society and the Construction of Peace*. London: Palgrave.
Vickers, Miranda (2000). Kosovo the Illusive State. In Buckley, William Joseph (ed.), *Kosovo: Contending Voices on Balkan Interventions* (pp. 97–100). Cambridge: Wm. B. Eerdmans Publishing Co.
Walker, R. B. J. (1987). Realism, Change and International Political Theory. *International Studies Quarterly* **31**, 1, pp. 65–86.
—— (1993). *Inside/Outside: International Relations as Political Theory*. Cambridge: Cambridge University Press.
Wæver, Ole (1989a). Beyond the "Beyond" of Critical International Theory. 1. Copenhagen: COPRI.
—— (1989b). Tradition and Transgression in International Relations: A Post-Ashleyan Position. 24. Copenhagen: COPRI.
—— (1995a). Securitization and Desecuritization. In Lipschutz, Ronni (ed.), *On Security* (pp. 46–86). New York: Columbia University Press.
—— (1995b). What is Security? – The Securityness of Security. In Hansen, Birthe (ed.), *European Security 2000* (pp. 222–51). Copenhagen: Copenhagen Political Studies Press.
—— (1996). The Rise and Fall of the Inter-Paradigm Debate. In Smith, Steve, Ken Booth and Marysi Zalewski (eds), *International Theory: Positivism and Beyond* (pp. 149–85). Cambridge: Cambridge University Press.
—— (1997). Figures of International Thought: Introducing Persons Instead of Paradigms. In Wæver, Ole and Iver B. Neumann (eds), *The Future of International Relations: Masters in the Making* (pp. 1–37). London: Routledge.
—— (2000). Europæisk Sikkerhed og integration: En analyse af franske og tyske diskurser om stat, nation og Europa. In Torfing, Jacob and Torben Bech Dyrberg (eds.), *Diskursteorien på arbejde* (pp. 279–318). Roskilde: Roskilde Universitets Forlag.
—— (2003) Discursive approaches. In Wiener, Antje and Thomas Diez (eds), *European Integration Theory* (pp. 197–216). Oxford: Oxford University Press.
Walt, Stephen (1991). The Renaissance of Security Studies. *International Studies Quarterly* **35**, 2, pp. 211–39.
Waltz, Kenneth (1954). *Man, State, and War. A Theoretical Analysis*. New York: Columbia University Press.

Weber, Cynthia (1995). *Simulating Sovereignty: Intervention, the State and Symbolic Exchange*. Cambridge: Cambridge University Press.

—— (2000). IR: The Resurrection or New Frontiers of Incorporation. *European Journal of International Relations*, **5**, 4, pp. 435–50.

Weller, Marc (1999a). The Rambouillet Conference on Kosovo. *International Affairs*, **75**, 2, pp. 211–51.

—— (1999b). *The Crisis in Kosovo 1989–1999. From the Dissolution of Yugoslavia to Rambouillet and the Outbreak of Hostilities*. Cambridge: Cambridge University Press.

—— (2000). The US, Iraq and the Use of Force in a Unipolar World. *Survival*, **41**, 4, pp. 81–100.

Wendt, Alexander (1992). Anarchy is What States Make of it: The Social Construction of Power Politics. *International Organisation* **46**, 2, pp. 393–425.

Wheeler, Marc (1999a). The US, Iraq and the Use of Force in a Unipolar World. *Survival*, **41**, 4, pp. 81–100.

—— (1999b). On the Hazards of Foreign Travel for Dictators and Other International Criminals. *International Affairs*, **75**, 3, pp. 599–619.

—— (1997). Agency, Humanitarianism and Intervention. *International Political Science Review*, **18**, 1, pp. 9–25.

Wheeler, Nicholas and Justin Morris (1996). Humanitarian Intervention and State Practice at the End of the Cold War. In Fawn, Rick and Jeremy Larkins (eds), *International Society after the Cold War: Anarchy and Order Reconsidered* (pp. 135–71). London: Macmillan.

Williams, Michael C. (1998). Identity and the Politics of Security. *European Journal of International Relations*, **4**, 2.

Zizek, Slavoj (1999). Against the Double Blackmail. *New Left Review*, **234**, pp. 76–82.

—— (2000). *The Fragile Absolute. Or Why Is the Christian Legacy Worth Fighting for?* London and New York: Verso.

—— (2001). *Did Somebody Say Totalitarianism? Five Interventions in the (Mis)use of a Notion*. London: Verso.

Index

absolutism 80
Albright, Madeleine 52, 59, 67, 70, 74, 79, 80, 85–7, 97, 98
Algeria 3, 6, 25–34, 37–9, 42–3, 104–55, 156–62, 164–9
Amnesty International 41, 48, 50, 57, 63, 129, 134–5
analytical strategy 9, 23–5, 44
Annan, Kofi 32–3, 59, 65–7, 69, 71, 132–3, 161
archaeology 6, 15, 31, 39
atrocities 31, 45, 50, 59, 61, 82, 84–5, 87, 129, 130–3, 142, 149, 164, 168
Auschwitz 101
authority 10, 12, 19–20, 26, 67, 69, 71, 77, 94, 104, 144, 164, 168, 171
autonomy 13, 53, 57, 79, 80, 92, 151, 164, 165

Balkan war 88, 100
Balkans, the 27, 52, 68, 83, 87, 88, 93, 158, 159
Bartelson, Jens 8, 9, 13–17, 21, 22, 31, 32, 34, 77, 171
Blair, Tony 59, 75, 79–82, 86, 88, 98, 100–3
Bosnia 33, 43, 47–50, 52, 54, 55, 59, 61, 64, 65, 68, 71, 72, 76, 157, 159, 160
Bulgaria 89, 91
Burleigh 92
Bush, George 19, 20, 49, 109, 110, 171

Charette, Hervé de 52, 125–8, 130, 133
Chirac, Jacques 59, 70, 74, 81, 127, 128

civil war 86, 122, 125, 129, 137, 157, 159
Clinton, Bill 49, 68, 74, 75, 82, 83, 86–91, 93, 99–101, 103, 119, 123
Cohen, William 45, 64, 96, 98, 99, 102, 109
Cold War 100, 102, 158
community: Algerian 128, 146, 147, 151, 153, 166–8; domestic 6, 11, 19, 79; international 2, 11, 26, 28, 30, 32, 38, 45, 48, 50–8, 64, 65, 68–70, 72, 74, 76, 94–104, 106, 123, 129, 132–147, 149, 152, 157, 159–162, 164, 167–9; ethnic 86, 89, 93, 94; Yugoslavian 85, 90–4, 166
conditions of possibility 4, 6, 21, 22, 32, 35, 39, 78, 156, 163, 166
constitutionalism 80
constructivism 5–7
Contact Group 41, 42, 54, 56–8, 63, 66, 67, 73, 75, 96
Cook, Robin 56, 58, 62–4, 66, 67, 71–6, 78–82, 88–90, 100, 142, 143
critique 1, 4–6, 7, 8, 10, 15, 17, 19, 24, 25, 41
CSCE 47–51, 158

deconstruction 4, 9, 10, 13, 14, 22
democracy 12, 80, 89, 91–4, 100, 101, 103, 104, 106–14, 120, 121, 123, 125, 127, 128, 131, 137, 140, 245, 146, 150–2, 157–9, 165, 166, 168, 169, 171
depoliticizing 6, 81
Derrida, Jacques 1, 4, 6, 7, 10, 13, 38, 118
diachronic 15, 21, 22, 23, 29–31, 33–5, 38, 39, 42, 43, 46, 96, 156, 157

diplomacy 6, 29, 45, 63–5, 68, 69, 71, 76, 162
discourse: boundaries of 40–3; definition of 3; and change 31–5; monuments of 40; regularity of 40–3; statements of 15; strategies of 39

Eagleburger, Lawrence 86–8
epistemology 7, 26
ethic 5, 11, 17, 95, 96, 154, 167
ethnic cleansing 30, 33, 45, 56–63, 65, 68, 72, 74, 75, 77, 81, 83–7, 90, 97, 103, 149, 161
ethnic hatred 33, 78, 91
ethnic war 33, 46, 45, 56–63, 65, 68, 72–4, 76, 157, 158, 161
EU 41, 42, 52–5, 59, 109, 110, 113, 114, 118, 120, 123, 124, 127, 129, 131, 134, 140, 148, 150, 152, 158, 165
excesses of power 79
extrajudicial killings 26, 62, 104, 105, 136, 145, 156, 157, 163

Federal Republic of Yugoslavia 49, 51, 66, 79
FIS (Islamic Salvation Front) 106–8, 110–17, 120, 123, 125, 152, 158, 159
Foucault 1, 3–6, 8, 9, 14–17, 19, 22–4, 29–32, 35, 39–41, 43, 49, 171
foundationalism 8
France 6, 42, 70, 73, 106, 107, 109, 120, 122, 124–6, 133, 142, 150, 153, 157, 160
freedom 5, 6, 26, 47, 78–80, 87, 94, 101, 102, 131, 139, 146, 148–51, 154, 166, 169, 170
freedom of expression 86, 166
FRY 49–53, 55–61, 66, 69, 78, 81, 82, 86, 89, 90, 94–6, 158, 160
fundamentalism 106, 107, 109–12, 114, 119, 123, 151, 157–9, 167, 168

genealogy 15–17, 22, 29–31
genocide 33, 34, 45, 57, 77, 78, 80–83, 85, 86, 88, 94, 95, 100, 157, 159, 163, 164
Genocide Convention 82
GIA (Groupement Islamique Armé) 116, 117, 123, 153

Gulf War 2

Habermas, Jürgen 5, 60
Havel, Václav 98
Hitler, Adolf 79, 82, 88, 153
Holbrooke, Richard 57, 61, 63, 68, 69, 71, 75
Holocaust 2, 81–3, 88, 164
human rights: organizations of 26, 48, 84, 130, 144, 145, 148; and violations of 26, 32, 47, 48, 57, 84, 118–20, 135, 145, 156, 158, 159
humanitarian law 84
humanitarian values 98

idealism 2, 6, 11, 41, 135, 162
identity 5, 6, 10, 16, 26, 27, 39, 42, 74, 85, 86, 89–91, 93, 105, 117, 131, 140, 147, 148, 151, 153–5, 164–9
independence 26, 54, 57, 61, 89–92, 112, 122, 124, 150, 151, 159, 160, 164, 165, 167, 168
integration, European 40, 53, 90, 92, 93, 100
international community 2, 11, 26, 28, 30, 32, 38, 45, 48, 50–8, 64, 65, 68–70, 72, 74, 76, 94–104, 106, 123, 129, 132–47, 149, 152, 157, 159–62, 164, 167–9
International Criminal Tribunal for the Former Republic of Yugoslavia 85
international law 80, 94–6, 98, 104, 145, 167
international norms 98, 168
international politics 3, 4, 6, 9, 18, 27, 37, 38, 170
International Relations 1–3, 5–7, 9–13, 17, 18, 22–4, 36, 40, 41, 70, 170
intervention: legitimations of 5, 19, 21, 22, 26, 34–9, 43, 46, 76, 77, 162, 163, 169, 170; humanitarian 6, 69, 71, 162
Iraq 98
Islamists 43, 110, 111, 113, 117, 121–3, 125, 128, 131, 137, 141, 152–4, 158, 164, 166

Jospin, Lionel 42, 78, 88, 96, 100, 131, 133, 136

198   Index

Kant, Immanuel 4
KLA (Kosova Liberation Army) 46, 54–9, 63–5, 72–4, 82
Kosovar Albanians 27, 30, 46–8, 51, 54, 56–9, 61, 62, 67, 75, 81, 82, 84–6, 89, 149, 157, 159, 161, 165–6
Kosovo 6, 22, 25–31, 33–7, 39–41, 43, 45–76, 78, 80–4, 86–92, 95, 98–101, 103–6, 138, 139, 149, 154, 156–64, 166–70
Kuwait 2, 98

Laclau, Ernesto and Mouffe, Chantel 2, 24, 31, 32
law, confines of 78, 103, 163
legal definition 82, 164
legality 95, 148, 167, 170
legitimacy of force 94
limits to power 79

Macedonia 47–9, 63, 89
massacres 26, 32, 33, 72, 82–6, 104, 128–31, 133–8, 142, 148, 151, 156, 158, 161, 162, 167
method 8, 149
methodology 1, 8, 23–6, 40
Middle East 2, 112, 171
moral 5, 6, 28, 95, 96, 98, 99, 101, 102, 105, 130, 132–6, 141, 142, 146, 157, 162, 167, 168, 171
multi-ethnicity 86, 89–94, 165

national interest 3, 12, 42, 57, 94, 98, 99, 116
national politics 3, 4, 6, 9, 18, 27, 37, 38, 170
nationalism 88, 91, 101
NATO 45, 56, 60, 63, 64, 66, 68–70, 72–8, 82–6, 88, 91–104, 161, 162, 166–8
Nietzsche, Friederick 2, 5, 14, 15, 31
non–intervention 6, 18, 21, 22, 26, 27, 30, 31, 33, 34–9, 43, 97, 100, 103, 105, 126, 134, 136, 138, 139, 146, 154, 156, 160, 162, 163, 167, 169, 170

object: of concern 31, 33, 105, 106; of intervention 30, 31, 33, 34, 45, 46, 76, 156; of observation 31, 33, 45, 46, 54; of non–intervention 30, 31, 34, 105, 106, 136
ontology 7, 8

OSCE 41, 42, 52, 56, 75, 158
Other 11, 139, 151, 153–5, 167

particularity 10, 12, 36, 60, 135, 167, 169
Pasqua, Charles 114–16, 120, 121, 159
pluralism 8, 78, 89, 91, 92, 101, 103, 123, 125, 127, 128, 150, 165
poststructuralists 1–9, 14, 18, 22–6, 31, 32, 41, 151, 157
propaganda 82, 83

Racak killings 72, 161
Rambouillet Agreement/Talks 73–6, 161, 162
realism 2, 6, 9, 11, 135, 162
refugees 59, 60, 62, 65–8, 71, 84, 85, 92, 93, 112, 149
relativism 5
representation 4, 6, 9, 13, 15–17, 19, 20, 23, 39, 56, 58–61, 70, 72, 73, 76–8, 82–4, 85–8, 92, 94, 99, 114, 122, 137, 139, 149, 152, 157, 159, 161–4, 166, 170
repression 26, 47, 49, 56–9, 61, 63, 65, 67, 71, 72, 79, 82, 85, 86, 89, 94, 99, 104, 113, 118, 120, 131, 137, 149, 150, 157, 165, 166, 170
right to rule 78, 163
rights of the people 79
Romania 89, 91
Rugov, Ibrahim 53, 59, 62, 63

Saussure, Ferdinand de 31, 41
security 6, 29, 40, 41, 56, 57, 65, 66, 69, 115, 117, 120, 131, 134, 146, 149, 164, 165
self 11, 139, 144, 151, 153, 154, 155, 167
Serbia 27, 33, 47, 49, 50, 53, 54–9
Scharping, Rudolf 92
Solana, Javier 63, 72, 73, 88, 96
sovereign power 78–81, 94, 96, 103, 163
sovereignty; genealogy of 8, 13, 14; violation of 36, 39, 95, 103, 163
state power 77, 80, 81, 140, 163, 164
structuralist 41
synchronic 21–3, 29, 34–6, 39, 42, 43, 46, 139, 156, 162, 163

Talbott, Strobe 90

terrorism 6, 32, 54–8, 59, 63–7, 70, 71, 76, 105, 106, 109, 110, 112, 114–17, 119–23, 125, 128, 129, 133, 137, 144–6, 150–3, 158, 159, 163, 164, 166, 168
tolerance 45, 78, 89–93, 99–104, 165–9
truth 2, 4–6, 16, 19, 61, 66, 78–87, 94, 105–6, 129, 131–3, 139, 140, 144, 148, 149, 164, 166, 170

United Nations; and mandate 65, 69, 90, 94–96, 162, 168; Security Council 40, 41, 50, 52, 56, 57, 65–7, 69–71, 95–8, 161, 162, 168

Védrine, Hubert 64, 65, 67, 74, 75, 82, 83, 90, 96, 131, 135, 136, 140–3, 150, 151, 153

Walker, R. B. J. 1, 5–14, 17, 21–3, 32
Weber, Cynthia 1, 7, 10, 18–22, 32, 36, 37, 42
Wæver, Ole 5, 7, 24, 25, 41, 111

Yugoslavia 26, 46–8, 51, 52, 56–9, 61, 66, 76–80, 82, 85, 87, 88, 90–4, 96–8, 100, 103, 104, 149, 156–8, 165–7

For Product Safety Concerns and Information please contact our EU representative GPSR@taylorandfrancis.com
Taylor & Francis Verlag GmbH, Kaufingerstraße 24, 80331 München, Germany

www.ingramcontent.com/pod-product-compliance
Lightning Source LLC
Chambersburg PA
CBHW070646160426
43194CB00009B/1595